Shifting Centres of Gravity in Human Rights Protection

The protection of human rights in Europe is currently at a crossroads. There are competing processes which push and pull the centre of gravity of this protection between the ECHR system in Strasbourg, the EU system in Luxemburg and Brussels, and the national protection of human rights.

This book brings together researchers from the fields of international human rights law, EU law and constitutional law to reflect on the tug-of-war over the positioning of the centre of gravity of human rights protection in Europe. It addresses both the position of the Convention system vis-à-vis the Contracting States, and its positioning with respect to fundamental rights protection in the European Union. The first part of the book focuses on interactions in this triangle from an institutional and constitutional point of view and reflects on how the key actors are trying to define their relationship with one another in a never-ending process. Having thus set the scene, the second part takes a critical look at the tools that have been developed at European level for navigating these complex relationships, in order to identify whether they are capable of responding effectively to the complexities of emerging realities in the triangular relationship between the EHCR, EU law and national law.

Oddný Mjöll Arnardóttir is Professor of Human Rights Law at the University of Iceland and Chairperson of its Human Rights Institute.

Antoine Buyse is Professor of Human Rights and Director of the Netherlands Institute of Human Rights (SIM) at Utrecht University.

Routledge Research in Human Rights Law

Available titles in this series include:

Socio-Economic Rights in Emerging Free Markets
Comparative Insights from India and China
Surya Deva

The Right to Development in International Law
The Case of Pakistan
Khurshid Iqbal

Global Health and Human Rights
Legal and Philosophical Perspectives
John Harrington and Maria Stuttaford

The Right to Religious Freedom in International Law
Between group rights and individual rights
Anat Scolnicov

Emerging Areas of Human Rights in the 21st Century
The role of the Universal Declaration of Human Rights
Marco Odello and Sofia Cavandoli

The Human Right to Water and its Application in the Occupied Palestinian Territories
Amanda Cahill

International Human Rights Law and Domestic Violence
The effectiveness of international human rights law
Ronagh McQuigg

Human Rights in the Asia-Pacific Region
Towards Institution Building
Hitoshi Nasu and Ben Saul

Human Rights Monitoring Mechanisms of the Council of Europe
Gauthier de Beco

The Positive Obligations of the State under the European Convention of Human Rights
Dimitris Xenos

Vindicating Socio-Economic Rights
International Standards and Comparative Experiences
Paul O'Connell

The EU as a 'Global Player' in Human Rights?
Jan Wetzel

Regulating Corporate Human Rights Violations
Humanizing Business
Surya Deva

The UN Committee on Economic, Social and Cultural Rights
The Law, Process and Practice
Marco Odello and Francesco Seatzu

State Security Regimes and the Right to Freedom of Religion and Belief
Changes in Europe Since 2001
Karen Murphy

The European Court of Human Rights in the Post-Cold War Era
Universality in Transition
James A. Sweeney

The United Nations Human Rights Council
A Critique and Early Assessment
Rosa Freedman

Children and International Human Rights Law
The Right of the Child to be Heard
Aisling Parkes

Litigating Transnational Human Rights Obligations
Alternative Judgements
Mark Gibney and Wouter Vandenhole

Reproductive Freedom, Torture and International Human Rights
Challenging the Masculinisation of Torture
Ronli Noa Sifris

Applying an International Human Rights Framework to State Budget Allocations
Rights and Resources
Rory O'Connell, Aoife Nolan, Colin Harvey, Mira Dutschke and Eoin Rooney

Human Rights Law in Europe
The Influence, Overlaps and Contradictions of the EU and the ECHR
Kanstantsin Dzehtsiarou, Tobias Lock, Theodore Konstadinides and Noreen O'Meara

Nomadic Peoples and Human Rights
Jérémie Gilbert

Children's Lives in an Era of Children's Rights
The Progress of the Convention on the Rights of the Child in Africa
Afua Twum-Danso Imoh & Nicola Ansell

China's Human Rights Lawyers
Advocacy and Resistance
Eva Pils

The Right to Equality in European Human Rights Law
The Quest for Substance in the Jurisprudence of the European Courts
Charilaos Nikolaidis

Business and Human Rights in South East Asia
Risk and Regulatory Turn
Mahdev Mohan & Cynthia Morel

Indigenous Peoples, Title to Territory, Rights and Resources
The Transformative Role of Free Prior and Informed Consent
Cathal M. Doyle

Challenging Territoriality in Human Rights Law
Building Blocks for a Plural and Diverse Duty-Bearer Regime
Wouter Vandenhole

Comparative Executive Clemency
The Prerogative of Mercy in the Commonwealth
Andrew Novak

Shifting Centres of Gravity in Human Rights Protection
Rethinking relations between ECHR, EU, and national legal orders
Edited by Oddný Mjöll Arnardóttir and Antoine Buyse

Developing the Right to Social Security – A Gender Perspective
Beth Goldblatt

Forthcoming titles in this series include:
Jurisdiction, Immunity and Transnational Human Rights Litigation
Xiaodong Yang

Extraterritoriality and International Human Rights Law
The Spatial Reach of African Human Rights Treaties
Takele Soboka Bulto

Human Rights Law and Personal Identity
Jill Marshall

Human Rights and the Politics of Knowledge
Joanne Coysh

The Law and Practice of the European Social Committee
Francesco Seatzu & Amaya Ubeda de Torres

Reconciling Cultural Diversity and International Human Rights Obligations
The Compatibility Approach in the Practice of International Human Rights Institutions
Michael K. Addo

Social and Economic Rights in Theory and Practice
A Critical Assessment
Helena Alviar Garcia, Karl Klare & Lucy A. Williams

The Human Rights Approach to Disability
Cases and Materials
Andreas Dimopoulos

Capturing Caste in Law
The Legal Regulation of Caste Discrimination
Annapurna Waughray

Care, Migration and Human Rights
Law and Practice
Siobhán Mullally

The Protection of Vulnerable Groups under International Human Rights Law
Ingrid Nifosi-Sutton

Human Dignity and Degrading Treatment in the European Convention on Human Rights
The Ends of Article 3 of the European Convention on Human Right
Elaine Webster

The Istanbul Convention, Domestic Violence and Human Rights
Ronagh McQuigg

The Right to Truth in International Law
Victims' Rights in Human Rights and International Criminal Law
Edited by Melanie Klinkner and Howard Davis

Children's Rights Law in the Global Human Rights Landscape
Isolation, inspiration, integration?
Edited by Eva Brems, Ellen Desmet and Wouter Vandenhole

The Democratic Foundations of the European Convention on Human Rights
Sovereignty, Equality, Agency
Alain Zysset

Human Rights in the Media
Representation, Rhetoric, Reality
Edited by Michelle Farrell, Edel Hughes and Eleanor Drywood

Shifting Centres of Gravity in Human Rights Protection

Rethinking relations between the ECHR, EU and national legal orders

Edited by
Oddný Mjöll Arnardóttir and Antoine Buyse

Routledge
Taylor & Francis Group
LONDON AND NEW YORK

First published 2016
by Routledge

2 Park Square, Milton Park, Abingdon, Oxfordshire OX14 4RN
52 Vanderbilt Avenue, New York, NY 10017

Routledge is an imprint of the Taylor & Francis Group, an informa business

First issued in paperback 2020

British Library Cataloguing in Publication Data
A catalogue record for this book is available from the British Library

Library of Congress Cataloging in Publication Data
Shifting centres of gravity in human rights protection : rethinking relations between the ECHR, EU, and national legal orders / Edited by Oddný Mjöll Arnardóttir and Antoine Buys.
pages cm. -- (Routledge research in human rights law)
Includes bibliographical references and index.
ISBN 978-1-138-12124-9 (hbk) -- ISBN 978-1-315-65112-5 (ebk) 1. Human rights--Europe. 2. Human rights--European Union countries. 3. International and municipal law--Europe. 4. International and municipal law--European Union countries. I. Oddný Mjöll Arnardóttir, editor. II. Buyse, Antoine C. (Antoine Christian), 1977- editor.
KJC5132.S69 2016
342.2408'5--dc23
2015034991

ISBN: 978-1-138-12124-9 (hbk)
ISBN: 978-0-367-59701-6 (pbk)

Typeset in Galliard
by Taylor & Francis Books

Contents

PART II
'European rights' and national implementation: rethinking the status quo

Contributors

Oddný Mjöll Arnardóttir is Professor of Human Rights Law at the University of Iceland. She is Chairperson of the University of Iceland Human Rights Institute.

Nina-Louisa Arold Lorenz is visiting Senior Researcher at the Raoul Wallenberg Institute in Lund, Sweden. Prior to this she was Senior Lecturer at the Raoul Wallenberg Institute in Lund where she had also served as Managing Director of the Master Program in International Human Rights Law.

Davíð Þór Björgvinsson is Professor of Law at the University of Copenhagen and at the University of Iceland. In Copenhagen, he participates in iCourts, the Danish National Research Foundation's Centre of Excellence for International Courts. In 2013, Professor Björgvinsson completed his nine-year term as a judge at the European Court of Human Rights.

Antoine Buyse is Professor of Human Rights, Director of the Netherlands Institute of Human Rights of Utrecht University, and a member of the Young Academy of the Royal Academy of Arts and Sciences. He hosts a weblog about the European Convention on Human Rights.

Başak Çalı is Director of the Centre for Global Public Law and Associate Professor in International Law at Koç University.

Andreas Follesdal is Professor of Political Philosophy at the Faculty of Law at the University of Oslo. He serves as Co-director of the Norwegian Centre of Excellence PluriCourts for the Study of the Legitimate Roles of the Judiciary in the Global Order. He is Principal Investigator of the European Research Council Project MultiRights, on the Legitimacy of the Multi-Level Human Rights Judiciary.

Xavier Groussot is Professor of European Law at Lund University. At Lund he serves as Director of the LLB programme in EU Business Law and Vice Dean of the Faculty of Law. He is also a Visiting Professor at University Panthéon-Assas (Paris II).

Dóra Guðmundsdóttir is Adjunct Lecturer and Researcher at the Faculty of Law at the University of Iceland and a legal consultant. Previously she was legal secretary and ad hoc judge at the EFTA Court in Luxembourg.

Giuseppe Martinico is currently Associate Professor of Comparative Public Law at the Scuola Sant'Anna. Prior to joining the Scuola, he was García Pelayo Fellow at the Centro de Estudios Politicos y Constitucionales in Madrid and Max Weber Fellow at the European University Institute, Florence.

Gunnar Thor Petursson is Associate Professor at the School of Law, Reykjavik University. Gunnar Thor is a guest lecturer at the Faculty of Law, Panthéon-Assas (Paris II), France and at the Faculty of Law, University of Lund, Sweden. Since 2014 Gunnar Thor has been an Ad-Hoc College Member of the EFTA Surveillance Authority.

Niamh Nic Shuibhne is Chair of European Union Law at the University of Edinburgh. She is a joint editor of the *Common Market Law Review* and a Visiting Professor at the College of Europe in Bruges.

Björg Thorarensen is Professor of Constitutional Law, University of Iceland. She was Deputy Chairperson of the Negotiation Committee on Iceland's accession to the EU 2009–2013 and the Icelandic delegate in the CDDH Ad Hoc Negotiation Group on the accession of the EU to the ECHR 2012–2013. Since 2011 she has served as Chairperson of the Icelandic Data Protection Authority.

Geir Ulfstein is Professor of International law at the University of Oslo. He is Co-director of the PluriCourts Centre for the Study of the Legitimate Roles of the Judiciary in the Global Order, a Centre of Excellence at the University of Oslo. He also heads the Legal Research Team in the European Research Council project MultiRights.

Acknowledgement

This volume contains the reflections of 13 scholars on the theme of shifting centres of gravity in European human rights protection. The contributors have backgrounds in the fields of international human rights law, European law, constitutional law, political philosophy and political science. The participants in this project originally convened to discuss the theme of shifting centres of gravity at a conference hosted by the University of Iceland Human Rights Institute in March 2014, when EU accession to the ECHR still seemed likely. We are very grateful to them for bringing their varied backgrounds and collected expertise to bear on the topic, and for staying with the moving target of centres of gravity throughout the eventful time that has passed since. This has produced what we believe is a unique 360° view of current developments. We are also grateful to the University of Iceland Human Rights Institute and the Icelandic Research Fund for making the conference possible, for the support of the former institute and of the Netherlands Institute of Human Rights of Utrecht University in allotting us time to work on this project, and to Katherine Carpenter and Olivia Manley at Routledge for their professionalism in bringing it to fruition with us.

Antoine dedicates this book to the loving memory of his father and (step) mother, Jean and José, who both sadly passed away during the time in which this book was written.

Oddný Mjöll Arnardóttir and Antoine Buyse
Reykjavík and Utrecht, 2016

1 Introduction

Oddný Mjöll Arnardóttir and Antoine Buyse

In 2014, Dean Spielmann, the President at the time of the European Court of Human Rights (ECtHR), argued that '[t]he future imagined at Brighton is one where the centre of gravity of the Convention system should be lower than it is today, closer temporally and spatially to all Europeans, and to all those under the protection of the Convention'.[1] This book brings together researchers from the fields of international human rights law, European Union (EU) law and constitutional law to reflect on the tug-of-war over the positioning of the centre of gravity of human rights protection in Europe, addressing not only the position of the Convention system vis-à-vis the Contracting States, but also its positioning vis-à-vis fundamental rights protection in the EU. The aim is, first, to analyse how current developments reflect conflicting trends with regard to the positioning of this centre of gravity, and to assess the implications thereof for the future of European human rights protection. Having thus set the scene, the second and connected aim is to take a critical look at the tools that have been developed at the European level for navigating these complex relationships, with the aim of identifying whether they are capable of responding effectively to the complexities of emerging realities in the triangular relationship between the ECHR, EU law and national law.

The metaphor of shifting gravity reflects not just constant changes in the European human rights architecture, but also – and this is important both from a political and legal perspective – a battle over which actor has the final say in human rights matters. Is it one of the two regional Courts, the one in Strasbourg or the one in Luxembourg, or is it national highest courts or legislatives? Even if state parties to both the EU's treaties and the European Convention on Human Rights and Fundamental Freedoms originally perceived themselves as masters of the treaties, the dynamics of European integration and the key role of the two European courts have greatly changed this traditional perception and even affected reality, in the sense that European and national judges are informally and formally – through their case law – influencing and reflecting upon each other's jurisprudence. National ministries of foreign affairs or justice are no longer the only conduits of communication.

1 Dean Spielmann, 'Whither the Margin of Appreciation' (2014) 67 CLP 49, 65.

The gravity metaphor is not intended to convey any idea of inevitability: for Newton the apple may only have fallen from the tree to the ground due to the Earth's greater gravity with no other trajectory possible; in human rights protection the direction of pull-and-push movements can directly be influenced by the actors involved. This is done by the conscious creation of mechanisms which foster interaction, such as the preliminary reference procedure within the EU and the partly similar possibility for national judges to ask the ECtHR for an advisory opinion under Protocol 16. But it is also done by processes of trial and error, as shown by judicial dialogue – whether in comity or conflict – and the creation of the pilot judgment procedure in Strasbourg. Finally, it is in our view key to see constantly evolving doctrines of judicial restraint by courts as part of these shifting gravities. To put it differently, it is not just the institutional frameworks but also the doctrinal ones that influence where the final say on matters of human rights protection can be found. And it is not just a question of judicial dialogue between courts,[2] but also very often of a *monologue intérieur* within courts, both national and international, for example on the question of how much leeway international courts leave to domestic ones or, the other way around, how domestic judges deal with competing European human rights pronouncements coming from Strasbourg and Luxembourg. This volume endeavours to explore these dynamics by addressing the claim that there is nothing 'natural' about changes in gravity; rather, it is very often the result of conscious choices, as the quote from President Spielmann above illustrates, sometimes with unintended results.

The protection of human rights in Europe is currently at a crossroads as there are competing processes which push and pull the centre of gravity of this protection between the ECHR system in Strasbourg, the EU system in Luxemburg and Brussels, and the national protection of human rights.

In Strasbourg, the ECtHR currently faces severe challenges. The Brighton Declaration of 2012 addresses the problems the Court is facing in terms of efficiency, and in terms of the legitimacy dilemma created by the backlog of cases and increased criticism of the quality and consistency of the Court's case law.[3] While 'Brighton' mostly offers only minor adjustments to the current control mechanism, it also places a more serious long-term review of the Court's fundamental nature and role on the agenda for the coming decade. Substantively, 'Brighton' highlights the political momentum for bringing responsibility for the protection of ECHR rights 'home' to the Contracting States. The focus placed on the principle of subsidiarity and the margin of appreciation has already been concretised in Protocols 15 and 16 to the Convention, which are intended to emphasise the Court's subsidiary role vis-à-vis the Contracting States' prerogatives. While neither of the two Protocols has taken effect, recent case law and extrajudicial

2 See, famously, Anne-Marie Slaughter, 'A Global Community of Courts' (2003) 44 *Harvard Intl LJ* 191.

3 High Level Conference on the Future of the European Court of Human Rights Brighton Declaration, 19–20 April 2012 (the 'Brighton Declaration'), <www.echr.coe.int/Documents/2012_Brighton_FinalDeclaration_ENG.pdf> accessed 21 August 2015, paras 11–12 ('Brighton Declaration').

commentary[4] indicate that the Court is already on the path towards realising that goal. However, despite the emphasis on subsidiarity and margins, the Brighton Declaration is still firmly based on the premise of the ECtHR's continued 'key role in the system for protecting and promoting human rights in Europe'.[5] This was indeed also reflected in the Draft Agreement on the Accession of the EU to the ECHR, which positioned the ECtHR as the 'supreme' European human rights court through making its judgments (in cases to which the EU is party) binding on the EU and its courts.[6]

In Brussels and Luxembourg, however, forces seem to be pulling in a somewhat different direction. The EU is increasingly bringing its weight to bear upon the field of fundamental rights, most notably through giving the Charter of Fundamental Rights (CFR) the status of primary law. Further, since the Charter was proclaimed, all secondary legislation aims to comply with it[7] and an increasing volume of secondary legislation implement particular Charter provisions. Contrarily to the ECHR emphasis on subsidiarity and margins, the EU may even aim to fully harmonise legislation in the field of fundamental rights protection, leaving no discretion of implementation to the Member States.[8] The strengthening of the EU mandate in the field of fundamental rights protection also seems to have had an effect on the relationship between the Luxembourg and Strasbourg Courts. Gráinne de Búrca has for example noted that since the coming into force of the CFR, the case law of the European Court of Justice (ECJ) has become increasingly self-contained instead of engaging as before with the case law of the ECtHR.[9] Most recently, in its opinion of 18 December 2014, the ECJ also found the Draft Accession Agreement incompatible with EU law for reasons related to the special character of the EU legal system and the positioning of the ECJ as the supreme arbiter of questions of EU law.[10] Instead of moving towards a unified and harmonious approach to human rights protection in Europe, this controversial ruling, characterised in initial commentary as a 'bombshell'[11] and an 'unmitigated

4 Spielmann (n. 1); Robert Spano, 'Universality or Diversity of Human Rights? Strasbourg in the Age of Subsidiarity' (2014) 14 HRLR 487.
5 Brighton Declaration (n. 3) para. 31.
6 Fifth Negotiation Meeting between the CDDH Ad Hoc Negotiation Group and the European Commission on the Accession of the European Union to the European Convention on Human Rights, 'Final Report to the CDDH', 47+1(2013)008rev2 <www.coe.int/t/dlapil/cahdi/Source/Docs2013/47_1_2013_008rev2_EN.pdf> accessed 21 August 2015, Appendix I ('Draft Accession Agreement').
7 See for example Communication from the Commission, 'Compliance with the Charter of Fundamental Rights in Commission legislative proposals' (COM (2005) 172 final).
8 Case C-399/11 *Stefano Melloni* v. *Ministerio Fiscal* (Judgment 26 February 2013).
9 Gráinne de Búrca, 'After the EU Charter of Fundamental Rights: The Court of Justice as a Human Rights Adjudicator' (2013) 20 *Maastricht Journal of European and Comparative Law* 168, 184.
10 Opinion 2/13, 18 December 2014.
11 Antoine Buyse, 'CJEU Rules: Draft Agreement on EU Accession to ECHR Incompatible with EU Law' (ECHR Blog, 20 December 2014) <http://echrblog.blogspot.nl/2014/12/cjeu-rules-draft-agreement-on-eu.html> accessed 21 August 2015.

disaster',[12] has therefore intensified the tug-of-war over the centre of gravity of human rights protection in Europe.

The literature in this field tends to address only one of the above developmental strands at a time or to focus on only one link in the ECHR–EU–Member State triangle. This coincides with the general tendency in legal scholarship to treat international human rights law, EU law and domestic law as separate legal islands, which each – to a certain extent – maintaining their own discourse on the issues raised. For example, at the level of institutional developments, the literature on EU accession has focused on analysing the issues in relative isolation from the situation and current reform of the ECtHR.[13] And, similarly, the literature on the reform of the ECtHR is mostly centred on discussing models of individual or constitutional justice, but the issues have been framed in isolation from the question of EU accession and the consequences of the ECJ's strengthened mandate in respect of fundamental rights protection.[14] Moreover, the implications of the ECJ's opinion on the Draft Accession Agreement and its consequences for the positioning of the centre of gravity of human rights protection in Europe and the relations between the ECHR, the EU and national legal orders, may be manifold and deserve attention.

At the normative level there has hitherto been a rather clear consensus in political and academic discourses that, while the CFR sometimes provides a higher level of protection, the goal is the 'parallel interpretation'[15] and gradual convergence between the standard of protection in the Strasbourg and Luxembourg jurisprudence, so that normative clarity and consistency between the two regimes

12 Steve Peers, 'The CJEU and the EU's accession to the ECHR: a clear and present danger to human rights protection' (EU Law Analysis, 18 December 2014) <http://eulawanalysis.blogspot.nl/2014/12/the-cjeu-and-eus-accession-to-echr.html> accessed 21 August 2015.

13 For example Paul Gragl, 'A Giant Leap for European Human Rights? The Final Agreement on the European Union's Accession to the European Convention on Human Rights' (2014) 51 CML Rev 13; Jörg Polakiewicz, 'EU Law and the ECHR: Will the European Union's Accession Square the Circle?' (2013) EHRLR 592; Christina Eckes, 'EU Accession to the ECHR: Between Autonomy and Adaptation' (2013) 76 MLR 254; Paul Mahoney, 'From Strasbourg to Luxembourg and Back: Speculating about Human Rights Protection in the European Union after the Treaty of Lisbon' (2011) 31 HRLJ 73.

14 For example Steven Greer and Luzius Wildhaber, 'Revisiting the Debate about "Constitutionalising" the European Court of Human Rights' (2013) 12 HRLR 655; Jonas Christoffersen, 'Individual or Constitutional Justice: Can the Power Balance of Adjudication Be Reversed?', in Jonas Christoffersen and Mikael Rask Madsen (eds), *The European Court of Human Rights between Law and Politics* (Oxford University Press, 2013) 181; Andreas Føllesdal, Birgit Peters and Geir Ulfstein, *Constituting Europe: The European Court of Human Rights in a National, European and Global Context* (Cambridge University Press, 2013).

15 Joint communication from Presidents Costa and Skouris, 24 January 2011 <http://curia.europa.eu/jcms/upload/docs/application/pdf/2011-02/cedh_cjue_english.pdf> accessed 21 August 2015, para. 1.

can be reached where relevant.[16] The ECJ's opinion on the Draft Accession Agreement has, however, to a certain extent exposed the complexities of this idealised vision for 'European' human rights protection, including the problematic issue of deciding where floors and ceilings of human rights protection lie.[17] In this context, it should be noted that the content of protected rights and the level of protection is to a large extent decided through application in concrete cases, heavily influenced by the ECHR margin of appreciation doctrine or similar methods of calibrating intensity of review in the EU context. As the relationship between the two European legal regimes on one hand and the national level on the other is governed by different principles and doctrines, it is mostly approached from the perspective of either EU law or the law of the ECHR. Studies adopting a common frame of reference for analysing the national relationship with both regimes are, accordingly, extremely few and far between.[18] Specifically, the margin of appreciation doctrine has not been analysed clearly from an ECHR–EU comparative perspective, which hampers a common understanding of how 'European' baselines are formed.[19] Also, although widely commented on in the literature, the key legal tools used to navigate the complex relationship between the respective actors (the principle of subsidiarity, the margin of appreciation (or similar techniques) and the ECtHR pilot judgment procedure) are underdeveloped theoretically,[20] and in need of some rethinking in light of the emerging landscape.

In light of all the above, this book is intended to take a critical look at the forces influencing shifting centres of gravity in European human rights protection and the implications thereof for the future of human rights protection in Europe; and to contribute to the rethinking of current doctrinal approaches to the navigation of the ECHR–EU–national triangle of human rights protection.

16 Draft Accession Agreement (n. 6), Preamble; Joint communication from Presidents Costa and Skouris (ibid.); Peter Van Elsuwege, 'New Challenges for Pluralist Adjudication after Lisbon: The Protection of Fundamental Rights in a Ius Commune' (2012) 30 NQHR 195, 216; Paul Gragl, '(Judicial) Love Is Not a One-Way Street: The EU Preliminary Reference Procedure as a Model for ECtHR Advisory Opinions under Protocol No. 16' (2013) 38 EL Rev 229, 237.

17 See Article 53 ECHR, Article 53 CFR and Case C-399/11 *Stefano Melloni* v. *Ministerio Fiscal* (Judgment 26 February 2013).

18 But see Giuseppe Martinico, 'Is the European Convention Going to Be the "Supreme"? A Comparative-Constitutional Overview of ECHR and EU Law before National Courts' (2012) 23 EJIL 401.

19 Janneke Gerards, 'Pluralism, Deference and the Margin of Appreciation Doctrine' (2011) 17 ELJ 80, uses elements of the ECHR doctrine as a 'source of inspiration' (102) for arguments on the development of a (different) margin of appreciation doctrine in the EU context, without much analysis of if and how current practices are comparable.

20 Andreas Follesdal, 'The Principle of Subsidiarity as a Constitutional Principle of International Law' (2013) 2 *Global Constitutionalism* 37; George Letsas, *A Theory of Interpretation of the European Convention on Human Rights* (Oxford University Press, 2007) 81; Jan Kratochvíl, 'The Inflation of the Margin of Appreciation by the European Court of Human Rights' (2011) 29 NQHR 324, 325.

The first part of the book focuses on interactions in the triangle from an institutional and constitutional point of view. The contributions reflect how the key actors are trying to define their position vis-à-vis one another in a never-ending process. Groussot, Arold Lorenz and Petursson in Chapter 2 address the *telos*, the goals of the two European courts and the extent to which they align or clash. Proceeding from the stance that accession to the ECHR is valuable for the EU in terms of a better protection of the rights of individual citizens, they examine the ECJ case law after six years of application of the EU Charter of Fundamental Rights and the situation after the delivery of Opinion 2/13, and ask whether the aim of the full protection of fundamental rights in Europe can be reconciled with the effectiveness of EU law. Addressing also the relationship between the two European rights regimes, Björgvinsson in Chapter 3 discusses the EU's increased engagement with fundamental rights, Opinion 2/13, the *Bosphorus Airways* 'presumption of Convention compliance' for EU law, and the environment of political and judicial resentment that currently exists in the ECtHR. He argues that these developments have weakened the Court's claim to continue to play a leading role in European human rights protection on a pan-European level, and that they signal a shift in the centre of gravity from Strasbourg to Luxembourg. Turning, more specifically, to the relationship of the ECtHR with national courts, Ulfstein in Chapter 4 argues that the Court is an international court with constitutional functions in the national legal orders and that it should therefore be subject to constitutional standards adapted to its status as an international court. On the back of this approach, his chapter moves on to address how the ECtHR and national courts act – and should act – as part of a constitutional system across the international–national division. Martinico continues with this theme in Chapter 5 and examines the place of the European Convention in national constitutional law from the perspective of the 'price of success'. This, he argues, manifests itself when national judges first comply with the procedural duty in domestic law to take the case law of the Strasbourg Court into account, but then decide to depart from the concrete results reached by the ECtHR. Finally, Thorarensen in Chapter 6 critically reviews an upcoming new tool which it was hoped would establish a more fruitful 'constitutional' interaction between national judges and the ECtHR: the advisory opinion procedure of Protocol 16 ECHR.

The second part of the book aims to rethink a number of both classic and more recent doctrines and tools which have helped to shape interactions within the triangle. Part II reflects many of the ways in which the various actors can show higher or lower degrees of restraint towards one another in their case law, where the underlying assumption seems to be that the more serious one actor performs its task, the more leeway it can 'earn' from the other actors in the triangle. In Chapter 7 Buyse looks at how these shifts may have worked in the pilot judgment procedure of the Strasbourg Court, which has partially led to realignments both between the European and national levels but also between various Council of Europe institutions as well as within domestic systems. Turning then to doctrines of judicial restraint, Nic Shuibhne in Chapter 8 argues that while the ECJ rarely refers explicitly to a 'margin of appreciation', it does apply a comparable margin of discretion method in situations where fundamental rights and EU free movement rights come into conflict. While she argues that these developments also fit with the Charter of Fundamental Rights, she cautions about the implications of permitted differentiation for the classical requirement of uniform application of EU law across all of the Member States. Çalı in Chapter 9 argues that the ECtHR has started to shift its flexible case-by-case approach towards a variable standard of judicial review which manifests itself in a 'responsible courts doctrine'. Under this doctrine, the Court exhibits more leniency to domestic courts that take the case law of the ECtHR seriously. She argues that while such a doctrine offers a way out of criticisms of the Court as micro-managing well-established judiciaries, it also entails some costs and risks. Moving on to a comparative perspective, Arnardóttir and Guðmundsdóttir in Chapter 10 compare the margin of appreciation doctrine at the European Court of Human Rights with the exercise of judicial restraint at the European Court of Justice. They elaborate a distinction between systemic and normative elements of restraint (the former is, for example, reflected in Çalı's responsible courts doctrine) and find that despite being differently situated in the respective legal systems, and despite presenting core issues in different terms, there are some striking similarities in approaches to judicial restraint across both courts. Finally, in Chapter 11 Follesdal places the whole issue of interactions between actors in a wider politico-philosophical perspective, arguing for a more justifiable 'person-centric' conception of subsidiarity to inform doctrines of judicial restraint and balance respect for the sovereignty of states with protection of the human rights.

We sincerely hope that this book will be of interest not just to legal scholars, but also to those who study human rights from other perspectives such as political science or European studies. It is an explicit attempt to bring together the perspectives of Strasbourg, Luxembourg and national legal orders by analysing their interactions. Gravity may lead to matters coming closer together, but may equally cause clashes. This book analyses both possibilities in the constantly evolving European human rights architecture.

2 The paradox of human rights protection in Europe: two courts, one goal?

Xavier Groussot, Nina-Louisa Arold Lorenz and Gunnar Thor Petursson

1 Introduction

Two international courts, two different personalities, two different procedures. One of these courts, the Court of Justice of the European Union (ECJ), is the highest judicial body of the European Union. The other, the European Court of Human Rights (ECtHR), is the high court that handles issues arising under the European Convention of Human Rights.[1] Already in 1953, in its draft treaty establishing a European Community, the ad hoc assembly of the European Coal and Steel Community provided for the integration of the substantive provisions of the ECHR in the Treaty. Yet, the

> Omission of a reference to fundamental rights in the ECSC and the EEC treaties was because, in the opinion of their authors, these were economic treaties with implications for the protection of fundamental rights. By contrast, when it came to founding a political community, the issue of protection of fundamental rights, returned to the forefront.[2]

In parallel to the debate on accession, it is well known that protection of fundamental rights developed mainly through the case law on general principles of the Court of Justice.[3] As a result of its unwritten and casuistic nature, the protection

1 See L. Friedman (foreword) in N.-L. Arold Lorenz, X. Groussot and G. T. Petursson, *The European Human Rights Culture: A Paradox of Human Rights Protection in Europe* (Nijhoff, 2013).

2 J. P. Jacqué, 'The Accession of the European Union to the European Convention on Human Rights and Fundamental Freedoms' (2011) 48 CML Rev 995.

3 See the Joint Declaration of the European Parliament, the Council and the Commission of 5 April 1977 [1977] OJ C103/1. This declaration indicates the importance of fundamental rights as part of the general principles of law recognised by EC law and emphasises the key role played by the ECHR. Initially, the protection of fundamental rights was believed to fall outside the scope of Union competences, and the ECJ refused to rule on that matter.

of fundamental rights in the European Union has often been a source of inconsistencies.[4]

The accession of the EU to the ECHR may put an end to these inconsistencies.[5] This accession is now required by Article 6(2) TEU of the Lisbon Treaty and it was on its way to become a reality until the somewhat surprising outcome of Opinion 2/13 in December 2014.[6] Accession is valuable for the Union as it means that the rights of individual citizens would be more closely protected. If this is truly the case, accession to the ECHR should then be viewed as a new shift in the protection of rights in the EU and a new dimension to inter-institutional judicial relationships. Arguably, with accession to the ECHR, there will be a shift in the centre of gravity of the protection of human rights in Europe. But what is the situation at this time in the CJEU case law after six years of application of the EU Charter of Fundamental Rights and also after the delivery of Opinion 2/13? From the summer of 2005 onwards, there has been an increase in human rights topics being invoked at Luxembourg. This is also noticed in the literature. Partly, this is caused by the parties in a procedure invoking human rights more frequently,[7] partly by judges themselves who are more inclined to invoke human rights issues. It is not only broader competences that explain such expected increase in human rights issues. Also the general awareness of human rights has grown and stimulates outside demand on the Court. Most judges found the increase in human rights issues in their own case law a natural development from the general principles of law.[8] The very existence of the Charter – a written norm for the protection of human rights in Europe – is certainly not foreign to such a development. Human rights have become the daily business at the ECJ. However, there are multiple recent examples where the Court seems to hide or refrain from the application of the EU Charter of Fundamental Rights – thus leading to an incoherent application of this now binding instrument. At the same time, the Court refers less and less to the ECtHR. So there is also a move towards an autonomous interpretation of the EU fundamental rights. Can this evolution be explained solely by a claim for autonomy vis-à-vis the ECHR? Or is this the

4 W. van Gerven, 'Toward a Coherent Constitutional System within the European Union' (1996) 2 *European Public Law* 81, 98.

5 See C. Timmermans, 'Will the Accession of the EU to the European Convention of Human Rights Fundamentally Change the Relationship between the Luxemburg and the Strasbourg Courts?', CJC DL 2014/01 – Centre for Judicial Cooperation.

6 Opinion 2/13, Delivered on 18 December 2014 (full court), nyr.

7 Arold Lorenz, Groussot and Petursson (n. 1) 152. 'I think first of all that there is a change in the arguments presented to us. In most cases the human rights question or argument is brought by the parties or the intervening parties and is not *ex officio* brought up by the Court itself' (interviewee J).

8 See interviewees A, B, C, D, E, G, J, L, ibid: 'I think certainly it will be inevitable that questions of fundamental rights will increase in our Court. So our Court will increasingly become a fundamental rights court due to many reasons. Because of the new areas of competences we gained, because of the expansion of the scope application of Community law, and therefore even of fundamental rights of the Community legal order with regard to 27 member states' (interviewee G).

result of the main goal of the ECJ: to ensure the respect of EU law (and therefore not to ensure the respect in particular of fundamental rights)?[9] The relationship between the EU and ECHR legal orders has always been a complicated one, whereas the protection of human rights in Europe should be effective. This is a paradox. Would the accession of the EU to the ECHR have solved this paradox by rendering this relationship less complicated and more coherent? And, in the current landscape, is there or should there be any impact of Opinion 2/13 on the relationship between the two courts?

2 The paradox of coherence and the Charter

With the entry into force of the Lisbon Treaty, the Charter has finally become a legally binding document, a core element of the Union's legal order and, more importantly to us, the starting point for the Court in Luxembourg for assessing the compatibility of acts with EU fundamental rights.[10] The general principles are, therefore, no longer the exclusive guiding norms to ensure the protection of fundamental rights within the EU. The argument to view the Charter as the new guiding norm (*leitnormen*) is not only confirmed by the text of Article 6 TEU but also by the recent case law of the ECJ such as *Volker-Schecke*,[11] *Test-Achats*[12] and *Digital Rights*.[13] In Case C-236/09 *Test-Achats*, a preliminary ruling from the Belgian Constitutional Court on the validity of Article 5(2) of Directive 2004/113, the ECJ assessed the EU secondary legislation in light of the principle of equality between men and women. It appears clear from its reasoning that the starting point of its inquiry is the Charter,[14] more precisely its Articles 21 and 23 that state that any discrimination based on sex is prohibited and that equality between men and women must be ensured in all areas. Since recital 4 to Directive 2004/113 expressly refers to Articles 21 and 23 of the Charter, the validity of

9 See AG Maduro in Joined Cases C-402/05 and C-415/05 *Kadi and Al Barakaat* [2008] ECR I-6351, para. 37.

10 Concerning the use of the Charter as a starting point in EU adjudication, see e.g. Opinion of AG Bot in Case C-108/10 *Ivana Skattolon* [2011] ECR I-7491. See also Joint Communication from Presidents Costa and Skouris, 24 January 2011, para. 1.

11 Joined Cases C-92/09 and C-93/09 *Volker und Markus Schecke and Eifert* [2010] ECR I-11163.

12 Case C-236/09 *Association Belge des Consommateurs Test-Achats ASBL and Others* [2011] ECR I-773.

13 Joined Cases C-293/12 and C-594/12 *Digital Rights Ireland and Seitlinger and Others* [2014] nyr.

14 *Test-Achats* (n. 12), paras 16 and 32. One should highlight here that the question put by the national court was formulated in light of Article 6(2) EU. As put by the Court, 'Article 6(2) EU, to which the national court refers in its questions and which is mentioned in recital 1 to Directive 2004/113, provides that the European Union is to respect fundamental rights as guaranteed by the European Convention for the Protection of Human Rights and Fundamental Freedoms and as they result from the constitutional traditions common to the Member States, as general principles of Community law. Those fundamental rights are incorporated in the Charter, which, with effect from 1 December 2009, has the same legal status as the Treaties.'

Article 5(2) of that Directive must be assessed in the light of those provisions.[15] It is also worth noting that although the facts of the *Test-Achats* case were prior to the entry into force of the Charter (the reference was lodged on 29 June 2009) and although the national court in its question does not mention the Charter, this did not constitute an obstacle to relying on the Charter as the starting point of the inquiry on the compatibility of the Directive in light of the Charter. The Charter has even been given a retroactive effect that confirms, in our view, its status as *leitnormen*.[16]

In a similar vein, *Digital Rights* concerned two references (one from the High Court in Ireland and the other from the Constitutional Court in Austria) for a preliminary ruling on the validity of Directive 2006/24 on the retention of data generated or processed in connection with the provision of publicly available electronic communications services or of public communications networks. These questions give the opportunity to decide on the circumstances in which it is constitutionally possible for the EU to impose a limitation on the exercise of fundamental rights within the specific meaning of Article 52(1) of the Charter by means of a directive and the national measures transposing it. The Directive 2005/24 (notably Articles 4, 5 and 8) derogates from the system of protection of the right to privacy established by Directives 95/46 and 2002/58 with regard to the processing of personal data since it requires the retention of the data and allows the national authorities to access those data. In that sense, Article 5 of the directive constitutes in itself an interference with the rights guaranteed by Article 7 of the Charter on the right to privacy.[17] Articles 4 and 8 laying down rules relating to the competent national authorities' accessing the data also constitute an interference with the rights guaranteed by Article 7 of the Charter. And Directive 2006/24 constitutes an interference with the fundamental right to the protection of personal data guaranteed by Article 8 of the Charter because it provides for the processing of personal data. The reasoning of the ECJ in *Digital Rights* is remarkable. Indeed, it relies on the Charter as the *leitnormen* to assess the validity of the data retention Directive and also refers to ECHR case law related to the right to privacy.[18] In the light of Article 52(1) of the Charter, the Court held that the retention of data for the purpose of allowing the competent national authorities to have possible access to those data, as required by Directive 2006/24, genuinely satisfies an objective of general interest, namely public security.[19] It then goes into the analysis of the proportionality of the interference. This principle entails that acts of the EU institutions be appropriate for attaining the legitimate

15 Ibid. para. 17. See also, to that effect, *Volker und Markus Schecke and Eifert* (n. 11), para. 46.
16 See Case C-555/07 *Kücükdeveci* [2010] ECR I-365, para. 22.
17 *Digital Rights Ireland* (n. 13), para. 34.
18 Ibid. para. 35. See, as regards Article 8 of the ECHR, *Leander* v. *Sweden* App. No. 9248/81 (ECtHR, 26 March 1987), para. 48; *Rotaru* v. *Romania* [GC] App. No. 28341/95 (ECtHR, 4 May 2000), para. 46; and *Weber and Saravia* v. *Germany* App. No. 54934/00 (adm dec, ECtHR 29 June 2006), para. 79.
19 Ibid. paras 41–44.

objectives pursued by the legislation at issue and do not exceed the limits of what is appropriate and necessary in order to achieve those objectives.[20]

The ECJ, relying again on ECHR case law, considers that the EU's legislative discretion should be limited due to the nature of the rights at issue guaranteed by the Charter, i.e. the protection of personal data strongly connected to the right to respect for private life,[21] and the extent and seriousness of the interference.[22] The judicial review of the EU measure must therefore be strict. This position is also verified by settled case law which states that derogations and limitations to the protection of personal data must apply only in so far as are strictly necessary.[23] By analogy to the Strasbourg case law on Article 8 ECHR,[24] the ECJ considers that the EU legislation at issue must lay down clear and precise rules governing the scope and application of the measure in question and impose minimum safeguards so that the persons whose data have been retained have sufficient guarantees to effectively protect their personal data against the risk of abuse and against any unlawful access and use of that data.[25] The need for such safeguards is all the more important where personal data are subjected to automatic processing and where there is a significant risk of unlawful access to those data as it is laid down in Data Retention Directive.[26] For the Court, the directive does not lay down clear and precise rules governing the extent of the interference with the fundamental rights enshrined in Articles 7 and 8 of the Charter and therefore the Court concludes that Directive 2006/24 entails a wide-ranging and particularly serious interference with those fundamental rights in the legal order of the EU, without such an interference being precisely circumscribed by provisions to ensure that it is actually limited to what is strictly necessary.[27] The EU legislature has exceeded the limits imposed by the principle of proportionality in the light of Articles 7, 8 and 52(1) of the Charter.[28]

But after six years of application by the ECJ, can we really say that the Charter is the true guiding norm? A rapid look at the CJEU case law allows us to conclude that reference to fundamental rights standards is not systematic in EU litigation.

20 Ibid. paras 45–46.

21 Ibid. para. 53. The Court noted that the protection of personal data resulting from the explicit obligation laid down in Article 8(1) of the Charter is especially important for the right to respect for private life enshrined in Article 7 of the Charter.

22 Ibid. paras 47–48. Here, the Court draws an analogy with the case law of the ECtHR on Article 8 ECHR (*S and Marper* v. *United Kingdom* App. Nos 30562/04 and 30566/04 (ECtHR, 4 December 2008), para. 102).

23 Ibid. para. 52. Referring to Case C-473/12 *IPI* [2013] nyr, para. 39.

24 See, by analogy, as regards Article 8 of the ECHR, *Liberty and Others* v. *United Kingdom* App. No. 58243/00 (ECtHR, 1 July 2008), paras 62 and 63; *Rotaru* v. *Romania* (n. 18), paras 57–59; and *S and Marper* v. *United Kingdom* (n. 22), para. 99.

25 Ibid. para. 54.

26 Ibid. para. 55. See, by analogy, as regards Article 8 of the ECHR, *S and Marper* v. *United Kingdom* (n. 22), para. 103, and *M. K.* v. *France* App. No. 19522/09 (ECtHR, 18 April 2013), para. 35.

27 Ibid. paras 58–65.

28 Ibid. para. 69.

Often the Court follows an orthodox approach of the *ultra petita* principle in action in judicial review under Article 263 TFEU whereas it could view EU fundamental rights as *moyen d'ordre public*. This lack of systematic use of EU fundamental rights is also detectable in preliminary ruling references. Three Grand Chamber cases offer in that sense an excellent illustration, i.e. *Römer*,[29] *Ruiz Zambrano*[30] and *Dominguez*.[31] In *Römer* and *Dominguez*, the CJEU failed to refer to respectively Article 21(1) Charter and Article 31(2) Charter in cases concerning the recognition of general principles of EU law. In *Ruiz Zambrano*, the CJEU in a cryptic reasoning focused merely on a citizenship provision (Article 20 TFEU) and failed to give guidelines on the right to family protection under Article 7 of the Charter. These cases reflect judicial minimalism in the context of EU fundamental rights.[32] Moreover, in the recent *Google* case from 2014, the ECJ should have in our view referred to Article 11 of the Charter on freedom to expression but failed to so in making merely reference to Article 7 and of the Charter.

These are examples of judicial minimalism,[33] which can be assessed as the result of the special dynamics established by the preliminary reference procedure. Sometimes the CJEU has the possibility to solve cases either from the angle of EU fundamental rights or in another manner.[34] For instance, *Ruiz Zambrano* was a judgment that could have been dealt with merely in terms of citizenship or free movement of persons, or on the grounds of the fundamental right to family life. In *Google*, it was enough for the Court to rely heavily on secondary legislation to show the 'vel of protection' of fundamental rights and not using Article 11 of the Charter in a balancing of interests with Article 7 and 8 of the Charter.[35] As underlined by Sarmiento:

> Minimalism plays an important role here, for it is the means through which the ECJ refrains from acting as a Court that *promotes* (and not only *guarantees*) the protection of fundamental rights, affecting, at the same time, the way in which the EC[t]HR reacts to cases under the scope of application of EU Law.[36]

Moreover, if the Charter is the true guiding (written) norm, the reference to (unwritten) general principles of EU law in the ECJ's case law should cease.

29 Case C-147/08 *Römer* [2011] ECR I-3591.
30 Case C-34/09 *Ruiz Zambrano* [2011] ECR I-1177.
31 Case C-282/10 *Dominguez* [2012] nyr.
32 D. Sarmiento, 'Half a Case at a Time: Dealing with Judicial Minimalism at the European Court of Justice', in P. Popelier, C. Van de Heyning and P. Van Nuffel (eds), *Human Rights Protection in the European Legal Order: The Interaction between the European and the National Courts* (Intersentia, 2011) 65.
33 See L. Pech, 'Between Judicial Minimalism and Avoidance Strategy: On the Court of Justice's Sidestepping of the Fundamental Constitutional Issues in the Cases of *Römer* and*Dominguez*' (2012) 49 CML Rev 1841. See *Dominguez* (n. 31), para. 16.
34 See Sarmiento (n. 32).
35 Case C-131/12 *Google Spain* [2014] nyr.
36 Ibid.

Looking at the text of Article 6 TEU, this situation is seen as perhaps the most coherent solution and the general principles could perform a more modest role, lying dormant in most situations. This is obviously not the situation when looking at the recent ECJ jurisprudence.[37] The general principles of EU law are still quite present in the Court's case law. It seems that the Court has had problems getting rid of its arsenal of general principles.[38] This reluctance is perhaps not so surprising given the flexibility of such unwritten norms. In that respect, Wimmer provides two main reasons for explaining such a situation: first, general principles are part of the 'argumentative budget' of the legal professions and enables an autonomous legal discourse. Second, the general principles serve as cement between various sources of law and are a factor of increasing coherence within the system. In other words, the main reason for keeping the general principles is to allow a sound balance between consistency and flexibility in the case law of the Court.[39] Problematically, the very existence of multi-norms of fundamental rights protection may lead to a divergent standard of protection. However, such a risk is in our view quite limited given the ruling in the *Åkerberg* case which arguably unifies the personal scope of protection of general principles and rights enshrined within the Charter. In the end, to come back to the main issue of this section and to paraphrase Cruz-Villalón, the Charter does not offer a glamorous presence and it is thus difficult to view it as a true guiding norm.[40]

3 The paradox of autonomy and the ECHR

Recently, some scholars criticised what they saw as a significant decrease in the ECJ's citation of the Convention text and case law, and cautioned against an

37 See Joined Cases C-29/13 and 30/13 *Global Trans Lodzhistik* [2014], nyr; para. 57. According to the Court, it must be noted that observance of the rights of the defence is a general principle of European Union law which applies where the authorities are minded to adopt a measure which will adversely affect an individual. See also Case C-206/13 *Siragusa* [2014] nyr, paras 33–34. According to the Court: 'It follows from all the foregoing that it has not been established that the Court has jurisdiction to interpret Article 17 of the Charter, (see, to that effect, Case C-245/09 *Omalet* [2010] ECR I-13771, para. 18; see also the Orders in Case C-457/09 *Chartry* [2011] ECR I-819, paras 25 and 26; Case C-134/12 *Corpul Național al Polițiștilor* [2012] ECR, para. 15; Case C-498/12 *Pedone* [2013] ECR, para. 15; and Case C-371/13 *SC Schuster & Co Ecologic* [2013] ECR, para. 18). As for the principle of proportionality, this is one of the general principles of EU law which must be observed by any national legislation which falls within the scope of EU law or which implements that law (see, to that effect, Case 77/81 *Zuckerfabrik Franken* [1982] ECR 681, para. 22; Case 382/87 *Buet and EBS* [1989] ECR 1235, para. 11; Case C-2/93 *Exportslachterijen van Oordegem* [1994] ECR I-2283, para. 20; and Joined Cases C-422/09, C-425/09 and C-426/09 *Vandorou and Others* [2010] ECR I-12411, para. 65).

38 See P. Cruz-Villalón, 'Rights in Europe: the Crowded House', King's College Working Paper 01/2012.

39 M. Wimmer, 'The Dinghy's Rudder: General Principles of European Union Law through the Lens of Proportionality' (2014) 20 *European Public Law* 331, 342.

40 Cruz-Villalón (n. 38).

isolated or autonomous interpretation of the Charter. For instance, de Búrca analysed that from December 2009 to December 2012, the ECJ referred to the Charter in 78 cases.[41] In these cases, the ECJ made only 15 references to the European Convention of Human Rights. Similarly the General Court at the same time made reference to the Charter in 26 cases with only six references to the ECHR.[42] It is also often the situation that when the Court refers to the ECHR, its reference to the ECtHR's case law is quite limited as is visible from judgments such as *ZZ* or *Melloni*.[43] One Advocate General (Interview G) also expressed the view that the Court is bound to change:

> The CJEU will more become a fundamental rights court. It should have a larger symmetry with the fundamental rights jurisprudence of the European Court of Human Rights, but with the expansion of the rules of the fundamental rights in our Community legal order, it is inevitable that there will probably be a pull toward a stronger autonomy in the case law of our Court with regard to fundamental rights. Not simply to follow the standard of Strasbourg.[44]

This analysis is confirmed by the recent case law of the ECJ in many Grand Chamber cases that do not explicitly mention the ECHR standards such as *Toshiba Corporations, Åkerberg, Sky Österreich, Google* or *Spasic*.[45] This situation also clashes with the obligation to take account of the case law of the ECHR in accordance with Article 52(3) of the Charter when the rights are corresponding between the ECHR and the Charter, as established in *Jaramillo*.[46] The lack of reference to the ECHR can be explained by the existence of the Charter which establishes a visible EU standard of fundamental rights protection. In *Otis* and *Chalkor*, the ECJ stated that because effective judicial protection is secured by Article 47 of the Charter, reference should be made *only* to that provision.[47] In

41 G. de Búrca, 'After the EU Charter of Fundamental Rights: The Court of Justice as a Human Rights Adjudicator?' (2013) 20 *Maastricht Journal of European and Comparative Law* 168, 171.

42 Ibid.

43 See Case C-300/11 *ZZ* [2013] nyr; and Case C-399/11*Melloni* [2013] nyr.

44 Arold Lorenz, Groussot and Petursson (n. 1) 152.

45 Case C-17/12 *Toshiba Corporations* [2012] nyr; Case C-617/10 *Åkerberg* [2013] nyr; Case C-283/11 *Sky Österreich* [2013] nyr; *Google* (n. 35); and Case C-129/14 PPU *Zoran Spasic* [2014] nyr.

46 AG Maduro in Case C-465/07 *Elgafagi* [2009] ECR I-921, para. 23; and Case C-334/12 RX-II *Jaramillo* [2013] nyr, para. 43. According to the Court, reference must be made to the case law of the ECtHR in accordance with Article 52(3) of the Charter.

47 Case C-199/11 *Otis* [2013] nyr; paras 46–47. C-386/10 P *Chalkor* [2011] ECR I-13085, paras 46–47. It must be borne in mind in that regard that the principle of effective judicial protection is a general principle of EU law, to which expression is now given by Article 47 of the Charter (see Case C-279/09 *DEB* [2010] ECR I-13849, paras 30 and 31; order in Case C-457/09 *Chartry* [2011] ECR I-819, para. 25; and Case C-69/10 *Samba Diouf* [2011] ECR I-7151, para. 49). Article 47 of the Charter

Radu, the Grand Chamber noted that 'the right to be heard, which is guaranteed by Article 6 of the ECHR and mentioned by the referring court in its questions, is today laid down in Articles 47 and 48 of the Charter. It is therefore necessary to refer to those provisions of the Charter.'[48] This autonomous interpretation of the Charter in isolation from the ECHR can also be explained by the specific nature of the rights enshrined in the Charter. In fact, we find rights which do not find an explicit expression in the ECHR, e.g. the principle of good administration under Article 41 of the Charter,[49] or rights which have a scope of protection different from the ECHR, e.g. the *ne bis in idem* principle under Article 50 of the Charter, which also covers cross-border situations.[50] It may also be so that the ECHR case law conflicts with an EU policy as can be the scenario in EU competition law, asylum policy, or mutual recognition of judgments in surrogacy matters.[51] The lack of reference to the ECtHR's case law could be viewed here as more instrumental and this reading is confirmed by Opinion 2/13.[52]

It is worth looking in more detail at two Grand Chamber cases of the ECJ delivered in 2014: *Google*[53] and *Spasic*.[54] In *Google*, Mr Costeja González lodged a complaint against a daily newspaper (*La Vanguardia*) with a large circulation, in particular in Catalonia (Spain). The complaint was based on the fact that, when an internet user entered his name in the 'Google Search', he would obtain links to two pages of *La Vanguardia*, on which his name appeared for a real-estate auction connected with attachment proceedings for the recovery of social security debts. Mr Costeja González requested both the newspaper and Google to remove or conceal the personal data relating to him. In this case, the ECJ had to interpret Directive 95/46 on the processing of personal data in commercial matters and assess the scope of protection of Articles 7 (right to privacy) and 8 (right to data protection) of the EU Charter of Fundamental Rights. It is worth noting that the Court did not refer to any Strasbourg case law and merely focused on the objective of Directive 95/46 which is accordingly to ensure the effective and complete protection of the fundamental rights and freedoms of natural persons, and in particular their right to privacy, with respect to the processing of personal data. It insists very clearly on the need to respect the right to privacy with respect to the

secures in EU law the protection afforded by Article 6(1) of the ECHR. It is necessary, therefore, to refer only to Article 47 (Case C-386/10 P *Chalkor* v. *Commission* [2011] ECR I-13085, para. 51).

48 Case C-396/11 *Radu* [2013] nyr, para. 32.

49 Case C-604/12 *H. N.* [2014] nyr.

50 *Spasic* (n. 45).

51 See e.g. Case C-17/12 *Toshiba Corporations* [2012] nyr. See L. Bay Larssen, 'Some Reflections on Mutual Recognition in the Area of Freedom, Security and Justice', in P. Cardonnel, A. Rosas and N. Wahl (eds), *Constitutionalising the EU Judicial System: Essays in Honour of Pernilla Lindh* (Hart, 2012) 139, 150–152. The ECJ judge questions the application of Article 8 ECHR in the context of mutual recognition of judgments in cases of child abduction and the application of Regulation No. 2201/2003.

52 See section 4 below on Opinion 2/13.

53 *Google* (n. 35).

54 *Spasic* (n. 45).

processing of personal data in the context of commercial and advertising activity. Relying on the text of the Directive, it shows that this right has 'special importance' and therefore cannot be interpreted restrictively.[55] The analysis does not take into consideration Article 11 of the Charter on the freedom of expression and information. There is no balancing realised by the Court between the right to privacy and the freedom of expression. For the Court, the level of protection seems to stem from the EU's secondary legislation. The *Google* case reflects, in that sense, a very autonomous interpretation of EU law. This is in sharp contrast with the Opinion of Advocate General Jääskinen in the same judgment. The Advocate General establishes a clear bridge between the provision of the Charter and the European Convention of Human Rights, particularly between Article 7 of the Charter and Article 8 ECHR, which 'must be duly taken into account in the interpretation of the relevant provisions of the Directive, which requires the Member States to protect *in particular* the right to privacy'.[56] For him, Article 8 ECHR also covers issues relating to protection of personal data. For this reason, and in conformity with Article 52(3) of the Charter, the case law of the ECtHR on Article 8 ECHR is relevant both to the interpretation of Article 7 of the Charter and to the application of the Directive in conformity with Article 8 of the Charter.[57] Moreover, the Advocate General balanced the right to privacy with the right of freedom of expression enshrined in Article 11 of the Charter and referred once again to ECtHR case law.[58] This 'pluralist' reasoning is strikingly dissimilar to the one of the ECJ.

The lack of references to the ECHR is also visible in the *Spasic* judgment.[59] The national court asks whether Article 54 of the Agreement Implementing the Schengen Convention (CISA), which subjects the application of the *ne bis in idem* principle to the condition that, upon conviction and sentencing, the penalty imposed 'has been enforced', is 'actually in the process of being enforced' or 'can no longer be enforced' ('the execution condition'), is compatible with Article 50 of the Charter, in which that principle is enshrined. As a preliminary point, it is important to emphasise that whereas Article 50 of the Charter applies both to

55 Ibid. para. 58.
56 Ibid. paras 111–114.
57 Ibid. paras 115–116.
58 Ibid. paras 120–123. In *Times Newspapers Ltd* v. *the United Kingdom (Nos. 1 and 2)* v. *United Kingdom* (App. Nos 3002/03 and 23676/03) ECHR 2009, para. 45, the ECtHR observed that internet archives make a substantial contribution to preserving and making available news and information: 'Such archives constitute an important source for education and historical research, particularly as they are readily accessible to the public and are generally free … However, the margin of appreciation afforded to States in striking the balance between the competing rights is likely to be greater where news archives of past events, rather than news reporting of current affairs, are concerned. In particular, the duty of the press to act in accordance with the principles of responsible journalism by ensuring *accuracy* [our emphasis] of historical, rather than perishable, information published is likely to be more stringent in the absence of any urgency in publishing the material.'
59 *Spasic* (n. 45).

internal and cross-border situations and whereas Article 54 CISA applies only in cross-border situations, Article 4 of Protocol 7 ECHR applies only to internal situations. It is well known that Article 54 CISA imposes an additional condition (the execution condition) different from Article 50 of the Charter.[60] Also, this condition does not correspond to the derogations authorised by Article 4 of Protocol 7 ECHR. The application of this condition could be seen as contrary to the ECHR case law if it occurred within the national context. Therefore a rigorous interpretation of the Charter in light of ECHR law will lead to a declaration of the execution condition as incompatible with Article 50 of the Charter. The ECJ in *Zoran Spasic* decided not so surprisingly to take another path more in line with the explanations of the Charter. Those seem to draw a distinction between purely national and cross-border situations when it comes to the application of the *ne bis in idem* principle.[61] Article 54 CISA must be regarded as respecting the essence of the *ne bis in idem* principle enshrined in Article 50 of the Charter.

However, it must be ascertained whether the restriction required by the execution condition referred to in Article 54 CISA is proportionate. In doing so, the Court pointed out that the execution condition enshrined in Article 54 CISA should be viewed in the light of its context, i.e. the EU's policy of ensuring a high level of security as laid down by Article 3(2) TEU and Article 67(3) TFEU.[62] In fact, the execution condition aims to prevent, in the area of freedom, security and justice, the impunity of persons definitively convicted and sentenced in an EU Member State. This constitutes an objective of general interest as required by Article 52(1) of the Charter.[63] For the Court, the execution condition laid down in Article 54 CISA does not go beyond what is necessary to prevent, in a cross-border context, the impunity of persons definitively convicted and sentenced in the European Union.[64] Therefore, the execution condition is compatible with Article 50 of the Charter.

The *Spasic* case shows the potential risk of conflict between an EU policy and the interpretation of an ECHR right. The reliance on the Charter by the Court allows an autonomous interpretation which does not irremediably undermine the EU policy. We can also ask ourselves whether this situation is a claim of autonomy towards the ECHR or whether it is merely a claim not to be a human rights court. As stressed by one judge (Interview B):

60 Ibid. para. 52.
61 See Opinion of AG Jääskinen in *Spasic* (n. 45), paras 70–72.
62 As can be seen from Article 67(3) TFEU, in order to achieve its objective of constituting an area of freedom, security and justice, the European Union endeavours to ensure a high level of security through measures to prevent and combat crime, and through measures for coordination and cooperation between police and judicial authorities and other competent authorities, as well as through the mutual recognition of judgments in criminal matters and, if necessary, through the approximation of criminal laws.
63 *Spasic* (n. 45), para. 65.
64 Ibid. para. 72.

> We are not a human rights court, and we are aware of that. This is not our main task, this a very important task for Europe, this is very important for the citizens of Europe and we do it but we do it as supreme court normally would do it and not as a human rights court would do it. Because a human rights court has exclusive competence to develop and to apply human rights. For us, we do it in the framework of our normal function; our normal function is to guarantee the uniform application of Community law, and this is the more important task of our Court.[65]

Here, the interviews at the ECJ provided clear reactions: the ECJ is not a human rights court, but human rights are part of several functions (interviewees D, I, P). Expressed in the words of an Advocate General (interviewee F): '[The ECJ] is no human rights court, only in extraordinary circumstances will human rights be invoked but in core it is an EU court.'[66] This vision of the ECJ court is powerfully confirmed by Opinion 2/13 which emphasises the crucial importance of respecting the autonomy of EU law.[67] A task endowed and only endowed to the ECJ.

4 The paradox of accession after Opinion 2/13

Opinion 2/13 – which comprises 258 paragraphs – was delivered on 18 December, only a few days before Christmas.[68] The Opinion of Advocate General Kokott was made public on the same day but written in June 2014.[69] While the Advocate General came to the conclusion that the accession was acceptable under certain conditions, the ECJ reached a negative conclusion. Before going into the reasoning of the ECJ and particularly its impact on the relationship between the two courts, it is worth noting that from our perspective the end result of Opinion 2/13 came as a surprise. In fact, all the Members States and the EU legislative institutions had agreed in principle on the compatibility of the accession. The Advocate General had convincingly opined on a conditional accession. The ECJ had participated actively in the negotiation process: first by issuing a position in 2010 and secondly by a joint declaration of Presidents Costa and Skouris. So everything seemed to point towards a positive (even if conditional) outcome on the accession of the EU to the ECHR. We were wrong. And the Court said no to the accession of the EU to the ECHR. An issue of crucial interest, in that respect, is whether we are dealing with a conditional no or a no *tout court*? It will be shown that the Court is saying no *tout court*. In our view, many of the conditional requirements suggested by the Court in Opinion 2/13 are simply unachievable.

65 Arold Lorenz, Groussot and Petursson (n. 1) 152.
66 Opinion 2/13 (n. 6).
67 See for a discussion on the relationship between ECHR and EU fundamental rights, K. Tuori, *European Constitutionalism* (Cambridge University Press, 2015) 99.
68 For an extensive comment on Opinion 2/13, see L. Halleskov Storgaard, 'EU Law Autonomy versus European Fundamental Rights Protection – on *Opinion 2/13* on EU Accession to the ECHR' (2015) 15 *Human Rights Law Review* 1.
69 The view of AG Kokott in Opinion 2/13 (n. 6) was delivered on 13 June 2014.

For Advocate General Kokott, in her view in Opinion 2/13, 'the devil is in the detail'.[70] In contrast, it may be said that for the ECJ, the devil seems to be everywhere.[71] The Court is particularly concerned by a clash of case law between the ECtHR and the CJEU. This clash is illustrated by the tension between the protection of human rights and the effectiveness of EU law. The general tone of the ECJ in the Opinion is very defensive and based on rhetoric of autonomy, exclusive jurisdiction and effectiveness. The *Melloni* case is at the heart of the reasoning of the Court,[72] which also goes very deep into the specific nature of EU law.[73] It is underlined that the EU constitutional framework is based on a particularly sophisticated institutional structure and a full set of legal rules to ensure its operation, which has consequences on the procedure for and conditions of accession to the ECHR.[74] As stated by the Court:

> These essential characteristics of EU law have given rise to a *structured network of principles,* rules and mutually interdependent legal relations linking the EU and its Member States, and its Member States with each other ... This legal structure is based on the fundamental premiss that each Member State shares with all the other Member States, and recognises that they share with it ... That premiss implies and justifies the existence of mutual trust between the Member States that those values will be recognised and, therefore, that the law of the EU that implements them will be respected.[75]

At the heart of this legal structure are the fundamental rights recognised by the EU Charter of Fundamental Rights. But the ECJ quickly refers to the need to respect the EU objectives which are closely connected to ensuring the effectiveness of the internal market and the process of integration.[76] So this setting gives the clear impression of a system of protection of fundamental rights limited by the broader EU legal order/system.

The reasoning of the ECJ in order to reject the accession to the ECHR is based on arguments which can be found not only within the Draft Accession Agreement such as the co-defendant mechanism and the prior involvement procedure; but also outside the explicit scope of the Draft Accession Agreement.[77] This last category enshrines in our view the strongest (policy) arguments against accession. Looking at the co-defendant mechanism, which has the aim of ensuring that

70 Ibid. The tone of the AG's view is positive, inclusive and constructive.

71 More precisely the devil seems to be in the case law related to the effectiveness of EU law, e.g. cases on Article 53 of the Charter and the issue of mutual trust, particularly entrenched in the freedom, security and justice area.

72 *Melloni* (n. 43).

73 Opinion 2/13 (n. 6), paras 153–172.

74 Ibid. para. 158.

75 Ibid. paras 167–168.

76 Ibid. paras 169–172.

77 It is important here to contrast AG Kokott's view, which focuses on the text of the DAA, particularly its Article 3.

proceedings brought before the ECtHR by non-Member States and individual applications are correctly addressed to Member States and/or the EU as appropriate, the Draft Agreement states that a contracting party is to become a co-defendant either by accepting an invitation from the ECtHR or by decision of the ECtHR upon the request of that contracting party. If the EU or Member States request leave to intervene as co-defendants in a case before the ECtHR, they must establish that the conditions for their participation in the procedure are fulfilled, with the ECtHR deciding on that request in the light of the plausibility of the reasons given. In carrying out such a review, the ECtHR would be required to test the rules of EU law governing the division of powers between the EU and its Member States as well as the criteria for the attribution of their acts or omissions.[78] The ECtHR could adopt a final decision in that respect which would be binding both on the Member States and on the EU. To consent to the ECtHR to adopt such a decision would risk adversely affecting the division of powers between the EU and its Member States.[79]

Furthermore, the ECJ expresses its position on the prior involvement procedure. First of all, it stresses that the question whether the Court has previously given a ruling on the same question of law as that at issue in the proceedings before the ECtHR can be resolved only by the competent EU institution, that institution's decision having to bind the ECtHR. To authorise the ECtHR to rule on such a question would be equivalent to confer on it jurisdiction to interpret the case law of the Court. Therefore, that procedure should be organised in such a way as to guarantee that, in any case pending before the ECtHR, the EU is completely and systematically informed, so that the competent institution is able to consider whether the Court has already given a ruling on the question at issue and, if not, to arrange for the prior involvement procedure to be initiated.[80] Second, the ECJ deems that the Draft Agreement excludes the possibility of bringing a matter before the Court in order for it to rule on a question of interpretation of EU secondary law by means of that procedure. Limiting the scope of that procedure exclusively to questions of validity irremediably affects the competences of the EU and the powers of the ECJ.[81]

The Court also raises four arguments outside the explicit scope of the Draft Accession Agreement: the first is connected to the relationship between Article 53 ECHR and 53 Charter; the second relates to the issue of mutual trust and effectiveness of EU law; the third considers the exclusive jurisdiction of the ECtHR in common foreign and security policy (CFSP) matters; the fourth concerns Protocol 16 to the ECHR. Concerning Protocol 16, the accession of the EU to the ECHR as envisaged by the Draft Agreement is capable of affecting the specific characteristics of EU law and its autonomy. Indeed, the ECJ expresses the view that a request for an advisory opinion made pursuant to Protocol No. 16 by a national

78 Opinion 2/13 (n. 6), paras 215–231.
79 Ibid. para. 234.
80 Ibid. paras 236–241.
81 Ibid. paras 242–247.

court of a Member State that has acceded to that protocol could trigger the procedure for the prior involvement of the Court of Justice, thus creating a risk of circumvention of the preliminary ruling procedure under Article 267 TFEU.[82]

For the ECJ, Article 53 ECHR – the so-called non-regression clause – should be coordinated with Article 53 of the Charter. The Court considers it should not be possible for the ECtHR to call into question the Court's findings in relation to the material scope of EU law, for the purposes, in particular, of determining whether a Member State is bound by fundamental rights of the EU. Referring to its *Melloni* judgment[83] it emphasises that Article 53 of the Charter is interpreted as meaning that the application of national standards of protection of fundamental rights must not compromise the level of protection provided for by the Charter or the primacy, unity and effectiveness of EU law.[84] Here, Article 53 Charter is interpreted as a 'limited best protection clause'.[85] According to the Court:

> In so far as Article 53 of the ECHR essentially reserves the power of the Contracting Parties to lay down higher standards of protection of fundamental rights than those guaranteed by the ECHR, that provision should be coordinated with Article 53 of the Charter, as interpreted by the Court of Justice, so that the power granted to Member States by Article 53 of the ECHR is limited – with respect to the rights recognised by the Charter that correspond to those guaranteed by the ECHR – to that which is necessary to ensure that the level of protection provided for by the Charter and the primacy, unity and effectiveness of EU law are not compromised.[86]

The Court considers that there is no provision in the Draft Accession Agreement to ensure such coordination.

The principle of mutual trust is a key element of Opinion 2/13.[87] The Court sees a tension between this fundamental principle of EU law and the Draft Accession Agreement.[88] As the Court phrases it:

> The approach adopted in the agreement envisaged, which is to treat the EU as a State and to give it a role identical in every respect to that of any other contracting party, specifically disregards the intrinsic nature of the EU and, in

82 Ibid. paras 198–200.
83 *Melloni* (n. 43), para. 60.
84 Opinion 2/13 (n. 6), paras 185–188.
85 For a more thorough discussion on Article 53 Charter, see X. Groussot and I. Olsson, 'Clarifying or Diluting the Application of the EU Charter of Fundamental Rights? The Judgments in *Åkerberg* and *Melloni* from the 26th of February 2013' (2013) *Lund Student EU Law Review* 1.
86 Opinion 2/13 (n. 6), para. 189.
87 See also para. 167 (ibid.). For a discussion on the principle of mutual trust, see K. Lenaerts, 'The principle of mutual recognition in the area of freedom, security and justice', Fourth Annual Sir Jeremy Lever Lecture, All Souls College, University of Oxford, 30 January 2015 (available online).
88 Opinion 2/13 (n. 6), para. 191.

particular, fails to take into consideration the fact that the Member States have, by reason of their membership of the EU, accepted that relations between them as regards the matters covered by the transfer of powers from the Member States to the EU are governed by EU law.[89]

This obligation of mutual trust is jeopardised by accession, which is liable to upset the balance of the EU and undermine the autonomy of EU law. Mutual trust is particularly present in the area of freedom, security and justice, where Member States are required, except in exceptional circumstances, to trust all the other Member States to be complying with EU law and particularly with the fundamental rights recognised by EU law.[90] This obligation based on automaticity may also conflict with the case-by-case analysis used in ECtHR cases to determine a breach of human rights.[91]

Finally, the Court examines the specific characteristics of EU law as regards judicial review in CFSP matters. It first notes that certain acts adopted in the context of the CFSP fall outside the ambit of judicial review by the Court of Justice. With accession as provided by the Draft Accession Agreement, the ECtHR would be empowered to rule on the compatibility with the ECHR of certain acts, actions or omissions performed in the context of the CFSP, and notably of those whose legality the Court of Justice cannot, for want of jurisdiction, review in the light of fundamental rights. As put by the Court, 'such a situation would effectively entrust the judicial review of those acts, actions or omissions on the part of the EU exclusively to a non-EU body, albeit that any such review would be limited to compliance with the rights guaranteed by the ECHR'.[92] Relying on Opinion 1/09, the ECJ concluded that jurisdiction cannot be conferred exclusively on an international court which is outside the institutional and judicial framework of the EU. The Draft Accession Agreement fails to take into consideration the specific characteristics of the EU.[93]

The two most problematic objections to get rid of if we wish to achieve accession in the future are in our view the 'CFSP' and 'Article 53' objections. Indeed, the argument based on Article 53 of the Charter imposes an interpretative diktat on the ECtHR as to the understanding of Article 53 ECHR. This is unacceptable. The 'CFSP' objection can only be solved by a reform of the Lisbon Treaty which would grant competence to the ECJ in 'CFSP' matters. The other arguments can quite easily be accommodated, even the tricky issue of mutual trust. Moreover, even if there is a willingness to consider all the objections of the ECJ, our position would be to refuse accession to the ECHR on a substantive basis. What would be the point in having an accession which grants a very specific status to the

89 Ibid. para. 194
90 See, to that effect, judgments in C-411/10 and C-493/10 *N. S. and Others* [2011] ECR I-13905, paras 78–80; and *Melloni* (n. 43), paras 37 and 63.
91 See e.g. App. No. 29217/12 *Tarakhel* [4 November 2014] and App. No. 14737/09 *Sneersone and Kampanella* [12 July 2011].
92 Opinion 2/13 (n. 6), para. 255.
93 Ibid. paras 256–257.

European Union and where the ECtHR would be extremely limited in reviewing EU acts? Should the effectiveness of EU law be taken into consideration by the ECtHR in its future judicial review? The adjudicative aim of the ECtHR in a scenario post accession should remain the same: the full protection of human rights in Europe. There is thus a danger of acceding to the ECHR by accepting all the conditions stipulated in Opinion 2/13.

In the present situation, many have argued that there is still an obligation to accede to the ECHR under Article 6(2) TEU. However, this obligation is conditioned by the willingness of the Council of Europe and the non-EU states to re-enter the negotiation. It is not crystal clear at this stage what will happen but one can imagine that Opinion 2/13 has certainly created muddied the waters. The President of the ECtHR Dean Spielmann has, for instance, openly stated that Opinion 2/13 was a great disappointment.[94] Some have also argued that the ECtHR may wish to retaliate by putting an end to the *Bosphorus* doctrine. Even if we may think that some judges at the ECtHR are tempted to argue so, we do not however think that this situation would become a reality – if only for political reasons.[95] We consider that the present situation is here to last for many years. If we are right, then Opinion 2/13 should also have an impact on the present ECJ case law on EU fundamental rights. As described earlier in this chapter, it appears that the ECJ uses a minimalist approach in relation to references both to the Charter and the ECtHR case law, e.g. in *Åkerberg*. In light of Opinion 2/13 leading to non-accession, it is of utmost importance that the ECJ systematically keeps the explicit references to the ECtHR case law, methodically uses the Charter as a true guiding norm and ensures that the corresponding rights to the ECHR as defined under Article 52(3) of the Charter are interpreted in harmony.

5 Conclusion: hierarchy, complexity and necessity?

In a speech delivered in January 2014 the President of the Bundesverfassungsgericht stated:

> The most striking of the ongoing transformations is the emerging formalisation of the relationship between the two Courts. The accession of the EU to the Convention will reshape the institutional architecture. European laws and judgments will be subject to the jurisdiction of the Strasbourg Court – an operation which our host, the President of the ECtHR Dean Spielmann, rightly praises as a high point of modern Europe's commitment to human rights. For accession to operate smoothly, it might once more be helpful to set the pyramid model aside and to focus on the mobile instead. Becoming

94 ECtHR, 2014 Annual Report, foreword by President Spielmann at 6. See also President Spielmann's speech at the opening of the judiciary year of the European Court of Human Rights, 20 January 2015, 4.

95 G. Butler, 'A Political Decision Disguised as Legal Argument? Opinion 2/13 and European Union Accession to the European Convention of Human Rights' (2015) *Utrecht Journal of International and European Law* 104.

> part of the Convention should not be thought of in terms of hierarchy, but in terms of specialisation. Strasbourg will not acquire the authority to assess the validity or the correct interpretation of EU law in a binding manner. Instead, accession means no more – and no less – than the external involvement of a specialised international human rights court. An involvement that will enhance the legitimacy and credibility of the system of human rights protection as a whole.[96]

However, even if some may agree with the former quote, it is in our view difficult to deny that fully-fledged accession (thus different from the vision of the ECJ in Opinion 2/13) would mean that the ECJ is in reality no longer the final arbiter of the meaning of EU fundamental rights overlapping with the ECHR as the ECtHR would exercise external control over the compatibility of EU acts to ensure that they comply with the ECHR, in the same way as for any other contracting party. And, in that sense, one may understand the rationale lying behind Opinion 2/13.

In light of Opinion 2/13, the paradox of complexity will remain, but it is far from clear whether accession of the EU to the ECHR according to the rejected Draft Accession Agreement would have fully resolved this paradox in any case. The system of protection of human rights will always remain complex in relation to multiple rights-based claims, i.e. claims based on rights contained within the ECHR/Charter and also enshrining rights only protected by the Charter. In this situation, the ECtHR will have the final say as to rights contained in the Convention, while the ECJ remains authoritative in relation to rights that go beyond those in the ECHR. But what is the dividing line between these two species of rights? Moreover, the Draft Accession Agreement establishes a very complex procedure with the co-defendant mechanism and the prior involvement procedure. The procedural measures established by the Draft Accession Agreement reflect also its complex logic placing the EU legal order in a privileged position since there is no analogous mechanism for the highest courts of other contracting parties to the Convention. This is contrary to the inner logic of accession based on equality. Nevertheless it seems that this is the price to pay for the EU becoming a party to the ECHR and ensuring the respect of Protocol 8 of the Lisbon Treaty on the specificity of the EU legal order as emphasised in Opinion 2/13. The system of human rights protection in Europe may change with accession but the goals of the two Courts should remain the same, i.e. different. If all the objections raised by the ECJ in its Opinion 2/13 are accepted, there is a risk for the whole system of human rights protection in Europe.

96 A. Voßkuhle, President of the Bundesverfassungsgericht, 'Pyramid or mobile? Human rights protection by the European Constitutional Courts', opening of the Judicial Year 2014 at the European Court of Human Rights Strasbourg, 31 January 2014.

3 The role of the European Court of Human Rights in the changing European human rights architecture

Davíd Þór Björgvinsson

1 Introduction

In the invitation to the conference where these reflections were originally presented, it was stated that the protection of human rights in Europe is at a crossroads. The reason is that the European Union (EU) is increasingly prioritising fundamental rights, for example by giving the Charter of Fundamental Rights (the Charter) the status of primary law and through the treaty-based obligation of accession to the European Convention on Human Rights (ECHR).[1]

Accession, if it ever takes place, will on the one hand extend the mandate and competences of the European Court of Human Rights (ECtHR) in the sense that the decisions of the ECtHR, in cases involving the EU will, as stipulated in Article 46 ECHR, be binding on the EU. But on the other hand there are also signs that the position of the ECtHR as a leading force in European human rights protection is being weakened due to the political momentum for bringing the responsibility for the protection of ECHR rights 'home' to the Member States and maybe also to the EU.[2] This situation presents an occasion for reflection on what this may

1 See Draft revised agreement on the accession of the European Union to the Convention for the Protection of Human Rights and Fundamental Freedoms. In Opinion 2/13 of the CJEU (Full Court) of 18 December 2014, the CJEU found the draft agreement incompatible with Article 6(2) TEU or with Protocol No. 8 EU. The opinion will be considered further below.

2 High Level Conference on the Future of the European Court of Human Rights. Brighton Declaration (19 and 20 April 2012) <www.echr.coe.int/Documents/2012_Brighton_FinalDeclaration_ENG.pdf> accessed 2 December 2014. The declaration stated in part B (12) that the conference: 'a) Welcomes the development by the Court in its case law of principles such as subsidiarity and the margin of appreciation, and encourages the Court to give great prominence to and apply consistently these principles in its judgments; b) Concludes that, for reasons of transparency and accessibility, a reference to the principle of subsidiarity and the doctrine of the margin of appreciation as developed in the Court's case law should be included in the Preamble to the Convention and invites the Committee of Ministers to adopt the necessary amending instrument by the end of 2013, while recalling the States Parties' commitment to give full effect to their obligation to secure the rights and freedoms defined in the Convention.' This is now reflected in Protocol No. 15 amending the Convention for the Protection of Human Rights and Fundamental Freedoms (adopted 24 June 2013)

mean for the ECtHR as a, so far, leading force in human rights protection at the pan-European level.

2 The scope of the Charter as compared to the ECHR

The scope of the Charter is defined in Article 51, stating:

> (1) The provisions of this Charter are addressed to the institutions and bodies of the Union with due regard for the principle of subsidiarity and to the Member States only when they are implementing Union law. They shall therefore respect the rights, observe the principles and promote the application thereof in accordance with their respective powers.
> (2) This Charter does not establish any new power or task for the Community or the Union, or modify powers and tasks defined by the Treaties.

These provisions aim to establish clearly that the Charter applies primarily to the institutions and bodies of the Union and to situations in which national authorities apply EU legislation on the home front, in compliance with the principle of subsidiarity. They were drafted in line with Article 6(2) of the Treaty on European Union, which requires the Union to respect fundamental rights. Most importantly for the purposes of this chapter, it would seem clear that the Charter does not apply to all areas of national law or action, but only to those that fall within the scope of EU law. It follows that the Charter does not apply to all areas of national law where civil and political rights are potentially engaged, whereas, by contrast, the ECHR does. On the basis of the explanations of the Charter[3] Koen Lenaerts uses the case law of the Court of Justice of the European Union (CJEU) predating the Charter to interpret the meaning of its provisions.[4] He finds that this case law includes two situations in which the Charter imposes obligations on the Member States, in accordance with Article 51 of the Charter. The first is when there is an EU obligation that requires the Member States to take action. The second is when a Member State derogates from EU law. When the Member States

CETS No. 213, where Article 1 adds to the Preamble to the Convention the following: 'Affirming that the High Contracting Parties, in accordance with the principle of subsidiarity, have the primary responsibility to secure the rights and freedoms defined in this Convention and the Protocols thereto, and that in doing so they enjoy a margin of appreciation, subject to the supervisory jurisdiction of the European Court of Human Rights established by this Convention.'

3 Explanations Relating to the Charter of Fundamental Rights: *Official Journal of the European Union* 14.12.2007, C 303/17, see in particular explanations to Article 51 of the Charter.

4 Koen Lenaerts, 'Exploring the Limits of the EU Charter of Fundamental Rights' (2012) 8 *European Constitutional Law Review* 375 (see esp. 377–378). See in particular the following cases: Judgment of 13 July 1989, Case 5/88 *Wachauf* [1989] ECR 2609; judgment of 18 June 1991, Case C-260/89 *ERT* [1991] ECR I-2925; judgment of 18 December 1997, Case C-309/96 *Annibaldi* [1997] ECR I-7493; judgment of 13 April 2000, Case C-292/97 *Karlsson* [2000] ECR I-2737 (para. 37).

implement legislation which does not follow from an EU law obligation, the Charter is not applicable. Article 51, paragraph 2, together with the second sentence of paragraph 1, confirms that the Charter may not have the effect of extending the competences and tasks which the Treaties confer on the Union. Explicit mention is made of the logical consequences of the principle of subsidiarity and of the fact that the Union only has those powers which have been conferred upon it.

This means that at the domestic level the Charter applies only where the respective actions of the Member State and/or national law falls 'within the scope of EU law'. Therefore, before a right provided for in the Charter can be invoked in national proceedings, it has to be determined whether the act complained of is within the scope of EU law.

In this regard it is of relevance that the CJEU has shown to be willing to interpret the 'scope of EU law' widely and that the threshold to engage EU law is relatively low. An example of this is the case of *Åkerberg Fransson*.[5] In the proceedings of that case, the CJEU was invited to answer questions relating to the *ne bis in idem* principle in Article 4 of Protocol No. 7 ECHR[6] and Article 50 of the Charter.[7] In the judgment, the CJEU addresses Article 51 of Charter. The Swedish Government and others disputed the admissibility of the questions referred for a preliminary ruling, as they did not concern EU law. It was argued that the Court would have jurisdiction to answer them only if the tax penalties, imposed on Mr Åkerberg Fransson, and the criminal proceedings brought against him, arose from implementation of EU law. It was submitted that this was not so in the case of either the national legislation, on whose basis the tax penalties were ordered to be paid, or the national legislation upon which the criminal proceedings were founded. In accordance with Article 51(1) of the Charter, those penalties and proceedings therefore did not fall under the *ne bis in idem* principle secured by Article 50 of the Charter. The Court rejected this argument by taking advantage of the fact that a relatively small part of the dispute related to the breaches of Mr Åkerberg Fransson's obligations to declare VAT. This was enough for the Court to engage Articles 2, 250(1) and 273 of Council Directive 2006/112/EC of 28 November 2006 on the common system of value added tax[8] and Article 4 (3) TEU as well as Article 325 TFEU. Then the Court stated in paragraph 31:

> It follows from the foregoing considerations that the Court has jurisdiction to answer the questions referred and to provide all the guidance as to

5 Judgment 26 February 2013 in Case C-617/10 *Åklagaren* v. *Hans Åkerberg Fransson*.
6 Article 4 (1) of Protocol No. 7 to the ECHR states: 'No one shall be liable to be tried or punished again in criminal proceedings under the jurisdiction of the same State for an offence for which he has already been finally acquitted or convicted in accordance with the law and penal procedure of that State.'
7 Article 50 of the Charter reads as follows: 'No one shall be liable to be tried or punished again in criminal proceedings for an offence for which he or she has already been finally acquitted or convicted within the Union in accordance with the law.'
8 OJ 2006 L347, 1.

interpretation needed in order for the referring court to determine whether the national legislation is compatible with the *ne bis in idem* principle laid down in Article 50 of the Charter.

It has moreover been argued that, when it comes to defining the necessary connection to trigger the application of the general principles of EU law, *inter alia* the Charter, the case law of the CJEU is unclear.[9] It would seem that, from the *Åkerberg Fransson* case, it can be inferred that the dispute only needs to be connected in part to EU law obligations regarding collection of VAT and that the Charter is engaged regardless of the fact that the relevant national legislation was adopted long before Sweden acceded to the EU.[10] In any case, and without going into too much depth in analysing the case law, it would seem to be possible to draw the conclusion that the phrase 'scope of EU law' may be interpreted expansively by the CJEU. Another more general point is that the phrase 'scope of EU law' has itself very unclear limits as it relates to many different sectors of society. It may at least safely be contended that it is not always clear when and whether national authorities are acting within the scope of application of EU law and that the meaning of this concept, as elaborated by the CJEU, is ambiguous.[11] Thus, it is certainly a matter of controversy as to what limitations Article 51 in reality imposes on the scope of application of the Charter. It may be argued that the threshold to engage EU law is relatively low, although it would also seem to be clear that in cases concerning purely domestic situations it will not apply.[12] As Hancox puts it: 'Drawing a limit is not easy due to a persistent tension between two opposing forces. On the one hand, centralizing forces push the EU towards becoming a more mature and comprehensive constitutional system; on the other, there is a desire to maintain a diversified and multifaceted constitutional system.'[13]

3 The relationship between the EU Charter and the ECHR

From the point of view of the EU, the relationship between the ECHR and the Strasbourg Court on the one hand and the Charter and the CJEU on the other is mainly regulated by Article 52(3) (scope of guaranteed rights) and 53 (level of protection) of the Charter, stating:

9 See for example Emely Hancox, 'The Meaning of "Implementing" EU Law under Article 51(1) of the Charter: *Åkerberg Fransson*' (2013) 50 CML Rev 1411, see esp. 1421.
10 See also Case C-555/07 *Kücükdeveci* [2010] ECR I-365.
11 Xavier Groussot, Laurent Pech and Gunnar Thor Petursson, 'The Scope of Application of Fundamental Rights on Member States Actions: In Search of Certainty in EU Adjudication' (Eric Stein, Working Paper No. 1/2011, Czech Society for European and Comparative Law, Prague, Czech Republic) <http://papers.ssrn.com/sol3/papers.cfm?abstract_id=1936473> accessed 4 December 2014, 1.
12 House of Commons European Scrutiny Committee, *The Application of the EU Charter of Fundamental Rights in the UK: A State of Confusion* (Forty-third Report of Session 2013–14), see esp. 43–47.
13 Hancox (n. 9) 1426.

> Article 52 (3): In so far as this Charter contains rights which correspond to rights guaranteed by the Convention for the Protection of Human Rights and Fundamental Freedoms, the meaning and scope of those rights shall be the same as those laid down by the said Convention. This provision shall not prevent Union law providing more extensive protection.
>
> Article 53: Nothing in this Charter shall be interpreted as restricting or adversely affecting human rights and fundamental freedoms as recognised, in their respective fields of application, by Union law and international law and by international agreements to which the Union, the Community or all the Member States are party, including the European Convention for the Protection of Human Rights and Fundamental Freedoms, and by the Member States' constitutions.

These provisions are intended to ensure the necessary consistency between the Charter and the ECHR, without thereby adversely affecting the autonomy of EU law and that of the CJEU. They affirm that the level of protection maintained under EU law could never be lower than that guaranteed by the ECHR. The provisions, however, would seem to be formulated in such a way that they allow the Union to guarantee more extensive protection. Lenaerts argues that a combined reading of Articles 52(3) and 53 of the Charter demonstrates a threat towards the autonomy of EU law in situations when the ECtHR either raises the level of protection of fundamental rights, or determines to expand the scope of application in a way that the level of protection overtakes that guaranteed by EU law. In those matters the CJEU is obliged to reinterpret the Charter in order to attain the level of protection guaranteed by the ECHR.[14] Moreover he asserts that such a combined reading of Articles 52(4) and 53 confirms that the Charter is not designed to define fundamental rights in accordance with 'the smallest common denominator'. It is rather meant to interpret fundamental rights in a way that ensures a high level of protection, which according to Lenaerts, is adapted to the nature of EU law and is in harmony with the national constitutional traditions.[15]

The foregoing suggests that the wording of the Charter means for example that the autonomy of EU law could mainly be grounded on the principle 'of the more extensive protection' compared to the ECHR. In other words, that the level of protection within the EU law can never be lower than that offered by Strasbourg. In that sense, the autonomy of EU law may be seen to be challenged when the ECtHR raises the level of fundamental human rights above EU standards or when it widens the protection to new situations by way of interpretation through case law. In such situations it would seem to be implied in Article 53 that the CJEU must follow Strasbourg.[16] In retrospect, these reflections by Judge Lenaerts may be seen as a prelude to Opinion 2/2013 of the CJEU which is discussed in the next section.

14 Lenaerts (n. 4) 394.
15 Ibid. 397.
16 Ibid. 394.

4 Opinion 2/2013 CJEU[17]

A major development has occurred by a way of Opinion 2/2013 of the CJEU in which the draft agreement on accession was rejected as incompatible with Article 6 (2) TEU or with Protocol No. 8 EU. In the Opinion, the CJEU found a series of flaws in the Agreement which mainly concern safeguarding the autonomy of EU law as well as its own jurisdiction.

The main features of the reasoning revolve around the concepts of autonomy, supremacy and effectiveness of EU law in the Member States, in line with Lenaerts's article cited above. It is noted in the Opinion (para. 180) that, as a result of accession, the ECHR, like any other international agreement concluded by the EU, would be binding upon the institutions of the EU and on its Member States, and would therefore form an integral part of EU law. In that case, the EU, like any other Contracting Party, would be subject to external control to ensure the observance of the rights and freedoms provided for by the ECHR. The EU and its institutions would thus be subject to the control mechanisms provided for by the ECHR and, in particular, to the decisions and judgments of the ECtHR. The Court goes on to state that it is indeed inherent in the very concept of external control that, on the one hand, the interpretation of the ECHR provided by the ECtHR would be binding on the EU and all its institutions and that, on the other hand, the interpretation by the Court of Justice of a right recognised by the ECHR would not be binding on the ECtHR. However, the Court states that this cannot be the case as regards the interpretation of EU law, including the Charter, provided by the Court itself.[18] The CJEU points out in particular that, in so far as the ECHR gives the Contracting Parties the power to lay down higher standards of protection than those guaranteed by the ECHR, the ECHR should be coordinated with the Charter. Where the rights recognised by the Charter correspond to those guaranteed by the ECHR, the power granted to Member States by Article 53 of the ECHR must be limited to that which is necessary to ensure that the level of protection provided for by the Charter and the primacy, unity and effectiveness of EU law are not compromised. In the Opinion, the Court found that there is no provision in the draft agreement to ensure such coordination (paras 180–190).[19] It would seem to be inherent in the Opinion on this point that the ECtHR can never raise the standard of protection provided for by the Charter, which would seem to defy the objective and purpose of the ECHR, at least with regard to the present Contracting parties.

17 Opinion 2/13, Pursuant to Article 218(11) TFEU, ECLI:EU:C:2014:2454.

18 This seems to be a misunderstanding, as the ECtHR would always refrain from interpreting EU law and the Charter, as in the case of domestic law of the Contracting States. It would only assess whether the legislation as interpreted by the relevant institutions and as applied in the circumstances of the case is compatible with the ECHR. Abundance of case law from the ECtHR supports this point.

19 Logically this means that the ECtHR can never raise the standard of protection provided for by the Charter.

The CJEU also sees a flaw in the fact that the EU is treated as any other state party to the ECHR. This, in the view of the CJEU, disregards the intrinsic nature of the EU, as it does not take account of the fact that, as regards the matters covered by the transfer of powers to the EU, the Member States have accepted that their relations are governed by EU law to the exclusion of any other law. This, the CJEU found, is liable to upset the underlying balance of powers within the EU and to undermine the autonomy of EU law (paras 191–195).

The next problem detected by the CJEU is Protocol No. 16 to the ECHR, signed on 2 October 2013. The Protocol permits the highest courts and tribunals of the Member States to request the ECtHR to give advisory opinions on questions of principle relating to the interpretation or application of the rights and freedoms guaranteed by the ECHR or the protocols thereto. The CJEU found that, in the event of accession, the mechanism established by that Protocol could affect the autonomy and effectiveness of the preliminary ruling procedure provided for by the FEU Treaty, notably where rights guaranteed by the Charter correspond to rights secured by the ECHR. It found that it could not be ruled out that a request for an advisory opinion made pursuant to Protocol No. 16 by a national court or tribunal could trigger the procedure for the 'prior involvement' of the Court thus creating a risk that the preliminary ruling procedure might be circumvented (paras 196–200).

Next the CJEU points out that the draft agreement allows for the possibility that the EU or Member States might submit an application to the ECtHR concerning an alleged violation of the ECHR by another Member State or the EU in relation to EU law. The Court found that the very existence of such a possibility undermines the requirements of the FEU Treaty. In those circumstances, the draft agreement could be compatible with the FEU Treaty only if the ECtHR's jurisdiction were expressly excluded for disputes between Member States, or between Member States and the EU, regarding the application of the ECHR in the context of EU law (paras 205–214). In addition the CJEU recalls that the draft agreement provides that a Contracting Party is to become a co-respondent either by accepting an invitation from the ECtHR or by decision of the ECtHR upon the request of that Contracting Party. If the EU or Member States request leave to intervene as co-respondents in a case before the ECtHR, they must prove that the conditions for their participation in the procedure are met. In carrying out the test of whether the conditions are met, the ECtHR will be required to assess the rules of EU law governing the division of powers between the EU and its Member States as well as the criteria for the attribution of their acts or omissions. The ECtHR could adopt a final decision in that respect which would be binding both on the Member States and on the EU. To permit the ECtHR to adopt such a decision would risk adversely affecting the division of powers between the EU and its Member States (paras 215–225).

Then the Court addresses the procedure for the prior involvement of the Court. It notes, first, that by this procedure the ECtHR is permitted to rule on such a question. This is in the view of the Court tantamount to conferring on the ECtHR jurisdiction to interpret the case law of the CJEU. Consequently, that procedure should be set up in such a way as to ensure that, in any case pending before the ECtHR, the EU is fully and systematically informed, so that the competent institution is able to assess whether the Court has already given a ruling on the question at issue and, if not, to arrange for the prior involvement procedure to be initiated. Second, the Court observes that the draft agreement excludes the possibility of bringing a matter before the Court in order for it to rule on a question of interpretation of secondary law by means of that procedure. Limiting the scope of that procedure solely to questions of validity adversely affects the competences of the EU and the powers of the Court (paras 236–248).

Lastly, the Court analyses the specific characteristics of EU law as regards judicial review in matters of the common foreign and security policy (CFSP). It notes that, as EU law now stands, certain acts adopted in the context of the CFSP fall outside the ambit of judicial review by the CJEU. Nevertheless, on the basis of accession as provided for by the draft agreement, the ECtHR would be empowered to rule on the compatibility with the ECHR of certain acts, actions or omissions performed in the context of the CFSP, notably those whose legality the Court cannot, for want of jurisdiction, review in the light of fundamental rights. Such a situation would effectively entrust, as regards compliance with the rights guaranteed by the ECHR, the exclusive judicial review of those acts, actions or omissions on the part of the EU to a non-EU body. In this sense the draft agreement fails to have regard to the specific characteristics of EU law with regard to the judicial review of acts, actions or omissions on the part of the EU in the area of the CFSP (paras 249–257).

In the light of all the flaws identified, the CJEU concluded that the draft agreement on the accession of the European Union to the ECHR is not compatible with EU law. This Opinion is a big blow for the accession process and for the ECtHR. There is hardly a doubt that some of the points raised may be very difficult to accommodate within the very nature and object of the ECHR and the role of the ECtHR. Many have raised objections to the legal argumentation in the Opinion. This, however, will not be done here. The underlying motivation and the consequences of the Opinion are of more interest for the purpose of this chapter. In essence, the consequence of the first argument is that the CJEU requires that the ECtHR does not raise the level of protection of human rights as provided for in the Charter as interpreted by the CJEU, as this may be a threat to the supremacy and effectiveness of EU law in the Member States. If this were to be accepted by the Contracting States to the ECHR, it would clearly marginalise the ECtHR when it comes to defining the standard of fundamental rights protection in the application and interpretation of EU law on behalf of the Union and by the Member States. Indeed this is tantamount to a reservation made by a state party to the ECHR which requires that the interpretation of ECHR rights by the ECtHR must not go further than the protection offered under domestic law (constitution) as interpreted by its national courts. This defies the whole object and purpose of the ECHR and is a condition which would seem to be impossible to meet. Indeed it could be argued that the Opinion represents a certain resistance to the idea that ECtHR is the frontrunner when it comes to defining the standards of human rights protection within the European Union. It rather insists that the CJEU takes the lead in defining human rights in relation to the implementation and application of EU legislation. This will bring forward a new set of challenges for the ECtHR. It is hardly an option to have to have one set of standards derived from the ECtHR and another derived from the EU and CJEU. A judge in a national court in one of the EU Member States, regardless of whether he is dealing with EU legislation or purely national legislation, will naturally first and foremost be inclined to look at the jurisprudence of the CJEU for guidance. Whether Opinion 2/13 in this regard is deliberate is hard to say, but, certainly with time, the CJEU will be given an opportunity to strengthen its position with regard to the case law on the Charter of Fundamental Rights. This will not only be relevant when it comes to the implementation and interpretation of the compatibility of European Union law with human rights, but also for the protection of human rights in the EU Member States. Consequently there will be less need for the ECtHR.

This may mean that the ECtHR will be marginalised within the EU, and further raises the question as to what effect this may have for the future of the ECtHR in non-EU Member States who are a party to the ECHR. This is an interesting question as the ECtHR has a particular way of approaching the EU. The *Bosphorus* doctrine, further discussed below, with its presumption of Convention compliance is a telling example. Moreover, recent case law, as related below, suggests that the ECtHR will be inspired by the CJEU, even when it is defining the minimum standards of fundamental rights for non-EU Member States.

A further consideration in this regard is the fact that many of the Contracting States to the entire Strasbourg system can also be seen as future Member States of the European Union. In their choices of foreign policy and external relations the EU is a major issue. Even when the ECtHR makes a decision against non-EU Member States, in theory it also has implications for EU Member States because this is the case law that will be referred to when defining human rights standards in these countries. This is in fact one of the problems identified by the CJEU in Opinion 2/13, and one of the reasons that the Draft Accession Agreement was rejected, because it doesn't work the other way around. It may follow from all this that the ECtHR may have some difficulty in the years to come to being accepted as the highest authority for the protection of human rights, and this may be the case even within states that are not EU Member States, as many of them strive to become Member States. One of the conditions of EU membership is that human rights are adequately protected, and in order to fulfil that condition these states are in practical terms more likely to seek guidance from the Charter and the case law of the CJEU rather than from the ECHR and the ECtHR.

As to the more political aspect of the issue, the Opinion in all likelihood means that the accession project will be dormant for some time. Perhaps several more years are needed before all the issues raised by the CJEU can be adequately addressed. The requirements that transpire from the Opinion will be very difficult to achieve, legally, and not least politically. During the negotiation process, there was already some resentment about the concessions given to the EU in the Draft Accession Agreement as it stood in the negotiating rounds concluded in April

2013. It would be no surprise if some parties to the Council of Europe, particularly larger ones who are non-EU Member States, under the present political circumstances might not be so eager to give in to any special concessions to the EU if negotiations were to be reopened. They might even be tempted to insist that the EU must follow the Strasbourg rules just like any other Contracting Party. This a card to be played in the much larger political game that is ongoing between the East and the West in Europe.

5 Case law of the ECtHR

A further indication of the reduced role of the ECtHR may be detected in the case law of the ECtHR in matters related to the application and interpretation of EU legislation. There are signs that Strasbourg will in any case, when engaged with the implementation and application of EU law in the EU's Member States or in cases involving the EU directly, be very cautious in raisings its standards for the protection of human rights above EU standards and even more cautious before going into direct confrontation with EU law and the CJEU. This is clearly manifested in the *Bosphorus Airways* judgment of the ECtHR, in which the Court came to the conclusion that there was a 'presumption of Convention compliance' built into the EU system.[20] The judgment deserves further attention.

The case concerned an application brought by an airline charter company registered in Turkey, Bosphorus Airways. In May 1993 an aircraft, leased by the company from Yugoslav Airlines ('JAT'), was seized by the Irish authorities when it was in Ireland. Before the ECtHR, Bosphorus Airways complained that the manner in which Ireland implemented the sanctions regime to impound its aircraft was a reviewable exercise of discretion within the meaning of Article 1 of the Convention and a violation of Article 1 of Protocol No. 1 of the Convention.

In relation to Article 1 of Protocol No. 1 and the legal basis for the impoundment of the aircraft, the Court made several interesting statements, *inter alia* in paragraph 148 where it found that the impugned interference was 'not the result of an exercise of discretion by the Irish authorities, either under Community or Irish law, but rather amounted to compliance by the Irish State with its legal obligations flowing from Community law and, in particular, Article 8 of Regulation (EEC) no. 990/93'.

This finding formed the basis for the final conclusion of non-violation of Article 1 of Protocol No. 1 of the Convention by Ireland. From the judgment it seems that this finding was based on the following special features of the Community legal order. First, the regulation was 'generally applicable' and 'binding in its entirety'. The Court moreover emphasised that the regulation was 'directly applicable' and that it became a part of the domestic legal order without the need to implement special legislation to that effect. The ECtHR therefore held that the Irish authorities rightly considered themselves obliged to impound any departing aircraft that

20 *Bosphorus Hava Yollari Turizm* v. *Ireland ve Ticaret Anonim Şirketi* App. No. 45036/98 (ECtHR, 30 June 2005).

fell under Article 8 of the Regulation. Second, the Court referred to the rights and duties under Article 234 TEC (now Article 267 TFEU) to refer matters of interpretation of EU legislation to the CJEU. In this regard it was pointed out that pursuant to Article 10 TEC (now, substantively, Article 4, para. 3 TEU) the duty of loyal cooperation required the state to appeal the High Court judgment to the Supreme Court in order to clarify the interpretation of the EU Regulation. Moreover, the Court found that the Supreme Court of Ireland had no discretion in the matter as the Supreme Court of Ireland had to make the preliminary reference, the ruling of the CJEU was binding on the Supreme Court and the ruling of the CJEU effectively determined the domestic proceedings by concluding that the regulation applied to the aircraft.

As to the question of whether the impoundment of the aircraft was justified, the Court first described the general approach and stressed that there must be a reasonable relationship of proportionality between the means employed and the aim pursued and that a fair balance has to be struck between the demands of the general interests of society and the interests of the individual company concerned. It also emphasised that the state enjoys a wide margin of appreciation in this regard. However, it also stressed that the Convention as such did not prevent Contracting Parties from transferring sovereign powers to international organisations for the purpose of cooperation in certain fields. Furthermore, as stated in paragraph 158, the Court examined whether it could be *presumed* that Ireland complied with its Convention requirements in fulfilling such obligations and whether any such presumption has been rebutted in the circumstances of the case.

In assessing whether such a presumption of Convention compliance could be made at the relevant time, the Court described the main features for the protection of fundamental rights within the Community legal order. It was found that repeated references by the CJEU to the Convention provisions and the Court's jurisprudence, specific treaty provisions referring to protection of such rights and the Charter, as well as the control and enforcement mechanism offered by the Union, allowed the Strasbourg Court to conclude the following (para. 165):

> In such circumstances, the Court finds that the protection of fundamental rights by EU law can be considered to be, and to have been at the relevant time, 'equivalent' (within the meaning of paragraph 155 above) to that of the Convention system. Consequently, the presumption arises that Ireland did not depart from the requirements of the Convention when it implemented legal obligations flowing from its membership of the EC.

In its reasoning, the Court stressed that such a presumption of Convention compliance could be rebutted if, in a particular case, it was considered that the protection of Convention rights was manifestly deficient. However, the Strasbourg Court did not find so in this case.

The case of *MSS* v. *Greece and Belgium* is also of importance for understanding the current relationship between the EU Charter and the ECHR. It would seem that the judgment reinforces the main principles of the *Bosphorus* judgment, as the ECtHR stated in paragraph 338:

> The Court notes the reference to the Bosphorus judgment by the Government of the Netherlands in their observations lodged as third-party interveners ... The Court reiterated in that case that the Convention did not prevent the Contracting Parties from transferring sovereign powers to an international organisation for the purposes of cooperation in certain fields of activity (see *Bosphorus*, cited above, § 152). The States nevertheless remain responsible under the Convention for all actions and omissions of their bodies under their domestic law or under their international legal obligations (ibid., § 153). State action taken in compliance with such legal obligations is justified as long as the relevant organisation is considered to protect fundamental rights in a manner which can be considered at least equivalent to that for which the Convention provides. However, a State would be fully responsible under the Convention for all acts falling outside its strict international legal obligations, notably where it exercised State discretion (ibid., §§ 155–57). The Court found that the protection of fundamental rights afforded by Community law was equivalent to that provided by the Convention system (ibid., § 165). In reaching that conclusion it attached great importance to the role and powers of the Court of Justice of the European Union (CJEC) – now the CJEU – in the matter, considering in practice that the effectiveness of the substantive guarantees of fundamental rights depended on the mechanisms of control set in place to ensure their observance (ibid., § 160). The Court also took care to limit the scope of the *Bosphorus* judgment to Community law in the strict sense – at the time the 'first pillar' of European Union law (§ 72).[21]

Although, the ECtHR stresses that the Contracting States remain responsible under the Convention for all actions and omissions of their bodies under their domestic law or under their international legal obligations, the judgment is a still confirmation of the presumption of Convention compliance. This is rather committal and gives an indication that the Strasbourg Court will be reticent in challenging the findings of the CJEU. However, having said that and in light of Opinion 2/13, the interesting question arises as to whether the ECtHR will maintain the position taken in these cases. Undoubtedly, some judges at the ECtHR will be tempted to overturn the *Bosphorus* judgment. It will not happen overnight, but the Court might be inclined to move away from it slowly but surely, and to take a more assertive position when it comes to defining the standards of human rights in the application of EU legislation by the Member States. After all, the states are responsible for upholding Convention rights regardless of the origin of the relevant legislation, and this is also clear in *Bosphorus.*

Having said that, other judgments also indicate that in some situations human rights are interpreted in conformity with EU law and standards. An example of

21 *MSS* v. *Belgium and Greece* App. No. 30696/09 (ECtHR, 21 January 2011).

this is the principle of *ne bis in idem*. Thus for example in *Sergey Zolotukhin* v. *Russia* the concept of '*idem*' was interpreted in conformity with the case law of the CJEU in order to facilitate a convergent interpretation of the wording of the *ne bis in idem* principle.[22] Clearly, the Strasbourg Court is inclined to adapt its understanding of rights in at least some situations to the nature of EU law and in harmony with the national constitutional traditions of the Member States.[23]

6 The problems facing the ECHR

There are some further signs that the ECtHR will have problems with asserting its position as a decisive force in this new environment of protection of human rights in Europe. This is particularly true when it comes to the implementation and application of EU law in the Member States, but also, in the longer run as regards human rights in general in these countries because the level of protection must be the same regardless of the origin of the legislation or its cross-border nature. The relevant arguments for this assertion broadly fall into two categories. The first category relates to the general judicial and political environment in which the ECtHR operates (section 6.1). The second category relates to the problems that the ECtHR is suffering from as an institution; problems that may weaken its claim

22 *Sergey Zolotukhin* v. *Russia* App. No. 14939/03 (ECtHR, 10 February 2009), see esp. para. 79. It should be mentioned that the ECtHR does not only refer to EU law, namely Article 50 of the Charter of Fundamental Rights of the European Union and the Convention Implementing the Schengen Agreement which prohibits prosecution for the 'same acts' but also to other instruments incorporating the *non bis in idem* principle, namely the United Nations Covenant on Civil and Political Rights and the American Convention on Human Rights. In para. 38, the ECtHR refers in particular to the judgment of the CJEU in *Norma Kraaijenbrink*, Case C-367/05, 18 July 2007, concerning the application of the *non bis in idem* principle where further references to other cases are also to be found.

23 There are more cases indicating a tendency towards harmonisation with the approaches of EU law and the CJEU. An example is *D. H. and Others* v. *Czech Republic* of 2007. It may be argued that in this case the Court adapted its approach to the concept of indirect discrimination to EU law (paras 184 and 187) where an EU directive is referred to, arguably raising the standard of protection under the ECHR up to that of the EU. See, on the other hand, where it can be argued that the ECtHR is levelling down to the EU standards, *Peterka* v. *Czech Republic* App. No. 21990/08 (adm dec, 4 May 2010), where the list of discrimination grounds in Article 21 of the Charter was referred to in order to support a restrictive reading of the protective scope of Article 14 by excluding those discrimination grounds that are not based on core personal choices or personal characteristics (non-personal discrimination grounds). Yet another case of interest is the *Ullens de Schooten and Rezabek* v. *Belgium* App. Nos 3989/07 and 38353/07 (ECtHR, 20 September 2011). The applicants complained that the Court of Cassation had refused their request to obtain a preliminary ruling from the Court of Justice. In the second case, Mr Ullens de Schooten complained that the Conseil d'Etat had failed to consider the manifestly unlawful nature of Article 3 of the decree and had refused to refer the question to the Court of Justice for a preliminary ruling. The applicants relied on Article 6 § 1 ECHR. It could be argued that the ECtHR levelled its requirements under Article 6 as regards the reasoning for refusal to the criteria laid down in the *CILFIT* case law of the CJEU.

to lead the way for protection of human rights within the EU in the years to come (section 6.2).

6.1 The political and judicial environment

Let us start with what may perhaps be termed as a lack of political interest in the Council of Europe. Obviously, the centre of gravity in the foreign policy in the EU Member States is the Union. This has been so for a long time for the old Member States of the EU (or the Community) and it is obviously the trend in the newer Member States as well. The political focus has been moving from Strasbourg to Brussels and will without much doubt continue to do so in the near future. The lack of real political commitment to the Council of Europe and the Court is, for example, manifested in the budgetary policy of 'zero-growth' for many years in spite of the increased influx of cases.[24] As far as the Council of Europe and the ECtHR is concerned, this may lead to doubts as to the Contracting States' commitment to these institutions at the present. Thus, there is a political resentment, almost to the level of hostility in some countries, as for example the United Kingdom, as is manifested in the reaction to some of the judgments of the Court. An example is the reaction to the *Hirst* judgment on prisoners' voting rights.[25] So far, the legislation in the UK has not been amended to enforce this ruling and there are clear signs of a lack of political willingness to do so.[26] It has been argued that the ECtHR has never, in its 50-year history, been subject to such a 'barrage of hostile criticism, as that which occurred in the United Kingdom in February 2011.[27] This has been referred to as 'Strasbourg-bashing', providing an example of growing conflict over the role and place of international courts.[28] Such attitudes, though not quite so deeply felt as in the UK, are present in other countries. An example is Russia's dragging its feet in ratifying Protocol 14 for a very long time.[29]

24 The Court does not have a separate budget from the rest of the Council of Europe as follows from Article 50 of the Convention, stating: (Expenditure on the Court) 'The expenditure on the Court shall be borne by the Council of Europe'. As such it is subject to the approval of the Committee of Ministers of the Council of Europe in the course of their examination of the overall Council of Europe budget.

25 Case of *Hirst* v. *United Kingdom (No. 2)* App. No. 74025/01 (ECtHR, 6 October 2005).

26 On 22 November 2012 the government published a draft Bill, the Voting Eligibility (Prisoners) Draft Bill, for pre-legislative scrutiny by a joint Committee of both Houses. The Committee published its report on 18 December 2013 and recommended that the government should introduce legislation to allow all prisoners serving sentences of 12 months or less to vote in all UK parliamentary, local and European elections. The Lord Chancellor and Justice Secretary, Chris Grayling, made a brief response to the Committee's report on 25 February 2014; but the government has not responded substantively and did not bring forward a Bill with the 2014 Queen's Speech.

27 Michael O'Boyle, 'The Future of the European Court of Human Rights' (2011) *German Law Journal* 1862–1877, 1862.

28 M. R. Madsen, 'The Legitimization Strategies of International Judges: The Case of the European Court of Human Rights' (*iCourts Working Paper Series* no. 12, 2014), 4.

29 In November 2010 Valery Zorkin, the Chairman of the Constitutional Court, warned the European Court of Human Rights that it shouldn't teach Russians how to live.

There is also a widespread judicial resentment within the EU countries as well as in countries outside the EU. This is reflected in the reaction of the judicial profession in Germany to the first *Hannover* judgment concerning the balancing of Article 8 and 10 rights under the ECHR.[30] The German courts had tilted the balance in favour of Article 10 ECHR.[31] However, the ECtHR disagreed. Although the German courts have largely followed the case law of the ECtHR, this specific decision of the court met serious opposition from German lawyers.[32] The core element in the criticism is that the ECtHR had not left enough discretion to the domestic courts. The role of the ECtHR should be only to guarantee minimum standards for the protection of human rights and leave the remainder to the national jurisdictions.[33] The judgment of the ECtHR in the case of *Görgülü* v. *Germany*[34] on visiting rights led to further reactions from the German Constitutional Court as regards the status of the Convention and the rulings of the ECtHR in particular.[35] In Paulus's interpretation[36] the case law of the German Constitutional Court is that that Court usually considers itself to be bound by the ECtHR's interpretation of the ECHR. This is subject to limitations, the main limitation being that the decision of the ECtHR cannot violate the German Constitution.[37]

Our courts, he said, have a better knowledge of what Russian people need because they understand the 'cultural, moral and religious code' of the nation. And if the ECtHR doesn't listen, he added, Russia may ignore the Court's decisions and even leave its jurisdiction completely. See Russian Law Online (3 February 2011) 'Meet Judge Nussberger': <www.russianlawonline.com/meet-judge-nussberger>.

30 *Hannover* v. *Germany* App. No. 59320/00 (ECtHR, 24 June 2004).

31 See the judgment of the German Federal Constitutional Court (Bundesverfassungsgericht) of 15 December 1999. The Caroline case: BVerfGE 101, 361.

32 A. Paulus, 'Germany', in D. Sloss (ed.), *The Role of Domestic Courts in Treaty Enforcement* (Cambridge University Press, 2009) 230. As regards the criticism of the decision of the ECtHR, see for example, S. Mückl, 'Kooperation oder Konfrontation?– *Das Verhältnis* zwischen Bundesverfassungsgericht und Europäischen Gerichtshof für Menschenrechte, (2005) 44 *Der Staat* 403, and D Grimm, 'Discussion Statement' (2007) 66 *Veröffentlichungen der Vereinigung der Deutschen Staatsrechtslehrer* 427–428.

33 Ibid. 230–231.

34 *Görgülü* v. *Germany* App. No. 74969/01 (ECtHR, 26 February 2004).

35 See judgments of the German Federal Constitutional Court (Bundesverfassungsgericht): BVerfGE 111, 307 and BVerfGE, Decision 1 BvR 2790/04 Dec. 2004.

36 Paulus (n. 32) 233.

37 See further on the situation in Germany: D. Richter, 'Does International Jurisprudence Matter in Germany? The Federal Constitutional Court's New Doctrine of "Factual Precedent"'(2006) 49 *German Yearbook of International Law* 51, 68ff., where openness is advocated and where, what she calls the vague concept of international jurisprudence as 'factual precedent', is criticised. Rather, such jurisprudence should be used to reveal the real meaning of an international treaty. See also R. Hofmann, 'The German Federal Constitutional Court and Public International Law: New Decisions, New Approaches?' (2004) 47 *German Yearbook of International Law* 9, 13ff., where the German approach is criticised for its reluctance to truly open its jurisprudence and the German domestic legal order to international norms.

The Court is being criticised by many for lack of efficiency, for having too many young and inexperienced judges and for lacking democratic legitimacy by for example not respecting the margin of appreciation, the principle of subsidiary and thereby undermining state sovereignty.[38]

All this is noted with concern by the judges and other officials in Strasbourg. The danger is that, as a consequence, the Court shows signs of being less assertive and less willing to take a principled position on many human rights issues seen as politically controversial and even backing out from earlier positions. Some cases may be mentioned to substantiate this. The case of *Scoppola* (*No. 3*), has been interpreted as a retreat from the position taken in the aforementioned *Hirst* judgment.[39] Another example, albeit not as clear, is *Von Hannover* v. *Germany (No. 2)* where the Court is retreating from its strict assessment in balancing Article 8 and Article 10 rights under the Convention, to give the national courts a margin of appreciation.[40] Even the well-known 'consensus argument' is giving way to more emphasis on the margin of appreciation and subsidiarity as can be inferred

38 There are many examples, in particular from the UK: 'European Court Undermining British Sovereignty' stating e.g. 'An ever-expanding list of controversial rulings issued by the European Court of Human Rights (ECHR) are fueling accusations that unelected judges at the pan-European court are usurping the judicial sovereignty of individual European nation states.' Moreover, in an interview with BBC Radio 4's *Today* programme on December 28, Lord Judge, who was the Chief Justice of England and Wales from 2008 to 2013, warned that allowing the ECtHR to set laws on social matters could pose a threat to parliamentary sovereignty: European Court of Human Rights 'risk to UK sovereignty'. See: <www.gatestoneinstitute.org/4134/echr-uk>.

39 *Scoppola* v. *Italy (No. 3)* App. No. 126/05 (ECtHR, 22 May 2012). The judgment has been criticised for being lacking in principle and for representing a retreat for 'politically' motivated purposes. See for example Javier R. Jaramillo, '*Scoppola* v. *Italy (No. 3)*: The Uncertain Progress of Prisoner Voting Rights in Europe' (2014) 36 B.C. Int'l & Comp. L. Rev. 32; Edward C. Lang, 'A Disproportionate Response: *Scoppola* v.*Italy (No. 3)* and Criminal Disenfranchisement in the European Court of Human Rights' (2013) 26 Am. U. Int'l. L. Rev. 835, who states in his conclusions (871): 'Not only is the judgment in that case inconsistent with the previous analysis of the Court in the Hirst v. United Kingdom (No. 2) case, it also demonstrates how the current analysis is inconsistent with an evolutive interpretation of the European Convention on Human Rights.' Moreover, see Marko Milanovic, 'Prisoner Voting and Strategic Judging' (EJIL Talk, 22 May 2012) <www.ejiltalk.org/prisoner-voting-and-strategic-judging> accessed 5 December 2014. He states: '*Scoppola* is thus hardly a decision born out of principle. But it will hopefully allow both the Court and the UK government to save face, with both learning something from their confrontation. All the UK government now needs to do to comply with *Hirst* is to pass some essentially cosmetic changes that would "strike the proper balance". Or, depending on how UK media and political elites react, rather than be defused the conflict may well escalate – we shall soon see.'

40 *Von Hannover* v. *Germany (No. 2)* ECHR 2012. See for example Kirsten Sjøvoll, 'Case Law, Strasbourg: *Von Hannover* v. *Germany (No. 2)* – Unclear Clarification and Unappreciated Margins' <http://inforrm.wordpress.com/2012/02/10/caselaw-von-hannover-v-germany-no-2-unclear-clarification-and-unappreciated-margins-kirsten-sjovoll> accessed 5 December 2014.

from judgments like *ABC* v. *Ireland* and *National Union of Rail, Maritime and Transport Workers* v. *United Kingdom*.[41]

6.2 Institutional problems of the ECtHR

The second set of arguments relate to the many problems and weaknesses of the Court in Strasbourg as an institution, which potentially make it increasingly difficult for it to fulfil and maintain its status as a front runner in the protection of human rights in Europe, and within the EU in particular. I will mention a few, some of which are obvious to the outside world, whereas others are more hidden.

First, the budgetary issues mentioned above. It has been suggested that it 'will not be possible endlessly to enhance the Court's human and financial resources on account of both lack of space and budgetary constraints' and that 'the current system (a single court for 800 million Europeans) has reached its limits and must therefore evolve further and possibly fundamentally'.[42] It cannot, however, be excluded that the commitment made in the Brighton Declaration to the long-term reform of the Court, and the currently ongoing work on this issue may lead to an improvement.[43]

Second, a lot of staff resources and the time of the judges is allocated to the handling of clearly inadmissible cases in single-judge formations (more that 90 per cent of the cases). Another big part of the Court's resources is assigned to routine repetitive cases on which well-established case law exists, such as those concerning length of proceedings, length of pre-trial detention and the like. This unavoidably limits personnel and resources that can be allocated to the handling and careful scrutiny of more 'worthy' cases, including even more serious cases and important new cases of principle. The order of the day over the last several years has been efficiency in terms of numbers of cases being disposed of. While this may please politicians, the danger is that this may seriously undermine confidence in the Court and in the quality of its work.

Third, and in relation to the second point, doubts can be raised as to whether some of the work the judges are supposed to do can be seriously considered to be true judicial work. An example of this is the handling of single-judge cases. As is well known, Protocol 14 came into force in June 2010 after its ratification by Russia. Among other changes, the Protocol created a single-judge formation empowered to reject obviously inadmissible applications and committees of three judges were empowered to adopt decisions and judgments where the underlying question in the case is subject to well-established case law. In a period of little

41 *A, B and C* v. *Ireland* ECHR 2010; *National Union of Rail, Maritime and Transport Workers* v. *United Kingdom* ECHR 2014.

42 The Right Honourable the Lord Woolf et al, 'Review of the Working Methods of the European Court of Human Rights' (December 2005) <www.echr.coe.int/Documents/2005_Lord_Woolf_working_methods_ENG.pdf> accessed 5 December 2014, 11.

43 High Level Conference on the Future of the European Court of Human Rights. Brighton Declaration (April 2012) <www.echr.coe.int/Documents/2012_Brighton_FinalDeclaration_ENG.pdf>.

more than a year (between 2012 and 2013) the single-judge formation of the Court managed to dispose of more than 81,000 applications at the admissibility stage, which helped in considerably reducing the overall number of pending cases. In addition, it is not uncommon for judges to serve as single judges in cases where the file is in a language they do not understand, thus being completely dependent on the lawyers in the registry. It is a valid question, therefore, as to whether these decisions can properly be called judicial. At the same time these judges are expected to deal with committee cases, Rule 39 requests, ordinary Chamber cases and Grand Chamber cases, together with administrative duties and responsibilities. This is indeed a monstrous task on any scale.

There is no doubt that the single-judge formation has been successful in the sense that it has made it possible for the Court to effectively dispose of thousands of cases and thereby to reduce its backlog. However, there is a price of another kind to pay for this effectiveness as the applicants are often left with limited explanations as regards the reasons why his or her application has been declared inadmissible. The obvious lack of reasons makes it impossible for the applicant to know the exact reasons for the Court's decision. The point has also been raised by the UN Human Rights Committee (HRC). In its views in the *Achabal* case, the HRC found that a case that earlier had been declared inadmissible as manifestly ill-founded by the ECtHR, on the basis that it did not find 'any appearance of violation of the rights and freedoms guaranteed by the Convention and its Protocols', was actually well founded. In its findings regarding the admissibility of the communication, the HRC expressed some serious criticism of the lack of reasoning of the Court's decision.[44] Moreover the HRC found a violation of Article 7 of the International Covenant on Civil and Political Rights as the applicant's claims of having been tortured while held in detention had not been investigated by the relevant authorities. It has been argued that the legitimacy of the Court's decisions is at stake here. It is asserted that while the Court imposes strict standards upon

44 *María Cruz Achabal Puertas* v. *Spain* (1945/2010), CCPR/C/107/D/1945/2010 (2013). In paragraph 7.3 the Human Rights Committee states: 'The Committee recalls its case law relating to article 5, paragraph 2 (a) of the Optional Protocol to the effect that, when the European Court bases a declaration of inadmissibility not solely on procedural grounds but also on reasons that include a certain consideration of the merits of the case, then the same matter should be deemed to have been "examined" within the meaning of the respective reservations to article 5, paragraph 2 (a), of the Optional Protocol; and it must be considered that the European Court has gone well beyond the examination of the purely formal criteria of admissibility when it declares a case inadmissible because "it does not reveal any violation of the rights and freedoms established in the Convention or its Protocols". However, in the particular circumstances of this case, the limited reasoning contained in the succinct terms of the Court's letter does not allow the Committee to assume that the examination included sufficient consideration of the merits in accordance with the information provided to the Committee by both the author and the State party. Consequently, the Committee considers that there is no obstacle to its examining the present communication under article 5, paragraph 2 (a), of the Optional Protocol.' See also Janneke Gerards, 'Inadmissibility Decisions of the European Court of Human Rights: A Critique of the Lack of Reasoning' (2014) 14 HRLR 148.

State Parties to the ECHR as regards the motivation of judgments and court decisions in both civil and criminal cases, it does not live up to the same standards itself. Arguably, the single-judge formation fails in fulfilling the requirements of procedural justice, which seriously undermines the legitimacy of its single-judge decisions and even the Court as a whole.[45]

As the fourth and final point, it should be mentioned, on top of being overburdened with work, that the organisation of the Court also raises questions. In Luxembourg the judges are a head of cabinet with legal assistants of their own choosing and other secretarial assistance. In comparison, the judges at the ECtHR have no personal legal assistance of their own choosing and share one secretarial assistant with one or even two other judges. All the lawyers in the registry work under the supervision and instructions from more senior registry members, but formally not directly from the judges. A further point is that the working conditions of the judges in Strasbourg have arguably contributed to the fact that it is more and more difficult for the Court to attract the most qualified people, reflected *inter alia* in the fact that the average age of the judges over the last ten years or so has dropped considerably. More people are being appointed under the age of 40 (even down to the age of 34). This has already (rightly or wrongly) given occasion for criticism. Dominic Raab, a Member of Parliament for the UK Conservative Party, for example has said that the inexperience and poor quality of the judges is 'undermining the credibility and value of the Court'.[46]

7 Concluding remarks

There is no doubt that the ECtHR's impressive corpus of case law stands out as a major contribution to the development of international human rights. However, as argued in this chapter, there are signs that the centre of gravity for the protection of human rights in Europe, and in particular within the EU Member States, will shift from Strasbourg to Luxembourg as the EU is increasingly prioritising fundamental rights. Opinion 2/13 means that accession of the EU to the ECHR is in all likelihood not going to be realised for years to come, if ever. And even if the draft agreement could be renegotiated and taking on board the considerations raised in the Opinion it would indeed leave the final saying in the protection of fundamental rights on the basis of the Charter to the CJEU. In addition, this process is likely to be driven forward by different factors: first, the ECtHR has afforded a very wide discretion to the EU by the statements in the cases of

45 Helena De Vylder, '*Stensholt* v. *Norway*: Why Single Judge Decisions Undermine the Court's Legitimacy' (Strasbourg Observers, 28 May 2014) <http://strasbourgobservers.com/2014/05/28/stensholt-v-norway-why-single-judge-decisions-undermine-the-courts-legitimacy-2> accessed 5 December 2014.

46 See '"Unelected" Euro judges "act beyond powers"' (Sky News, 21 April 2011) <http://news.sky.com/story/850249/unelected-euro-judges-act-beyond-powers> accessed 5 December 2014. This news item also stated the following: 'Unelected and inexperienced European judges risk triggering a constitutional crisis by acting outside of their agreed powers, a Tory MP has said.'

Bosphorus and *MSS* where the principle of 'presumption of Convention compliance' was established and reiterated. It remains to be seen whether this privileged treatment of EU law can be sustained if and when the EU becomes a Contracting Party, but at the time of writing this is the case law of the ECtHR. Other cases similarly show that the ECtHR has a great deal of good will when it comes to EU law and the case law of the CJEU. Moreover, as related above, the ECtHR is operating in an environment full of political and judicial resentments, i.e. reflected in a zero-growth policy that has been followed for many years and by politicians insistent on having reference to the concepts of 'subsidiarity' and 'margin of appreciation' inserted into the Preamble to the Convention. Related to this is the political and judicial criticism which has been directed at the Court over the last years, which has caused it to seek shelter in these concepts to avoid taking more principled decisions on present-day human rights issues and thereby risking provoking further political and judicial resentment. All of this, together with the other institutional problems mentioned above, weakens the Court's claim to continue playing a leading role in human rights protection on a pan-European level, in particular within the EU. At the same time, the centre of gravity is likely to move to Luxembourg.

4 The European Court of Human Rights and national courts: a constitutional relationship?*

Geir Ulfstein

1 Introduction

The European Court of Human Rights (ECtHR) has repeatedly characterised the European Convention on Human Rights (ECHR) 'as a constitutional instrument of European public order (ordre public)'.[1] Several authors have suggested that the ECtHR is – or should become – more like a constitutional court.[2]

But there has been criticism against a constitutionalisation of the ECtHR. The Secretary General of the Council of Europe, Torbjørn Jagland, said at the Interlaken Conference on the Future of the European Court of Human Rights:

> In recent years, there has been undefined talk of the Court becoming a 'Constitutional Court'. Although this has not yet led to any sort of agreement, let alone results, it has not been helpful. The Convention is not intended to

* This chapter was written under the auspices of ERC Advanced Grant 269841 MultiRights – on the Legitimacy of Multi-Level Human Rights Judiciary and the project Judicial Dialogues on the Rule of Law: Inter-action between national Courts and the European Court of Human Rights, financed by the Research Council of Norway/European Science Foundation (ECRP); and partly supported by the Research Council of Norway through its Centres of Excellence Funding Scheme, project number 223274 PluriCourts – the Legitimacy of the International Judiciary. I have benefited from comments by colleagues at the PluriCourts Centre and by the editors of this book.

1 *Loizidou* v. *Turkey* (Preliminary Objections) App. No. 15318/89 (1995) Series A 310, para. 75. See also e.g. *Al-Skeini and others* v. *United Kingdom* App. No. 55721/07 (ECHR 2011), para. 141.

2 See *inter alia* L. Wildhaber, 'A Constitutional Future for the European Court of Human Rights?' (2002) 23 *Human Rights Law Journal* 161; S. Greer, *The European Convention on Human Rights: Achievements, Problems and Prospects* (Cambridge University Press, 2006) 59; W. Sadurski, *Constitutionalism and the Enlargement of Europe* (Oxford University Press, 2012) 1, 44; A. Voβkuhle, 'Multilevel Cooperation of the European Constitutional Courts: Der Europäische Verfassungsgerichtsverbund' (2010) 6 *European Constitutional Law Review* 175, 181; S. Greer and L. Wildhaber, 'Revisiting the Debate about "Constitutionalising" the European Court of Human Rights' (2012) 12 *Human Rights Law Review* 655; A. S. Sweet, 'A Cosmopolitan Legal Order: Constitutional Pluralism and Rights Adjudication in Europe' (2012) 1 *Global Constitutionalism* 53.

> be a 'European constitution' and it is difficult to see how the Court could become like any existing national constitutional court.[3]

The ECtHR and national courts belong to two different legal orders, respectively the international and national order. The ECtHR reviews the 'conventionality' of governmental acts. National courts have the dual role of reviewing the conventionality of such acts, but they may also have the power to review their constitutionality.

On the other hand, the ECtHR has several constitutional implications (or 'functions'). First, the Court deals substantially with an essential constitutional issue, i.e. the protection of human rights. But the constitutional features go wider. The practice by the ECtHR may be an important factor in defining what is considered *lex superior* in national law, i.e. the content of the legal norms enjoying a constitutional status. Moreover, executive acts may be deemed unlawful if they violate ECtHR practice. Further, national legislation will generally be interpreted on the basis of ECtHR practice. National legislation in contradiction to ECtHR practice may even – depending on the relevant national system – be set aside. This means that ECtHR practice has constitutional functions both in influencing the interpretation of national constitutions, protecting individuals against governmental power, and serving as a basis for national judicial review of governmental acts.

The constitutional function of the ECtHR means that the Court should be subject to constitutional standards known from national constitutional law, especially the '[t]rinitarian mantra of the constitutionalist faith':[4] democracy, human rights and the rule of law. But the constitutional standards should be adapted to the special features of this relationship, where the principle of subsidiarity is of special relevance.

In this chapter I discuss how the ECtHR acts – and should act – as part of a constitutional system across the international–national division. While the constitutional debate has mainly focused on whether the ECtHR should have a constitutional function in empowering the Court to select cases that have a general legal interest – rather than dealing with all individual complaints – my focus is on the substantive aspects of the ECtHR's practice. I will also discuss the role of national apex courts and their interaction with the ECtHR from a constitutional perspective. The analysis is based on the practice by the ECtHR as well by national courts, but it also aims at developing constitutional thinking about the ECtHR: what should be the implications of a constitutional approach to the ECtHR.[5]

3 Quoted from A. Mowbray, 'The Interlaken Declaration – The Beginning of a New Era for the European Court of Human Rights?' (2010) 10 *Human Rights Law Review* 519, 523.

4 M. Kumm and others, 'How Large is the World of Global Constitutionalism?' (2014) 3 *Global Constitutionalism* 1, 3.

5 See a comparable approach in J. Klabbers, 'Setting the Scene', in J. Klabbers, A. Peters and G. Ulfstein (eds), *The Constitutionalization of International Law* (Oxford University Press, 2009) 1, 4–5.

Accession by the European Union (EU) to the ECHR may represent further constitutionalisation of the European legal order(s) by mandating ECtHR review of EU acts. It may also mean a stricter review by the ECtHR of Member States' implementation of EU acts than the current *Bosphorus* doctrine implies.[6] The possibility of accession in the near future, however, seems highly unlikely following the European Court of Justice's Opinion 2/13 of 18 December 2014. The potential effects of EU accession will therefore not be discussed in this contribution.

2 The role of the ECtHR

National apex courts will not necessarily review all aspects of other constitutional organs' acts with the same intensity – they may exercise different forms of deference. But what deference does and should be exercised by the ECtHR in reviewing governmental acts, and in what sense is it comparable to or different from deference practised by national courts undertaking constitutional review?

The ECtHR will under certain circumstances defer to decisions by national constitutional organs under reference to the doctrine of the margin of appreciation. The margin is clearly established in a long-standing practice of the ECtHR, and is now formalised in the new Protocol 15 (not yet in force), as an aspect of subsidiarity.[7] The principle of subsidiarity is aiming at the protection of national freedom by leaving decision-making to states, unless it is more effectively or efficiently performed at the international level.[8]

The margin of appreciation in the ECtHR context can, as suggested by George Letsas, on the one hand be understood as a 'substantive concept', which addresses 'the relationship between individual freedoms and collective goals'.[9] It can also

6 See O. De Schutter, '*Bosphorus* Post-Accession: Redefining the Relationships between the European Court of Human Rights and the Parties to the Convention', in V. Kosta, N. Skoutaris and V. P. Tzevelekos (eds), *The EU Accession to the ECHR* (Hart, 2014) 177–198; J. Callewaert, *The Accession of the European Union to the European Convention on Human Rights* (Council of Europe, 2014); S. Douglas-Scott, 'The Court of Justice of the European Union and the European Court of Human Rights after Lisbon', in S. A. de Vries, U. Bernitz and S. Weatherill (eds), *The Protection of Fundamental Rights in the EU After Lisbon* (Hart, 2013) 153; P. Craig, 'EU Accession to the ECHR: Competence, Procedure and Substance' (2013) 36 *Fordham International Law Journal* 1114.

7 Protocol No. 15 amending the Convention for the Protection of Human Rights and Fundamental Freedoms (adopted 24 June 2013) CETS No. 213.

8 See re subsidiarity: I. Feichtner, 'Subsidiarity', *Max Planck Encyclopedia of Public International Law* at <www.mpepil.com>; A. Føllesdal, 'Survey Article: Subsidiarity' (1998) 6 *Journal of Political Philosophy* 190; P. G. Carozza 'Subsidiarity as a Structural Principle of International Human Rights Law' (2003) 97 *American Journal of International Law* 38; M. Kumm, 'The Legitimacy of International Law: A Constitutionalist Framework of Analysis' (2004) 15 *European Journal of International Law* 907, 920–924; A. Føllesdal, 'The Principle of Subsidiarity as a Constitutional Principle in International Law' (2013) 2 *Global Constitutionalism* 37.

9 G. Letsas, *A Theory of Interpretation of the European Convention on Human Rights* (Oxford University Press, 2007) 80–81.

refer to the balancing of different human rights or to the same rights claimed by different persons. This aspect of the margin concerns the discretion accorded to the state through the openness of the substantive obligations. The second approach is what Letsas calls a 'structural concept', addressing 'the limits or intensity of the review of the European Court of Human Rights in view of its status as an international tribunal'.[10] This latter approach is the one that will be discussed here since we are interested in the relationship between national constitutional organs and the ECtHR, and not the discretion allowed by the ECHR's substantive obligations per se. The margin in this latter sense indicates a standard of review relevant for constitutional thinking, as it asks which deference the ECtHR as an international court should apply in reviewing domestic decisions, including those of national courts.

Andrew Legg proposes that the margin of appreciation is the practice of the ECtHR assigning weight to the respondent state's reasoning on the basis of three factors: (i) democratic legitimacy; (ii) the common practice of states; and (iii) expertise.[11] I agree that these are relevant factors to be taken into account. My focus is, however, on the interplay between the Court and different national constitutional organs. Consequently, the following discussion will be divided into a presentation of the general aspects of how the ECtHR deals with national constitutional organs, but subsequently the focus is on the particular aspects of review of, respectively, the national judiciary and the legislature.

2.1 General aspects

The Preamble of the ECHR refers to 'greater unity' between the Member States, not full harmonisation. Thus, while the ECtHR shall ensure equal respect for human rights as embodied in the ECHR, it shall also respect the differences between the Member States. The classic reference is the *Handyside* case (1976), leaving a margin of appreciation to the state where the freedom of expression is in tension with moral values.[12] Such a margin has also been applied to other ECHR obligations.[13]

It is worth noting that the Court in the *Handyside* case refers to 'State authorities' in general, without distinguishing between the different branches of national constitutional organs. The same generality is demonstrated in the *A* v. *United Kingdom* case (2009) which refers to 'domestic authorities'. But this case is also of importance in setting out that the margin applied by the Court is of a different nature than that applied at the national level.[14]

10 Ibid. 81.
11 A. Legg, *The Margin of Appreciation in International Human Rights Law: Deference and Proportionality* (Oxford University Press, 2012) 7.
12 *Handyside* v. *United Kingdom* App. No. 5493/72 (1976) Series A no. 24, para. 48.
13 D. J. Harris and others, *Harris, O'Boyle & Warbrick Law of the European Convention on Human Rights* (3rd edn, Oxford University Press, 2014) 15.
14 *A. and Others* v. *United Kingdom* App. No. 3455/05 (ECHR 2009), para. 184.

Hence, our point of departure is that the margin of appreciation applies to all national constitutional organs, but that the margin is not necessarily identical to the discretion allowed to the national legislature and the executive by national courts.

2.2 Review of national courts

The principle of subsidiarity establishes a presumption that decisions should be taken at the lower level, i.e. by national courts rather than by the ECtHR. But this presumption should be informed by the relationship between courts at the two levels.

First, national courts may be supposed to have greater expertise on the relevant facts of the case as well as the content of the applicable domestic law. This is acknowledged by the ECtHR in its insistence that it is not a court of 'fourth instance'.[15]

This means that the Court will only deal with errors of fact or of the application of national law to the extent it has significance for infringements of the ECHR. But also that it will exercise judicial self-restraint in the establishment of the facts of the case and the application of domestic law. While the element of closeness to the facts may have aspects comparable to deference exercised by national apex courts in relation to lower courts, the expertise of the ECtHR with respect to national law is clearly different from that of the highest national courts, which are not only supposed to have the best knowledge of national law, but in addition – in accordance with national constitutional law – may have the function of finally determining the interpretation of the constitution.

But there are other aspects where the ECtHR must be supposed to have greater expertise than domestic courts. The Court is in a better position to map any European consensus of relevance to the interpretation of the ECHR. The reason is that its Registry has the capacity as well as the competence to analyse domestic law in the 47 Member States. And, not least, the ECtHR is in a better position to interpret the ECHR. This is the day-to-day work of the Court while national courts are primarily concerned with domestic law (although ECHR law has become ever more important). This also relates to the special function of the ECtHR: it is supposed to have the final word on the interpretation and application of the ECHR. So, the greater expertise in this respect is supplemented by its function in this human rights system.

But, first, the ECtHR's deference will depend of the quality of the judgments by the national courts, as expressed by former ECtHR President Bratza:

> Secondly, the Strasbourg Court has, in my perception, been particularly respectful of decisions emanating from courts in the United Kingdom since the coming into effect of the Human Rights Act and this because of the very

15 Harris and others (n. 13) 17–18.

> high quality of the judgments of these courts, which have greatly facilitated our task of adjudication.[16]

This is reflected in the *Animal Defenders* case (2013) on political television advertising, where the Court said that it 'attaches considerable weight to these exacting and pertinent reviews, by both parliamentary and judicial bodies, of the complex regulatory regime governing political broadcasting in the United Kingdom and to their view that the general measures was necessary to prevent the distortion of crucial public interest debates and, thereby, the undermining of the democratic process'.[17]

Second, national courts will also stand a better chance to be allowed a wider margin of appreciation if they are able to convince the ECtHR that they have taken into account relevant principles for interpretation, such as the principle of proportionality, as applied by the ECtHR.[18] The Court stated for example in the *von Hannover (No. 2)* case (2012) that '[w]here the balancing exercise has been undertaken by the national authorities in conformity with the criteria laid down in the Court's case-law, the Court would require strong reasons to substitute its view for that of the domestic courts'.[19] This may be seen as an aspect of what Başak Çali has called a 'responsible courts doctrine' (see Chapter 9, this volume).

But, national courts may also try to convince the ECtHR about the proper interpretation of the ECHR. This requires that the national courts interpret the ECHR in a way that the ECtHR finds convincing and suited to application on a European basis. It is also helpful if the interpretation of the ECHR can convince other national courts in Member States.[20]

The *Al-Khawaja and Tahery* case (2011) has usually been seen as an example where the ECtHR has heeded the outcome from national courts.[21] In this case, the UK House of Lords insisted that allowing witness statements without the possibility of cross-examination in the particular circumstances was not in violation of the requirement of a fair trial. This was seen as a violation of the ECHR by the ECtHR Chamber, but was eventually accepted by the Grand Chamber.

16 N. Bratza, 'The Relationship between the UK Courts and Strasbourg' (2011) 5 *European Human Rights Law Review* 505, 507; R. Spano, 'Universality or Diversity of Human Rights?: Strasbourg in the Age of Subsidiarity' (2014) 14 *Human Rights Law Review* 487, 498–499.

17 *Animal Defenders International* v. *United Kingdom* App. No. 48876/08 (ECHR 2013), para. 116.

18 P. Mahoney, 'The Relationship between the Strasbourg Court and the National Courts' (2014) 130 *Law Quarterly Review* 568, 571.

19 *Von Hannover* v. *Germany (No. 2)* App. Nos 40660/08 and 60641/08 (ECHR 2012), para. 107.

20 M. Andenas and E. Bjorge, 'National Implementation of ECHR Rights', in A. Føllesdal, B. Peters and G. Ulfstein (eds), *Constituting Europe: The European Court of Human Rights in a National, European and Global Context* (Cambridge University Press, 2013) 181, 261.

21 *Al-Khawaja and Tahery* v. *United Kingdom* App. No. 26766/05 and 22228/06 (ECHR 2011).

But we have seen several cases where both national courts and the ECtHR have taken mutual account of each other's judgments and accommodated their practice. A prominent example involving the German Constitutional Court is the cases on freedom of expression in *von Hannover (No. 1) and (2)*.[22] This means that there may be a two-way interaction between the ECtHR and national courts, as opposed to a one-way influence of the ECtHR on the national judiciary.[23]

We can conclude that the margin of appreciation establishes a general presumption that decision-making should be left to state authorities, including national courts. But the application of the margin in relation to national courts should be informed by the constitutional functions of, respectively, national courts and the ECtHR. This means that the ECtHR is deferent to national courts' determination of the facts of the case and, not least, their interpretation of national law. On the other hand, the ECtHR has best expertise and, of special significance, has the particular function of being the ultimate interpreter of the ECHR.

National courts may be allowed a wider margin of appreciation if their judgments are of high quality and if they apply relevant principles of interpretation as developed by the ECtHR. But the ECtHR should also be open to well-reasoned interpretation of the ECHR by national courts. This means that the hierarchy between the two levels becomes less strict, and that the interaction is characterised by mutual trust and cooperation. These two aspects of the role of national courts, i.e. pronouncing judgments within the margin of appreciation and contribution to the interpretation of the ECHR, raise somewhat different constitutional issues.

The margin of appreciation may be seen as representing a de-constitutionalisation rather than a constitutionalisation of the relationship between national courts and the ECtHR if we consider that an essential aspect of a constitutional system is its legal consistency. The margin of appreciation may instead lead to legal fragmentation, allowing different application of the ECHR in different national jurisdictions.

This diversity distinguishes the ECHR system from a monolithic national legal system. But, first, elements of such diversity are not unknown in federal states which apply forms of subsidiarity in relation to their component parts.[24] Second, the forms and breadth of the margin is determined by the ECtHR, as the superior Court for interpretation and application of the ECHR.

The claim of de-constitutionalisation, further, does not apply to instances where the ECtHR considers national courts' well-reasoned opinion about the proper

22 *Von Hannover* v. *Germany (No. 1)* App. No. 59320/00 (ECHR 2004) and *Von Hannover* v.*Germany (No. 2)* (n. 19).

23 Voβkuhle (n. 2) 197; Mahoney (n. 18) 571; E. Bjorge, 'Bottom-up Shaping of Rights: How the Scope of Human Rights at the National Level Impacts upon Convention Rights', in E. Brems and J. Gerards (eds), *Shaping Rights in the ECHR: The Role of the European Court of Human Rights in Determining the Scope of Human Rights* (Cambridge University Press, 2013) 211.

24 D. Halberstam, 'Federalism: Theory, Policy, Law', in M. Rosenfeld and A. Sajó (eds), *The Oxford Handbook of Comparative Constitutional Law* (Oxford University Press, 2012) 577, 585; S. G. Breyer, *Making Our Democracy Work: A Judge's View* (1st edn, Knopf, 2010) 121–137.

interpretation of the ECHR. In such cases the issue is not whether to allow different interpretations in different national jurisdictions, but rather to find the best interpretation of the ECHR. Such openness from the ECtHR would not undermine legal consistency, but rather promote a sustainable interpretation of the ECHR which stands a better chance of being implemented by national courts. The ECtHR should, however, ensure that the views of all national courts pronouncing on a particular ECHR interpretation are taken into account in order to avoid that some national courts are in practice exercising hegemony in the interpretation of the ECHR.

The ECtHR has responsibility for upholding the rule of law in the interpretation of the ECHR. This principle may be threatened both at the national and international level – and in their interaction – by a more important role for national courts. This is of particular importance when the margin of appreciation and evolutive (dynamic) interpretation contribute to making human rights law less predictable for states as well as for individuals. More openness with respect to different interpretations of the ECHR by national courts will represent a challenge for the ECtHR in defining which interpretation to be considered authoritative. Finally, and not least, the ECtHR has the responsibility for ensuring respect for human rights as incorporated by the ECHR. This also sets limits for the use of the margin of appreciation and openness towards recognition of judgments by national courts.

2.3 Review of the national legislature

The importance of protecting political democracy as well as human rights is acknowledged in the preamble of the ECHR:

> Reaffirming their profound belief in those fundamental freedoms which are the foundation of justice and peace in the world and are best maintained on the one hand by an *effective political democracy* and on the other by a *common understanding and observance of the human rights* upon which they depend. [emphasis added]

But there may be a need to balance national democratic freedom and the protection of human rights.

The explicit acknowledgement of the significance of political democracy may be seen as strengthening the general margin of appreciation allowed to the national legislature. While also constitutional courts may attach some weight to parliaments' interpretation of the national constitution, the deference applied by the ECtHR is of a somewhat different character.

The President of the United Kingdom Supreme Court, Lord Neuberger, in a speech on 12 February 2014 reflecting on British sentiments towards Europe, said that the idea that the ECtHR can overrule parliamentary decisions is 'a little short of offensive to our notions of constitutional propriety'.[25] This raises the question

25 L. Neuberger, 'The British and Europe', *Cambridge Freshfields Annual Law Lecture 2014* at <www.privatelaw.law.cam.ac.uk/Documents/FreshfieldsLecture2014>.

of the appropriateness of 'constitutional' review of democratic decision-making, which at the national level has been discussed in terms of its 'counter-majoritarian' character.[26]

Review of the national legislators by international courts differs in several respects from review by national courts. On one hand, it may be seen as representing a more grave interference in national democracy, since the relevant legislature is not able to respond by amendment of the ECHR, as opposed to amendment of the national constitution. And we have no international democratic organ (except for non-binding decisions by the Council of Ministers and the Parliamentary Assembly) which can give the Court guidance on how competing interests and values should be balanced. The relevant avenue would therefore be amendment of the ECHR – which requires consent by all Member States. Or the state may take the dramatic step of withdrawing from the ECHR altogether.

On the other hand, the state has through its democratic organs delegated powers to the Court to make binding judgments on the interpretation and application of the ECHR (Article 46). Second, national authorities are left some discretion on the basis of the margin of appreciation. Third, the ECtHR will in designing remedies in cases where it has found a violation generally leave some room for national decision-making with respect to how judgments should be implemented.[27]

Finally, the ECtHR cannot declare national legislation null and void. It can only establish that a violation of the ECHR has occurred, and determine remedies, at the international level. If we see it through the prism of national law, it is up to the state to determine the effects of the ECtHR judgments in national law. National courts may find that implementing a judgment would represent a violation of the constitution or of ordinary legislation, and thus not to be enforced at the national level. National courts in EU Member States have, for example, claimed that EU law would not be recognised in national law if it infringes the 'constitutional identity' of Member States.[28] Such non-recognition would be a

26 See J. Waldron, 'The Core of the Case against Judicial Review' (2006) 115 *Yale Law Journal* 1346; R. Bellamy, *Political Constitutionalism: A Republican Defence of the Constitutionality of Democracy* (Cambridge University Press, 2007); R. H. Fallon Jr, 'The Core of an Uneasy Case for Judicial Review' (2008) 121 *Harvard Law Review* 1693; M. Tushnet, 'How Different Are Waldron's and Fallon's Core Cases for and against Judicial Review?' (2010) 30 *Oxford Journal of legal Studies* 49. See on the ECHR: A. Føllesdal, 'The Legitimacy of International Human Rights Review: The Case of the European Court of Human Rights' (2009) 40 *Journal of Social Philosophy* 595; A. Føllesdal, 'Why the European Court of Human Rights Might Be Democratically Legitimate – A Modest Defense' (2009) 27 *Nordic Journal of Human Rights* 260; R. Bellamy, 'The Democratic Legitimacy of International Human Rights Conventions: Political Constitutionalism and the European Convention on Human Rights' (2014) 25 *European Journal of International Law* 1019.

27 Harris and others (n. 13) 29.

28 A. Peters and U. K. Preuss, 'International Relations and International Law', in M. V. Tushnet, T. Fleiner and C. Saunders (eds), *Routledge Handbook of Constitutional Law* (Routledge, 2013) 33, 39; Voβkuhle (n. 2) 191.

breach of the international legal obligations, but could be in perfect harmony with national law. Hence, the interference in national democratic decision-making is less intrusive than that of national constitutional courts.[29]

The Court has indicated its willingness to listen to the national legislature. In the *Hirst* case (2005) on prisoners' voting rights, the Grand Chamber stated that 'there is no evidence that parliament has ever sought to weigh the competing interests or to assess the proportionality of a blanket ban on the right of a convicted prisoner to vote'.[30] The assumption would be that the ECtHR would have accorded weight to the legislature if it had sought to weigh the competing interests and assessed the proportionality of prohibiting prisoners from voting.

This is supported by cases where the Court has emphasised a parliament's thorough examination of interferences in human rights. In the *Animal Defenders* case on political television advertising (2013) the Court, as referred to above, attached 'considerable weight to these exacting and pertinent reviews, by both parliamentary and judicial bodies'.[31]

In *SAS* v. *France* (2014), the *burqa* case on wearing in public clothing that conceals face, the Court emphasised the importance of its subsidiary role in light of the democratic legitimacy of national authorities. The Court stated that '[i]n matters of general policy, on which opinions within a democratic society may reasonably differ widely, the role of the domestic policy-maker should be given special weight'.[32]

Hence, the general margin of appreciation also applies to acts by the national legislature. Indeed, the Preamble of the ECHR indicates a special role for the legislature as the organ for 'political democracy'. Furthermore, such a role is supported by the fact that democratic organs are nationally based, while we do not have as representative organs at the international level – the European Parliament and the Parliamentary Assembly of the Council of Europe coming closest.

The Court should therefore pay due respect to the fact that the democratic legitimacy of policy choices between different values and interests lies primarily with the national legislatures. This means that national legislatures should be allowed more discretion in such choices than what is allowed for both the executive and national courts – to the extent the latter organs make such choices. But it should be kept in mind that there is no common standard of deference to the legislature across different national jurisdictions – and the United Kingdom is an example of a state without any constitutional review by national courts.

Furthermore, the ECtHR should respect diversity of political decision-making in the different legislatures of the European Member States. Therefore, different

29 However, we also have national courts undertaking a 'weak' constitutional review, such as the Canadian Supreme Court, see A. H. Chen and M. P. Maduro, 'The Judiciary and Constitutional Review', in M. V. Tushnet, T. Fleiner and C. Saunders (eds), *Routledge Handbook of Constitutional Law* (Routledge, 2013) 97, 103.

30 *Hirst* v. *United Kingdom (No. 2)* App. No. 74025/01 (ECHR 2005), para. 79.

31 *Animal Defenders International* v. *United Kingdom* (n. 17), para. 116.

32 *SAS* v. *France* App. No. 43835/11 (ECHR 2014), para. 129.

ways of implementing the ECHR based on democratic decision-making must be allowed – which is also different from constitutional review in a national context.

The national legislature should be given a special discretion if their decisions are the result of democratic procedures that have taken due account of ECHR principles as developed by the Court. Such control raises, however, several dilemmas. First, it may be asked whether the ECtHR has sufficient knowledge about the considerations and procedures applied by the national parliaments. But as regards democratic procedures, an even more important dilemma is the diversity of procedures applied in different countries, and to what extent the Court should determine that one or some of the procedures are more democratic than others. Applying such determinations might also be seen in contradiction to the principle of sovereign equality in international law. This is very different from national constitutional review and there are good reasons for the Court to be cautious in declaring some procedures as more democratic than others.

Acknowledging a wide margin of appreciation would represent a danger of fragmentation rather than constitutionalisation, as discussed above in relation to national courts. But it is the ECtHR that determines the content of the margin. Moreover, the Court has the final word on the interpretation of the ECHR beyond the margin of appreciation, and it must uphold both the rule of law and effective protection of human rights as embodied in the ECHR.

3 The role of national courts

What about the role of national courts: do they interact with the ECtHR in what should be considered a constitutional manner, and what are – and should be – the features of such interaction?

National authorities have an international legal obligation to implement ECtHR judgments where they have been parties to a case (Article 46). But national courts go far beyond what is required by judgments against the particular state. They take account of the general practice of the ECtHR.[33] This should be seen as an aspect of constitutionalisation: national courts and the ECtHR act generally as a consistent legal system, with the ECtHR as the ultimate interpreter of the ECHR.

On the other hand, national courts may choose to ignore interpretations applied by the ECtHR and rely on their own status as the final arbiters of the content of domestic law. But then they risk review by the ECtHR. National courts may instead, as discussed above, through the quality of their judgments and by applying methods of interpretation developed by the ECtHR seek to widen their margin of appreciation. But they may also choose a more active approach – possibly in concert with other national courts – by seeking to influence the Court's interpretation of the ECHR.

33 D. Spielmann, 'Jurisprudence of the European Court of Human Rights and the Constitutional Systems of Europe', in M. Rosenfeld and A. Sajó (eds), *The Oxford Handbook of Comparative Constitutional Law* (Oxford University Press, 2012) 1232.

While lower courts may generally try to convince national apex courts about the proper interpretation of national legislation, including national constitutions, the role of national courts in relation to the ECtHR is of a somewhat different character. Such active interaction by national courts would give flesh to the principle of subsidiarity in the sense that national courts would participate in the interpretation of the ECHR as a joint enterprise. It could even place national courts in the leading role of interpreting the ECHR.[34] This would represent a 'bottom up' approach in line with the principle of subsidiarity.[35] It could even be a sign of the 'age of subsidiarity'.[36]

National courts could in this way be mediators between the national and the international legal system. They could also mediate between different national legal systems. In this way they would combine the pursuit of vertical and horizontal interaction. Active participation in future ECHR interpretation would assumedly benefit both the Member States and the system as a whole, in mutual learning and of finding the best solutions.[37] But this requires that national courts are familiar with and respect the methods of interpretation applied by the ECtHR. Second, it would require that national courts are sufficiently self-confident. Furthermore, the ECtHR should give guidance and be the ultimate guardian of the rule of law and of effective protection of human rights.

4 Conclusion

The ECtHR and national constitutional organs interact – and should interact – as part of a two-way common legal enterprise, with the ECtHR as the ultimate interpreter of the ECHR. This system should be guided by applicable constitutional principles, i.e. democracy, the rule of law, protection of human rights and subsidiarity. These principles should be adapted to the special relationship between the ECtHR and national constitutional organs.

The ECtHR applies a margin of appreciation in relation to national constitutional organs, allowing them certain discretion. But this doctrine is informed by relevant constitutional principles. The ECtHR pays – and should pay – particular respect to national courts when it comes to evaluation of the relevant facts of the case and interpretation of national legislation. The Court should also allow a wide margin of appreciation to national courts if their judgments are of a high qualitative standard and if they apply the methods of interpretation of the ECHR as developed by the ECtHR. Furthermore, the Court should be open to well-reasoned interpretations of the ECHR by national courts, and even more so if they reflect a consensus among different national courts.

As regards the national legislatures, the Court should acknowledge that they are – in the absence of comparable international democratic organs – the legitimate

34 See Mahoney (n. 18) 584.
35 See Bjorge (n. 23).
36 Spano (n. 16).
37 Voßkuhle (n. 2) 198.

democratic organs when it comes to policy choices. Their choices, if they are based on genuine democratic processes and respect for the principles embodied in the ECHR as interpreted by the ECHR, should be given significant weight. But both in relation to national courts and national legislatures, the ECtHR should protect the rule of law as well as ensuring effective protection of human rights.

National courts should continue to take account of the practice developed by the ECtHR. But national courts should be more active in their engagement with the Court, including in the proper interpretation of the ECHR. They should act as mediators both between the national and international level, and between different national systems. This would reflect an application of the principle of subsidiarity adapted to the special constitutional setting represented by the interaction between the ECtHR and national constitutional organs.

5 National courts and judicial disobedience to the ECHR: a comparative overview*

Giuseppe Martinico

1 Introduction

Openness and resistance are essential keywords to understanding the nature of the so-called post-totalitarian constitutionalism.[1] It is possible to find this element in many constitutions 'born from the Resistance',[2] which have been the product of a political compromise among very different democratic forces that had rejection of totalitarian experiences as their only common point. These constitutions are characterised by a strong programmatic character, inspired by the sincere denial of the features of the previous regime and by the need for an entirely different society. By 'constitutions born from the Resistance', Mortati also referred to other texts such as, for instance, the French (IV Republic) and the German constitutions. As Carrozza more recently noticed, today we could include within this group the Portuguese, Spanish and Greek constitutions that were promulgated during the 1970s.[3]

Openness is precisely one of the most evident features that characterises these texts, and it is possible to find the roots of this phenomenon even earlier, looking back at what, in the 1930s, Mirkine-Guetzévitch called the 'internationalization of modern constitutions'.[4] In other words, openness seems to belong to the core of the 'nouvelles tendances du droit constitutionnel'.[5] Something similar might be argued with regard to the connection between flexibility (in this context understood as ability to adapt) and constitutionalism, as I have tried to argue elsewhere (especially looking at what scholars term 'evolutionary constitutionalism').[6]

* Thanks to Giuseppe Bianco and Leandro Mancano for comments and to Oddný Mjöll Arnardóttir and Antoine Buyse for their help.

1 P. Carrozza, 'Constitutionalism's Post-modern Opening', in M. Loughlin and N. Walker (eds), *The Paradox of Constitutionalism: Constituent Power and Constitutional Form* (Oxford University Press, 2007) 169, 180–182.
2 C. Mortati, *Lezioni sulle forme di governo* (Cedam, 1973) 222.
3 Carrozza (n. 1) 180.
4 B. Mirkine-Guetzévitch, *Les Nouvelles tendances du droit constitutionnel* (Giard, 1931) 48.
5 Ibid.
6 G. Martinico, *Lo spirito polemico del diritto europeo. Studio sulle ambizioni costituzionali dell'Unione* (Aracne, 2011) 27.

In this chapter I explore the importance that such openness has had to provide the European Convention on Human Rights (ECHR) with a super-legislative authority and, above all, what one could call the unexpected consequences of such a success. As we will see, over the years national courts have developed a number of techniques to disobey the case law of the European Court of Human Rights (ECtHR) and this has created conflicts sometimes (by conflicts I mean interpretative disagreements). I am not interested in all these types of conflicts; rather, I will focus on those disagreements that are due to constitutional openness towards the ECHR. In other words, I am interested in those cases where national judges first comply with the procedural duty to take the case law of the Strasbourg Court into account but then decide to depart from the concrete results reached by the ECtHR, by giving arguments in support of their decision.[7]

As for the structure of this chapter, I recall what I mean by constitutional openness. In a second moment, I explore the super-legislative authority of the ECHR and, finally, I offer some examples of national disobedience. When looking at these particular kinds of conflicts my argument is that these interpretative disagreements should be seen as a natural consequence of constitutional openness rather than as a symptom of constitutional closure. Usually cooperation and conflict are understood as antithetical concepts, but in this chapter I try to look at some episodes of conflictual interactions that can trigger an exchange of arguments, i.e. a dialogue[8] (conceived as the most important type of cooperative interactions). Indeed, two interlocutors can have an exchange of view even if the result of this does not lead to a full agreement: if you take the argument of your interlocutor into account and give reasons explaining your disagreement, it is possible to define this exchange as dialogue; this is pluralism in action which is fed by that constitutional openness described in the first part of this chapter.

2 Openness and internationalisation

As pointed out by Mortati the openness and internationalisation of constitutions after the Second World War should be seen as a direct reaction to the legal nationalism that had characterised the totalitarian regimes.[9] This should not be surprising; as Bobbio pointed out in his essays, law and politics can be considered as two sides of the same coin, with politics as the dynamic side of political power.[10]

7 On the distinction between *interpretationa* and argumentation, see, among others, R. Alexy, 'Interpretazione giuridica', in *Enciclopedia delle Scienze sociali* (Treccani, 1996), available at <www.treccani.it/enciclopedia/interpretazione-giuridica_%28Enciclopedia_delle_scienze_sociali%29>.

8 A. Torres Pérez, *Conflicts of Rights in the European Union: A Theory of Supranational Adjudication* (Oxford University Press, 2009) 118–130.

9 Mortati (n. 2).

10 N. Bobbio, 'Diritto', in N. Bobbio, N. Matteucci and G. Pasquino (eds), *Dizionario della Politca* (UTET, 1976) 334.

By openness, in this chapter, I mean a constitutionally established friendliness towards legal sources that are, from a formal point of view, external to those governed by the national system; or, in other words, sources that are not produced by the national actors (and, as such, are not traceable to the general will of the people) in charge of the law-making functions according to the constitution. This kind of constitutional openness might present different forms: it can be limited to what we call general international law (international customary law) or even extended to international treaties. Concerning this second case, there are constitutions that present a wider openness with regard to human rights treaties, because of the continuity that exists between the their axiological contents and the substance of these treaties.

Openness, as has been studied by several scholars,[11] may perform an important function of constitutional relevance. It may contribute to reinforcing the original pact codified in the constitution by offering new arguments to reinforce those rights enshrined in the *Verfassung* or by making the constitutional text more flexible and adaptive to new needs of society. This elasticity of the original text knows some limitations, of course, because many of these constitutions are also characterised by the existence of a group of principles that may not be jeopardised, because their violation would imply the denial of the axiological basis on which the relevant legal order is founded. At the national level, constitutional law scholars describe this set of principles in different ways, e.g. the 'Republican form' ('forma repubblicana') in Italy and the eternity clause ('Ewigkeitsklause') in Germany.[12]

This openness is represented by some constitutional provisions that govern not only the effects of external norms in the local territory, but also the national participation in and contribution to the international community. All of these norms are based on the existence of an axiological continuity between the principles and values that govern the life of a given polity within its own boundaries and those that should characterise the international community. In other words, these constitutions have never accepted the limitation of the promotion of their values to the domestic boundaries, and indeed, even when the wording of their provisions refers to 'citizens', their constitutional courts have frequently extended the substance of these norms to non-citizens, at least in the field of fundamental rights.[13] These constitutions have also attempted to govern the action of domestic actors even beyond the national territory, promoting their values even beyond the national

11 A. Peters, 'Compensatory Constitutionalism: The Function and Potential of Fundamental International Norms and Structures' (2006) 19 *Leiden Journal of International Law* 579.

12 Article 139 of the Italian Constitution ('The form of Republic shall not be a matter for constitutional amendment') and Article 79, Paragraph (3) of the Basic Law (Grundgesetz-GG) of the Federal Republic of Germany ('Amendments to this Basic Law affecting the division of the Federation into Länder, their participation on principle in the legislative process, or the principles laid down in Articles 1 and 20 shall be inadmissible').

13 This is the Italian case, for instance, see Italian Constitutional Court, decision no. 432/2005, available at <www.cortecostituzionale.it>.

arena. The Italian experience is emblematic from this point of view, but is also part of a broader trend.[14]

As a consequence of that constitutional openness, today, national constitutions make reference to international and supranational law to ensure the protection of certain constitutional goods.[15] For instance, in the Italian case, it has been argued that the general clause of protection of fundamental rights that is contained in Article 2 of the Constitution is to be considered an 'open' norm.[16] This reading of Article 2 has allowed the Constitutional Court to recognise and guarantee the so-called new rights (the right to know, the right to privacy, environmental rights) and to keep the constitution up to date with respect to the need to protect the 'person' (*principio personalista*).

The cases of the Portuguese, Spanish and Italian constitutions share the same spirit of openness, as recalled, among others, by Cassese and Stein.[17] These constitutions introduced a fundamental distinction: that between the general category of international treaties and that particular group of international treaties devoted to human rights. As for Portugal, the fundamental provision is Article 16 of the Constitution, which recognises that international human rights treaties have a complementary role to it.[18] This provision accords an interpretative role to the Universal Declaration of the Rights of Human Rights, seemingly excluding other conventions like the ECHR, but the Portuguese Constitutional Court has often used the ECHR as an important auxiliary hermeneutic tool for interpreting the Constitution, leaving the matter unresolved.[19]

The most important confirmation of human rights treaties' special ranking in Spain is Article 10.2 of the Spanish Constitution, which acknowledges that they provide interpretive guidance in the application of human rights-related

14 See A. Cassese, 'Modern Constitutions and International Law' *Recueil de Cours* (Brill, 1985) 331.

15 A. Saiz Arnaiz, *La apertura constitucional al derecho internacional y europeo de los derechos humanos. El artículo 10.2 de la Constitución Española* (CEPC, 1999).

16 Article 2 Constitution: 'The Republic recognises and guarantees the inviolable rights of the person, both as an individual and in the social groups where human personality is expressed.'

17 Cassese (n. 14) 351. Another interesting case study is that of the Central-Eastern European constitutions, on which see E. Stein, 'International Law in Internal Law: Toward Internationalization of Central-Eastern European Constitutions?' (1994) 88 *American Journal of International Law* 427, 429.

18 Article 16 Constitution: '1. The fundamental rights enshrined in this Constitution shall not exclude such other rights as may be laid down by law and in the applicable rules of international law. 2. The provisions of this Constitution and of laws concerning fundamental rights shall be interpreted and construed in accordance with the Universal Declaration of Human Rights.'

19 Portuguese Constitutional Court, decision 345/99, available at <www.tribunalconstitucional.pt>. On this, see F. Coutinho, 'Report on Portugal', in G. Martinico and O. Pollicino (eds), *The National Judicial Treatment of the ECHR and EU Laws: A Comparative Constitutional Perspective* (Europa Law Publishing, 2010) 351, 360.

constitutional clauses (even if the Constitutional Court has specified that this does not implicate that human rights treaties have a constitutional *status*).[20]

3 The super-legislative authority of the ECHR

In this section we will see how the ECHR has benefited from the constitutional openness described in the previous section. The literature has underscored the variety of national constitutional provisions regarding the ECHR.[21] Indeed, looking at these provisions one can see the diversity of national approaches with respect to the domestic authority of the ECHR.[22] Despite these differences, it has been noted that European jurisdictions are progressively converging about the recognition of a super-legislative 'position' of the ECHR in the hierarchy of sources.[23] This convergence is the final outcome of different national pathways; sometimes, national legislators must be credited, in other circumstances it is rather constitutional or supreme courts, or even common judges.[24] This is irrespective of the formal position set out in the Constitution, or of the dualism or monism classification.[25] The ECHR is generally acknowledged to be a supra-legislative force, but its relationship with constitutional supremacy is more controversial and this explains the disagreement existing between national courts (especially supreme and constitutional courts) and the ECtHR.

To understand the essence of this super-legislative authority it is helpful to recall two judicial practices that are emblematic of the indirect and direct effects of the ECHR within the national legal orders (respectively, the interpretative priority given to the ECHR and the possible disapplication of national legal norms conflicting with the Convention).

The first judicial practice is the interpretative priority/*favor* granted to the ECHR resulting in the duty – for national judges – to interpret national provisions in light of and in conformity with the ECHR. This can be explained with reference to (a) constitutional provisions (Spain, Romania, Bulgaria); (b) legislative provisions (UK); (c) constitutional courts' doctrines (Italy and Germany) and is a

20 Article 10 Constitution: (2) 'The norms relative to basic rights and liberties which are recognised by the Constitution shall be interpreted in conformity with the Universal Declaration of Human Rights and the international treaties and agreements on those matters ratified by Spain.' See also Tribunal Constitucional, Judgment 30/1991, available at <www.tribunalconstitucional.es>.

21 H. Keller and A. Stone Sweet (eds), *A Europe of Rights: The Impact of the ECHR on National Legal Systems* (Oxford University Press, 2009); G. Martinico and O. Pollicino, *The Interaction between Europe's Legal Systems: Judicial Dialogue and the Creation of Supranational Laws* (Elgar, 2012); Martinico and Pollicino (n. 19).

22 For an overview, see Martinico and Pollicino (n. 19).

23 H. Keller and A. Stone Sweet, 'Assessing the Impact of the ECHR on National Legal Systems', in Keller and Stone Sweet (n. 21) 683ff.

24 By common judges I mean civil, criminal and administrative law courts. They are called 'giudici comuni' in Italian and in Spanish. See also L. Montanari, *I diritti dell'uomo nell'area europea fra fonti internazionali e fonti interne* (Giappichelli, 2002).

25 This conclusion is also supported by Keller and Stone Sweet (n. 23) 685–686.

reflection of the constitutional variety described above. Sometimes the language of domestic constitutions conveys a message of reaction to totalitarian experiences, e.g. in the form of an increased openness to international law and the acknowledgement of peace as a fundamental constitutional principle, not simply as a strategic foreign policy option (Spain, Article 10.2; Portugal, Article 16 of the respective constitutions). Similar provisions can be found in Article 20, Paragraph 1 of the Romanian Constitution.[26] In other cases, the duty to interpret national law consistently with ECHR provisions is sometimes based on ordinary legislative provisions, such as under the UK Human Rights Act (HRA). In 1998, the ECHR was incorporated in the HRA, which entails a selective incorporation of ECHR rights (the so-called 'Convention rights'). Section 3 provides the obligation to interpret domestic law 'so far as is possible' in conformity with the Convention.[27] Even in the absence of express written provisions (either constitutional or statutory) the duty to interpret national law in light of the ECHR can sometimes derive from the Constitutional Court's case law, as in Germany and Italy. In Germany, the Second Senate of the Bundesverfassungsgericht (BvG) clarified in 2004 the relationship between the BvG and the ECtHR[28] and somehow followed up on the Strasbourg Court's decision in *Görgülü* v. *Germany* (no. 74969/01).[29] From a formal point of view the ECHR was ratified as ordinary law, and therefore it can be derogated by any subsequent ordinary statute and cannot serve as a standard of constitutional review (i.e. one cannot claim the violation of Convention rights before the BvG). Moreover, in that decision the BvG recalled the open character of the German Constitution (Articles 23 and 24), obliging national judges to take into account the law and case law of the Convention and to interpret domestic norms in the light thereof, but only if this is possible (and providing reasons when failing to do so). In May 2011,[30] the BvG held preventive detention unconstitutional, basing its expansive interpretation of the *Grundgesetz* on the case law of Strasbourg

26 Article 20, Constitution of Romania: 'Constitutional provisions concerning the citizens' rights and liberties shall be interpreted and enforced in conformity with the Universal Declaration of Human Rights, with the covenants and other treaties Romania is a party to.'

27 Section 3 '(1) So far as it is possible to do so, primary legislation and subordinate legislation must be read and given effect in a way which is compatible with the Convention rights.'

28 See order 2 BvR (German Constitutional Court) no. 1481/04, available at <www.bundesverfassungsgericht.de>.

29 *Görgülü* v. *Germany* App. No. 74969/01 (ECtHR, 26 February 2004). As noted, this decision must be connected to another instance of judicial conflict between the two courts: *Von Hannover* v. *Germany* (App. No. 59320/00) ECHR 2004-VI. On that occasion, the two courts had interpreted the right to privacy differently. The BvG thus in 2004 seized the occasion to bring some clarity: the ECHR and the ECtHR's case law bind the Federal Republic only as a public international law subject. F. Palermo, 'Il Bundesverfassungsgericht e la teoria selettiva dei controlimiti' (2005) 25 *Quaderni Costituzionali* 181.

30 No. 2 BvR (German Constitutional Court) 2365/09, available at <www.bundesverfassungsgericht.de>. On this case, see E. Bjorge and M. Andenas, 'German Federal Constitutional Court – Preventive Detention – Relationship between International and

judges.[31] In Italy, with two fundamental decisions of 2007, the Constitutional Court clarified the position of the ECHR in the domestic legal system.[32] According to the Italian Constitutional Court, the Convention has a super-primary value (i.e. its normative ranking is halfway between statutes and constitutional norms). This is confirmed by the fact that, in some cases, the ECHR can serve as an 'interposed parameter' for the constitutional review of primary laws, since the conflict between them and the ECHR can entail an indirect violation of the Constitution, namely of its Article 117, Paragraph 1, which reads: 'Legislative power belongs to the state and the regions in accordance with the Constitution and within the limits set by European Union law and international obligations.' Since Article 117 recalls international obligations, a conflict between a national piece of legislation and the ECHR can be solved by considering the ECHR as an external part of the standard employed by the Corte costituzionale to review the constitutionality of domestic norms. In other words, by interposed norm ('norma interposta') scholars mean those norms that are sub-constitutional from a formal point of view but somehow indirectly recalled by a constitutional provision and thus able to 'complement' the constitutional text, in the sense that their violation by a legislative provision can amount to an indirect violation of the Constitution. Since Article 117 of the Constitution recalls that the legislator has to respect international obligations, a breach of the ECHR may lead to an indirect violation of Article 117.

The constitutional *favor* accorded to the ECHR implies the obligation to interpret national law in light of the ECHR's norms. At the same time, this does not imply that the ECHR has a constitutional value; on the contrary, the ECHR has to respect the Constitution. As we will see when dealing with the second judicial practice, according to the Italian Constitutional Court the ECHR cannot be treated domestically like EU law.[33] It is not always clear whether the duty to interpret national law in light of the ECHR includes the necessity of taking into account the case law of the ECtHR. In this respect, there are different answers. Formally, the Constitutions mentioned are silent on this, while the UK HRA expressly provides (Section 2) that: 'A court or tribunal determining a question which has arisen in connection with a Convention right must take into account any – (a) judgment, decision, declaration or advisory opinion of the ECtHR.' In Italy and Germany, as seen above, it was the Constitutional Court that gave instructions to this effect. Finally, it should be noted that the constitutional

National Law – European Convention on Human Rights' (2011) 105 *American Journal of International Law* 768.

31 For instance *M* v. *Germany* (App. No. 19359/04) ECHR 2009.

32 Corte Costituzionale (Italian Constitutional Court), decision nos 348 and 349/2007, available at <www.cortecostituzionale.it>.

33 For a detailed analysis of the judgments, see F. Biondi Dal Monte and F. Fontanelli, 'The Decisions No. 348 and 349/2007 of the Italian Constitutional Court: The Efficacy of the European Convention in the Italian Legal System' (2008) 7 *German Law Journal* 889; O. Pollicino, 'Italy – Constitutional Court at the Crossroads between Constitutional Parochialism and Co-operative Constitutionalism. Judgments No. 348 and 349 of 22 and 24 October 2007' (2008) 4 *European Constitutional Law Review* 363.

provisions providing for the duty of consistent interpretation mentioned above do not distinguish between the ECHR and other international treaties on human rights, whereas when this doctrine is based on legislation and judicial decisions the ECHR enjoys a special treatment.

The second important evidence of the super-legislative authority given to the ECHR consists in the possibility of disapplying national provisions conflicting with ECHR norms. In some countries there exist constitutional provisions empowering national judges to disapply national law that conflicts with international treaties. In France (where the Constitution stipulates the superiority of treaties), there are no specific provisions concerning human rights treaties, and all the Constitution's Title VI provisions – regarding the entry into force of international treaties – are applicable to the ECHR. The domestic super-legislative ranking of international treaties is inferable from Article 55, which provides that ratified treaties are superior to domestic legislation. The review of conformity of national law with international treaties (control of 'conventionnalité') is entrusted to national judges. Unlike France, many Eastern European countries have conferred this control on Constitutional Courts, causing a certain degree of convergence between the control of constitutionality and that of 'conventionnalité'.[34] A similar mechanism – with the important difference of the absence of the judicial review of legislation – is the Dutch model, based on Article 94 which empowers national judges to review the conventionality of national law, even though they are not allowed to review the constitutionality of the statutory norms, under Article 120 of the *Grondwet*. In essence, in both France and the Netherlands the convergence between EU and ECHR law is due to a set of constitutional instructions which seem not to distinguish between public international law and EU law.[35] In other countries (for instance in Italy) the possibility of disapplying domestic norms conflicting with the ECHR has been matter of dispute between the Constitutional Court and lower courts (with an attempt at involving the CJEU),[36] while there are other cases where, in principle, a power to disapply national provisions conflicting with the ECHR could be derived from the wording of the relevant constitutions.[37] Referring to other more

34 On jurisdiction of the national constitutional courts in this field, see Bulgaria Article 149.4; Poland Article 188; Czech Republic Article 87; Slovenia Article 160.

35 G. Betlem and A. Nollkaemper, 'Giving Effect to Public International Law and European Community Law before Domestic Courts: A Comparative Analysis of the Practice of Consistent Interpretation' (2003) 14 *European Journal of International Law* 569: 'there is no fundamental divide between the application of public international law and EC law'.

36 Case C-571/10 *Kamberaj*, available at <www.curia.europa.eu>. G. Bianco and G. Martinico, 'Dialogue or Disobedience? On the Domestic Effects of the ECHR in Light of the *Kamberaj* Decision' (2014) 20 *European Public Law* 435.

37 In Portugal, theoretically, it can be argued that Articles 204 and 8 of the Constitution, combined, entitle national judges to disapply national law conflicting with constitutional and international law, but scholars describe this possibility as a sort of a 'sleeping giant' that has never woken up ('Although authorized by the Portuguese Constitution, I could not find cases where Portuguese judges had directly invoked the ECHR to put aside conflicting national law' (Coutinho (n. 19) 364)). On the domestic effects of the

detailed works on this issue,[38] from this comparative overview it is possible to argue that in many European jurisdictions the Convention is apparently provided, at least, with a sort of 'direct effect'.[39] Moreover, there are also countries where the ECHR has been used as (direct or indirect) part of the standard employed to review the constitutionality of national norms. This is the Austrian case, for instance, where a constitutional rank is attributed to the Convention.[40]

Having recalled the essence of what can be termed the 'super-legislative authority' of the ECHR in the domestic systems of its Member States, in section 4 I present some examples of national judicial disobedience based on a constructive exchange of arguments between some national constitutional courts and the ECtHR. I start by recalling the contents of an inspiring talk given by the former President of the Italian Constitutional Court, Franco Gallo, before moving to an

ECHR, another interesting provision is Article 96 of the Spanish Constitution, the meaning of which is a matter of debate: does it empower judges to disapply national legislation in conflict with ECHR provisions? Granted, according to the Constitutional Tribunal, Spanish judges may disapply national laws conflicting with international treaties: Tribunal Constitucional, 49/1988, FJ 14; Tribunal Constitucional 180/1993, both available at <www.tribunalconstitucional.es>, although the possible disapplication of national law for conflict with human rights treaties like the ECHR appears to be more problematic, and the Constitutional Tribunal has never pronounced on this issue. Since the Constitutional Tribunal has demonstrated its willingness to take the ECHR into account – via Article 10.2 of the Constitution – scholars suggested that ordinary judges should refer a question to the Constitutional Tribunal when conflict arises, rather than disapplying national law (V. Ferreres Comella, 'El juez nacional ante los derechos fundamentales europeos. Algunas reflexiones en torno a la idea de diálogo', in A. Saiz Arnaiz and M. Zelaia Garagarza (eds), *Integración Europea y Poder Judicial* (Instituto Vasco de Administración Pública, 2006) 231). This view also hinges upon the distinction between normal international treaties (Article 96) and human rights Treaties (Article 10). Finally, there are states where disapplication is forbidden: in the UK, for instance, in case of conflict between primary legislation and the Convention, judges can only adopt a 'declaration of incompatibility' (on this declaration, see K. Ewing and J. Tham, 'The Continuing Futility of the Human Rights Act' (2008) *Public Law* 668), which does not influence the validity and the efficacy of the domestic norm. After such a declaration 'if a Minister of the Crown considers that there are compelling reasons for proceeding … he may by order make such amendments to the legislation as he considers necessary to remove the incompatibility' (Section 10) (see also A. Bradley and K. Ewing, *Constitutional and Administrative Law* (Longman, 2007) 436).

38 Martinico and Pollicino (n. 21).

39 See also the Austrian case: Keller and Stone Sweet (n. 23) 684. See also G. Martinico, 'Is The European Convention Going to Be "Supreme"? A Comparative Constitutional Overview of ECHR and EU Law before National Courts' (2012) 23 *European Journal of International Law* 401.

40 As Cede pointed out: 'The ECHR has a double status in Austria. In addition to its character as an international treaty, it has been transformed, on the domestic level, into a law with the rank of a constitutional act. This has a twofold implication. First, the ECHR grants individual rights that are directly actionable before all courts and authorities. Given their status as constitutional law, these rights may be relied upon before the CC' (P. Cede, 'Report on Austria and Germany', in Martinico and Pollicino (n. 19) 63). Partially different, as we saw, is the Italian case after decisions 348 and 349/2007, both available at <www.cortecostituzionale.it>.

analysis of some techniques present in the case law of some constitutional courts. Generally, I try to show that these episodes of conflicts are the direct offspring of the constitutional openness described above, rather than episodes of constitutional closure.

4 The price of success: raising barriers against the ECHR

The 'super-legislative status' of the ECHR has produced reactions at national level and this is inevitably the price of the success that this international instrument has had over the years and consequently of its invasiveness in the domestic boundaries. However, some of these reactions deserve special attention, since they do not come from negative prejudice against the instrument of the Convention.

Once, when commenting upon the critical discourses triggered by some decisions against the UK, Mahoney said:

> This urging of a principled, even robust, attitude to the Strasbourg jurisprudence is not a clarion call for rebellion, civil disobedience and unbridled activism on the part of national courts. Rather, it is a plea that the relationship between the Strasbourg Court and the national courts should not be taken to be a straitjacket. Ideally, it should be perceived on both sides as being a flexible, open-minded co-operation directed towards enabling the national courts to resolve human rights issues, so as to obviate the need for recourse to Strasbourg, but with the Strasbourg Court having the last word in the event of interpretive disagreement. It is essential to preserve a feeling of respect between Strasbourg judges and national judges, a sense of partnership.[41]

Trying to build on these lines, it is interesting to explore this issue, starting with an analysis of an emblematic speech given by a former member of the Italian Constitutional Court.

As Justice Gallo, former President of the Italian Constitutional Court, wrote in a text prepared for a meeting in Brussels held on 24 May 2012, recently the exchange of views between the Italian Constitutional Court and the Strasbourg Court has become more and more frequent.[42] In principle this gives an added value to the protection of fundamental rights in Europe. However, as Justice Gallo pointed out: 'the work of transposition of the case-law of the ECtHR into the national legal order has not been easy'.[43]

These words represent a certain tension that has emerged over recent years: the openness shown towards the ECHR and the case law of the ECtHR by the Constitutional Court in 2007 has been a sort of boomerang for the Consulta,

41 M. Mahoney, 'Strasbourg and the National Courts' (*Inner Temple Yearbook 2014–2015*) 116, available at <www.innertemple.org.uk/yearbook-2014/#1/z>.

42 F. Gallo, 'Rapporti fra Corte costituzionale e Corte EDU', Brussels, 24 May 2012, available at <www.cortecostituzionale.it/documenti/relazioni_internazionali/RI_BRUXELLES_2012_GALLO.pdf>.

43 Ibid.

since it has been employed to justify *expressis verbis* almost any form of disagreement with the interpretation of the Strasbourg Court. Since 2007 the Italian Constitutional Court has acknowledged a particular importance to the interpretative function played by the Strasbourg Court and this was a consequence of the particular *status* of the ECHR recognised by the Corte costituzionale. This way it also acknowledged a sort of procedural duty which is very similar to that known in the UK and consists of the obligation to take the case law of the ECtHR into consideration when interpreting the text of the European Convention, paying particular attention to the role played by the Strasbourg Court. At the same time, as many other constitutional courts do, the Italian Constitutional Court has sometimes found difficulty in 'transplanting' ('judicial transplant' is the formula employed by Justice Gallo in his speech) the solutions devised by the ECHR into the domestic systems and this has been explained in light of a number of important differences existing between the Italian Constitutional Court and the ECtHR as we will see later.

One could see the Italian case as particular in light of the uncertain position accorded to the ECHR (super-legislative but also sub-constitutional) but even in other jurisdictions the situation is pretty similar. Even in legal orders lacking a fully-fledged constitutional text, like the UK, judges have limited the openness granted to the ECHR.[44] Emblematically, in *Horncastle*, the Supreme Court[45] said that:

> [t]he requirement to 'take into account' the Strasbourg jurisprudence will normally result in this Court applying principles that are clearly established by the Strasbourg Court. There will, however, be rare occasions where this court has concerns as to whether a decision of the Strasbourg Court sufficiently appreciates or accommodates particular aspects of our domestic process. In such circumstances it is open to this court to decline to follow the Strasbourg decision, giving reasons for adopting this course. This is likely to give the Strasbourg Court the opportunity to reconsider the particular aspect of the decision that is in issue, so that there takes place what may prove to be a valuable dialogue between this court and the Strasbourg Court. This is such a case.[46]

44 See C. Murphy, 'Human Rights Law and the Challenges of Explicit Judicial Dialogue', Jean Monnet Working Paper 10/12 (2012), available at <http://jeanmonnetprogram.org/paper/human-rights-law-and-the-challenges-of-explicit-judicial-dialogue>. N. Bratza, 'The Relationship between the UK Courts and Strasbourg' (2011) 5 *European Human Rights Law Review* 505; more recently see also S. Lambrecht, 'Bringing Rights More Home: Can a Home-grown UK Bill of Rights Lessen the Influence of the European Court of Human Rights?' (2014) 15 *German Law Journal* 407.

45 On the impact of the ECHR on the activity of some national supreme courts, see E. Bjorge, 'National Supreme Courts and the Development of ECHR Rights' (2011) 9 *International Journal of Constitutional Law* 5.

46 UK Supreme Court, *R* v. *Horncastle and Others* [2009] UKSC 14, para. 11.

Even more clearly – and using rhetoric that recalls that of continental constitutional courts – the same court said, elsewhere:

> This Court is not bound to follow every decision of the [ECtHR]. Not only would it be impractical to do so: it would sometimes be inappropriate, as it would destroy the ability of the Court to engage in the constructive dialogue … which is of value to the development of Convention law. Of course, we should usually follow a clear and constant line of decisions … But we are not actually bound to do so or (in theory, at least) to follow a decision of the Grand Chamber … Where, however, there is a clear and constant line of decisions whose effect is not inconsistent with some fundamental substantive or procedural aspect of our law, and whose reasoning does not appear to overlook or misunderstand some argument or point of principle, we consider that it would be wrong for this Court not to follow that line.[47]

This language reminds us of the counter-limits[48] and *Solange*[49] doctrines, devised by the national constitutional courts to react to the problematic (in terms of protection of fundamental rights) jurisprudence of the European Court of Justice. Going beyond the mere negative reading of these decisions, Murphy has interestingly framed these decisions as examples of:

> explicit dialogue whereby the domestic judiciary have acknowledged that they are participants in transjudicial communication in the judgment of the court itself. This can be read, at its most ambitious, as an endorsement of the normative claim of constitutional pluralism. By endorsing the idea of a 'valuable dialogue' the UK Supreme Court is acknowledging the authority of the Strasbourg Court over the interpretation of human rights law. In doing so explicitly it may weaken its own authority.[50]

Apart from the perhaps intimidating tone used by the UK Supreme Court in those lines, what is interesting to us is the reference to a Strasbourg decision whose reasoning is based on a misunderstanding of the national scenario. In these cases,

47 UK Supreme Court, *Manchester City Council* v. *Pinnock* [2010] UKSC 45, para. 48 (emphasis added).

48 Corte costituzionale (Italian Constitutional Court), decision no. 183/1973, Frontini: [1974] 2 CML Rev 372; see also Corte costituzionale, decision no. 170/1984, Granital: [1984] CML Rev 756.

49 Starting with the famous *Solange I*: Bundesverfassungsgericht (German Constitutional Court), Case 2 BvG 52/71 Bundesverfassungsgericht: German Constitutional Court [1974] 2 CML Rev 540.

50 Murphy (n. 44): 'The explicit dialogue initiated by the UK Supreme Court in this saga may incorporate recognition of constitutional pluralism in the legal reasoning of UK human rights law. In doing so it may undermine the authority of both the UK Supreme Court and the legal system it serves.

in light of the pluralist spirit of the Convention, national courts may disagree with the ECtHR, by giving arguments in order to explain why they are going to depart from the concrete solution given by the Strasbourg Court. These cases are based on a distinction between interpretation and argumentation. In other words, even in these cases, national courts comply with the procedural duty to take into account the case law of the Strasbourg Court when interpreting national law, but this does not guarantee – in presence of reasonable arguments explained by the national court and based on the pluralistic spirit of the Convention – the same output in terms of solution devised for the case pending before the domestic judge.[51]

Going back to continental Europe, a similar approach has emerged in respect of the ECHR's penetration into the domestic legal order. The most telling example is BvG's order no. 1481/04, mentioned above, where the Karlsruhe judges ruled that, in case of unresolvable conflicts between ECHR and domestic law, the latter should prevail.[52] For the first time in its history, the BvG specified which matters are off-limits for the primacy of the ECHR: family law, immigration law and the law on protection of personality.[53] The BvG stressed the particularities of the proceeding before the ECtHR, which might lead to a different outcome in balancing between rights and values, and the latter is an element that we find even in the case law of other national constitutional courts. That case was seen as a reaction to another exchange which involved the German Constitutional Court and the ECtHR.[54]

In Austria, where the ECHR enjoys constitutional status, this Convention-friendliness cannot justify a violation of the Constitution.[55] In this sense, some authors[56] have compared the BvG's order no. 1481/04 to the *Miltner* case,[57] where the Austrian Constitutional Court stressed the possibility of departing from the ECtHR's case law, if adherence thereto could entail a violation of the Constitution. As we saw, the Italian Constitutional Court came to a similar conclusion in 2007 (decisions 348 and 349), where it clarified that the ECHR has a

51 For an interesting tripartition on how to interpret the formula 'take into account', see H. Fenwick, 'What's Wrong with s. 2 of the Human Rights Act?' (*UK Const. L. Blog*, 2012), available at <http://ukconstitutionallaw.org/2012/10/09/helen-fenwick-whats-wrong-with-s-2-of-the-human-rights-act>.

52 2 BvR (German Constitutional Court) 1481/04.

53 On this, see F. Hoffmeister, 'Germany: Status of European Convention on Human Rights in Domestic Law' (2006) 4 *International Journal of Constitutional Law* 722.

54 *Von Hannover* v. *Germany* (n. 29); *Von Hannover* v. *Germany (No. 2)* (App. Nos 40660/08 and 60641/08) ECHR 2012; *Von Hannover* v. *Germany (No. 3)* App. No. 8772/10 (ECtHR, 19 September 2013); *Axel Springer AG* v. *Germany* App. No. 39954/08 (ECtHR, 7 February 2012).

55 'In this case, even though the Convention has constitutional rank, the contrary rule of constitutional law would have to prevail by virtue of its lex specialis character' (Cede (n. 40) 70).

56 As N. Krisch says in 'The Open Architecture of European Human Rights Law' (2003) 2 *Modern Law Review* 183.

57 Austrian Constitutional Court, Miltner, VfSlg 11500/1987, available at <www.ris.bka.gv.at/vfgh>.

privileged position, but enjoys no 'constitutional immunity'; on the contrary, it must abide by all constitutional norms.

The Italian judges equated the ECHR with any source of international law and found, accordingly, that the 'constitutional tolerance' of the Italian system towards the ECHR is lower than towards EU law. This difference in degree is clearly visible: whereas the 'counter-limits' against the penetration of EU law are a subset of constitutional rights (which means that EU law prevails over non-core constitutional values), the Italian Court is stricter with the Convention, requiring its conformity with every constitutional norm. In conclusion, then, 'the need for a constitutionality test on the Convention norm excludes the possibility of having a limited set of fundamental rights that could serve as a counter-limit; indeed, every norm of the Constitution shall be respected by the international norm challenged'.[58]

Having presented an overview, let us return to Justice Gallo's speech, since, starting from that text, it is possible to detect some techniques employed by the Italian (and other) Constitutional (or Supreme) Courts to respectfully disagree.

5 Limits to following the European Court of Human Rights' case law: a focus on the Italian case

As recalled in section 4, Justice Gallo mentioned relevant differences between national constitutional courts and the ECtHR; in this section I look at these differences that might justify, according to Justice Gallo, disagreements between these courts.

The first diversity concerns the 'different relevance of the case'. While for the Italian Constitutional Court the case is the element connecting the legislative norm (i.e. the provision as concretely interpreted by the legal operator)[59] challenged and the reality, the question of constitutionality focuses on the abstract legislative provision. This way the concrete case triggers a decision that, in case of unconstitutionality, acquires an *erga omnes* effect. Contrarily, the decisions of the ECtHR are focused on the concrete case, since the Court would not aim at the 'universality of the pronouncement, but, on the contrary, delimit the possibility of generalizing the decision'.[60] Another difference pertains to the argumentative techniques employed by these two Courts. The Italian Constitutional Court uses formalism while the ECtHR has a more substantive approach, given its 'pragmatic syncretism', namely being more interested in the case and less interested in giving universalisable principles.[61] Moreover, according to Justice Gallo, since the decisions

58 Biondi Dal Monte and Fontanelli (n. 33) 915.

59 On provisions (*disposizioni*) and norms (*norme*) in the Italian legal scholarship, see V. Crisafulli, entry 'Disposizione e norma. Diritto costituzionale', in *Enc. dir.*, XIII (Rome, 1964) 195.

60 Gallo (n. 42).

61 J. P. Costa, 'Il ragionamento giuridico della Corte europea dei diritti dell'uomo' (2000) *Rivista internazionale dei diritti dell'uomo* 437, 440.

of the Italian Constitutional Court have annulment effects, when performing its role it also does a sort of impact assessment of its decisions. The ECtHR, instead, is the judge of a more pluralist context and its decisions are provided with a mere *inter partes* effect (from a formal point of view). A third difference relates to the use of the comparative argument. The ECtHR relies on it in an evident manner (and this is again connected to the pluralism characterising the ECHR system), while the Italian Constitutional Court rarely refers to comparative arguments (with some exceptions in the most recent case law of the Corte costituzionale). The fourth element identified by Justice Gallo is the 'manifestation of the process of decision-making'.[62] While the ECtHR can rely on the mechanism of the 'dissenting' and 'concurring opinions', these options do not exist in the case of the Italian Constitutional Court. Having listed such differences, Justice Gallo proceeded to recalling some recent novelties which seem to make them less pronounced. First of all the use of the pilot judgments that have contributed to the 'enlargement of the *thema decidendum* of a case, in order to deal, in a structural manner, with the issues of compatibility of a given discipline with the issue of the protection of fundamental rights'.[63] Justice Gallo further recalled some examples of *convergences* and *divergences* between the Italian Constitutional Court and the ECtHR. Within the first group Gallo recalled some instances where the Italian Constitutional Court accepted the judicial trend coming from Strasbourg, such as the *Dorigo* saga, the issue of expropriations and the problem of compensation of the damage produced by 'reverse accession'.[64] While the second case led to the famous decision no. 349/2007, the first has triggered a real saga (*Dorigo*), with two important decisions of the Italian Constitutional Court. In a first moment the Italian Constitutional Court saved the provisions at stake by sending a message to Parliament to intervene to deal with a situation that only a political intervention could resolve in an organic manner. In its second decision, given the inactivity of Parliament, the Italian Constitutional Court relied on the case law of the ECtHR and declared unconstitutional the provision at stake. The *Dorigo* saga[65] represents a perfect example of the impact of the ECtHR case law on the case law of the Italian

62 Gallo (n. 42).

63 Ibid.

64 '"[R]everse accession" (in Italian accessione invertita or occupazione appropriativa) refers to the operation in reverse of the normal rule that buildings accede to the land. In administrative law, reverse accession occurs, subject to the fulfilment of certain conditions, where the state occupies land without completing normal compulsory purchase procedures. The land, previously under private ownership, accedes to the buildings and any servitudes or burdens on the land cease to exist.' See the translator's note in the English translation of the Italian Constitutional Court's decision no. 349/ 2007, available at <www.cortecostituzionale.it/documenti/download/doc/recent_judgments/s349_2007_eng.pdf>. See also F. Saitta, 'Expropriation in Public Interest. Annual Report 2011. Italy' (*Ius Public Network Review*, December 2011), available at <www.ius-publicum.com/repository/uploads/29_02_2012_10_27_Saitta_UK.pdf>.

65 Italian Constitutional Court, decisions 129/08 and no. 113/11, both available at <www.cortecostituzionale.it>.

Constitutional Court.[66] Another example of a similar reception of the case law of the ECtHR[67] is given by the qualification of the confiscation by equivalent ('confisca per equivalente') as a measure analogous to a criminal sanction, with a consequent breach of the prohibition of retroactive application.[68]

However, as anticipated, there are also cases where convergence between the two Courts seemed to be impossible. For instance, as cases of disagreement we could refer to the *Cordova* saga concerning parliamentary immunities and the different approach to the issue of the 'functional nexus' ('nesso funzionale'),[69] which should be interpreted in a narrow sense according to the ECtHR.[70] Another example of disagreement is *Scoppola*,[71] concerning the different understanding of the principle of non-retroactivity of criminal laws. For instance, in decision no. 236/2011 the Italian Constitutional Court recalled *Scoppola II* and argued that the understanding of the equivalent principle of *lex mitior* under the ECHR does not correspond (entirely at least) to that of the Italian Constitutional Court. In these cases the Italian Constitutional Court recalled the ECtHR but also emphasised the differences existing in terms of contexts (by limiting this way the impact of a single case decided by the ECtHR).

In other circumstances the Italian Constitutional Court did the same by distinguishing for instance the type of balance to be struck by two courts: this is the case

66 On this, see G. Repetto (ed.), *The Constitutional Relevance of the ECHR in Domestic and European Law. An Italian Perspective* (Intersentia, 2013).

67 *Welch* v. *United Kingdom* (App. No. 17440/90) Series A 307-A.

68 Italian Constitutional Court, decision 301 and 97/2009, both available at <www.cortecostituzionale.it>.

69 The concept of 'functional nexus' 'refers to the relevance of a MP's opinion in carrying out his functions and in furthering the general political debate, regardless of the place where it has been voiced' (C. Fasone, 'The European Court of Human Rights finds Italy in violation of Article 6, s. 1 ECHR (Right to a fair trial), contradicting a previous ruling issued by the Italian Constitutional Court addressing parliamentary immunities (Constitutional Court, decision no. 305/2007; ECtHR, decision no. 46967/2007' (*Palomar*, April 2009)), available at <www3.unisi.it/dipec/palomar/italy006_2009.html#1>.

70 For instance in *Cordova I*, the ECtHR argued that: 'The Court takes the view that the lack of any clear connection with a parliamentary activity requires it to adopt a narrow interpretation of the concept of proportionality between the aim sought to be achieved and the means employed. This is particularly so where the restrictions on the right of access stem from the resolution of a political body. To hold otherwise would amount to restricting in a manner incompatible with Article 6 § 1 of the Convention the right of individuals to have access to a court whenever the allegedly defamatory statements have been made by a parliamentarian' (*Cordova* v. *Italy (No. 1)* (App. No. 40877/98) ECHR 2003-I).

71 *Scoppola* v. *Italy (No. 2)* App. No. 10249/03 (ECtHR, 19 September 2009). On the *Scoppola* saga, see E. Lamarque and F. Viganò, 'Sulle ricadute interne della sentenza Scoppola. Ovvero: sul gioco di squadra tra Cassazione e Corte costituzionale nell'adeguamento del nostro ordinamento alle sentenze di Strasburgo (Nota a C. cost. no. 210/2013)' (*Diritto penale contemporaneo*, 31 March 2014), available at <www.penalecontemporaneo.it/tipologia/0-/-/-/2950-sulle_ricadute_interne_della_sentenza_scoppola>.

for instance in decision no. 264/2012. In other words, while the Italian Constitutional Court quoted the Strasbourg Court (complying with the duty to take its case law into account) it also gave arguments to justify the different outcome of the case and the impossibility of transplanting the solution devised in Strasbourg. This distinction between interpretation (taking into account the case law of the ECtHR when dealing with fundamental rights) and argumentation (the mere fact of giving an interpretative weight to the ECtHR does not exclude different outcomes that are explained in light of the particularity of the context, reasoning, etc.) is crucial to understand the way in which the Italian Constitutional Court disobeys. Of course one can also read in these decisions a form of hidden criticism to the invasiveness of the Strasbourg Court. When commenting upon decision no. 264/2012 scholars stressed the language used by the Corte costituzionale which justified its conclusion on the basis of the alleged consistency with the 'essence of the European Court's decision'. Such a reference to the 'essence' of the ECHR's case law was seen as a way to mask a partial disagreement with the Strasbourg Court, by filtering only those elements of the ECtHR's case law that can be read consistently with the doctrine of the Italian Court.[72]

Another important example of disagreement is given by the different understanding of the principle of legitimate expectation. In *Agrati*,[73] concerning the so-called 'laws of authentic interpretation' ('Leggi di intepretazione autentica'), the Strasburg Court questioned the case law of the Italian Constitutional Court[74] by arguing that:

> la notion d'«utilité publique» est ample par nature. En particulier, la décision d'adopter des lois emportant privation de propriété implique d'ordinaire l'examen de questions politiques, économiques et sociales. Estimant normal que le législateur dispose d'une grande latitude pour mener une politique économique et sociale, la Cour respecte la manière dont il conçoit les impératifs de l'«utilité publique», sauf si son jugement se révèle manifestement dépourvu de base raisonnable.[75]

Indeed sometimes the problematic interpretation to be given to polysemous notions like 'utilité publique' triggers disagreements. In case 257/2011[76] the

72 A. Ruggeri, 'La Consulta rimette abilmente a punto la strategia dei suoi rapporti con la Corte EDU e, indossando la maschera della consonanza, cela il volto di un sostanziale, perdurante dissenso nei riguardi della giurisprudenza convenzionale ("a prima lettura" di Corte cost. no. 264 del 2012)' (*Diritti Comparati*, 14 December 2012) available at <www.diritticomparati.it/2012/12/la-consulta-rimette-abilmente-a-punto-la-strategia-dei-suoi-rapporti-con-la-corte-edu-e-indossando-l.html>.

73 *Agrati and Others* v. *Italy* App. Nos 43549/08, 5087/09, 6107/09 (ECtHR, 7 June 2011).

74 For instance see Italian Constitutional Court, decision no. 311/2009 available at <www.cortecostituzionale.it>.

75 *Agrati and Others* (n. 73).

76 Italian Constitutional Court, decision no. 257/2011, available at <www.cortecostituzionale.it>.

Italian Constitutional Court tried again to justify the presence of some exceptions to the principle of non-retroactivity of laws on the basis of the existence of a public interest. As the former President of the Italian Constitutional Court, Justice Franco Gallo, wrote,[77] there is an evident disagreement about the interpretation to be given to the notions of 'utilité publique' and 'public interest'.[78]

In other cases the Italian Constitutional Court marked the territory by excluding the ECHR from the constitutional standard employed to review the constitutionality of a piece of legislation when the domestic provisions offered a mature parameter of constitutionality: as in the case of decision 278/2013.[79] The case concerned a law providing that the choice to remain anonymous made by a biological mother, whose child had been adopted, retained irrevocable status for 100 years. The Italian Constitutional Court declared this provision unconstitutional without relying on the ECHR, thus showing the maturity of the national legal system in this respect. Similarly, in decision no. 162/2014,[80] by which the Italian Constitutional Court declared the prohibition on heterologous fertilisation unconstitutional. Scholars[81] have pointed out the omitted reference to the ECHR as a part of the constitutional standard, although the Italian Constitutional Court recalled the *S. H.* decision of the ECtHR.[82]

In all these cases the Italian Constitutional Court quoted, on the one hand, the case law of the Strasbourg Court but then decided to solve the issue relying exclusively on its constitutional provisions and – according to some commentators,[83] – thus showing proudly how a certain effect (the removal of an unjust provision) was the autonomous product of the Italian Constitution, without the need for the external help of the ECHR.

More recently, in decision no. 49/2015, the Italian Constitutional Court also developed another technique of disobedience. In this decision given at the end of March 2015, it clarified the content of the duty to take into account the case law of the ECtHR. First the Italian Constitutional Court recalled the pre-eminent interpretative function performed by the Strasbourg Court in the interpretation of the ECHR and the duty to interpret domestic law in a manner consistent with the latter. The openness established in 2007 – with decision nos 348 and 349/2007[84] – implies the duty to take into account the case law of the supreme interpreter of the Convention. However, in decision 49/2015,

77 Gallo (n. 42).

78 Ibid.

79 Italian Constitutional Court, decision no. 278/2013, available at <www.cortecostituzionale.it>.

80 Italian Constitutional Court, decision no. 162/2014, available at <www.cortecostituzionale.it>.

81 A. Ruggeri, 'La Consulta apre alla eterologa ma chiude, dopo averlo preannunziato, al "dialogo" con la Corte EDU (a prima lettura di Corte cost. no. 162 del 2014)' (*Forum costituzionale*, 2014), available at <www.forumcostituzionale.it>.

82 *S. H. and Others* v. *Austria* (App. No. 57813/00) ECHR 2011.

83 Lamarque and Viganò (n. 71).

84 Italian Constitutional Court, Decision nos. 348 and 349/2007, both available at <www.cortecostituzionale.it>.

the Corte costituzionale also stated that domestic judges are not 'passive recipients of an interpretative command issued elsewhere in the form of a court ruling, irrespective of the conditions that gave rise to it'. In order to clarify this point, the Italian Constitutional Court made a distinction between cases when the national judge has to deal with an established case law of the Strasbourg Court and cases where there is no established case law. This does not mean that judges are allowed not to follow the case law of the ECtHR; on the contrary, 'disregard the interpretation made by the Strasbourg Court, once it has become consolidated with a certain effect'.[85]

The distinction between 'established' and 'non-established case law' and the reminder concerning the legislative value of the law covering the effects of the ECHR has been seen as a return to the past and as a partial contradiction with the constitutional openness characterising the twin judgments of 2007.

6 Final remarks

In 2007 the Italian Constitutional Court had acknowledged some degree of openness to the ECHR and its judge, due to those constitutional preconditions recalled in section 1. However, such openness has sometimes come back as a boomerang. This has forced the Corte costituzionale to deal with the case law of the Strasbourg Court even in cases when the decisions coming from Strasbourg were in conflict with its way of understanding national law. This situation has also led the Corte costituzionale to devise techniques to justify a different outcome, in light of the particular national context, of the specific mandate of a constitutional judge, of the different type of balance struck by the Italian Constitutional Court, and given by the only partial overlapping between the values of the Convention and those of the Constitution. In other cases, the Court has demonstrated relying on (I would say proudly) national constitutional provisions only, when declaring the invalidity of national norms, also in those cases where the ECHR could have been used as added value. However, these decisions should not be seen as a step back when compared with decisions 348 and 349/2007. On the contrary, they follow the procedural pattern designed by the Italian Court on that occasion. The distinction between interpretation and argumentation is useful in this respect: indeed, even in cases where the Corte costituzionale decides differently, it always recalls the ECHR and the case law of the ECtHR, thus showing great deference to the latter's interpretative function. At the same time, this interpretative *favor* accorded to the ECtHR does not automatically guarantee convergence over the result. In order to explain its reasons, the Italian Court has to give arguments, by participating in a sort of dialogue with the ECtHR.[86]

85 Corte costituzionale, decision no. 49/2015, available at <www.cortecostituzionale.it>.

86 For a similar consideration on the case law of the UK Supreme Court see Murphy (n. 44).

Something similar happens in other jurisdictions, too. The argument that striking the balance before national constitutional courts and the ECtHR implies differences has been employed by the German Constitutional Court and other German judges. The very famous *Von Hannover* saga shows, for instance, that national courts sometimes construct the balancing (on that occasion: freedom of expression versus the right of public figures and celebrities to a private life) in a different manner from the Strasbourg Court. The saga was perceived as a clash, but actually triggered mutual influences on the judicial interlocutors and produced a change in the approach of domestic courts.[87]

This means that judicial disagreements or conflicts are not always negative. On the contrary, sometimes conflicts may trigger negotiation and dialogue, i.e. exchanges of arguments fed by that constitutional openness described in the first part of this chapter.

87 See *Von Hannover* v. *Germany (No. 2)* (n. 54): 'The Government submitted that up until the *Von Hannover* judgment the German courts had used the hard and fast concept of "figure of contemporary society par excellence", which attracted only limited protection under German law. Following the *Von Hannover* judgment, the Federal Court of Justice had abandoned that concept and developed a new concept of (graduated) protection according to which it was henceforth necessary to show in respect of every photo why there was an interest in publishing it. Furthermore, under the new approach adopted by the Federal Court of Justice the balancing of competing interests consisted in determining whether the publication contributed to a public debate. The information value of the publication was of particular importance in that respect. In sum, the new case-law of the Federal Court of Justice, endorsed by the Federal Constitutional Court, afforded greater weight to the protection of personality rights, as evidenced by the fact that an injunction was imposed on publication of two of the initial three photos' (para. 78).

6 The advisory jurisdiction of the ECtHR under Protocol No. 16: enhancing domestic implementation of human rights or a symbolic step?

Björg Thorarensen

1 Introduction

This chapter will focus on the aims and possible impact of Protocol No. 16, the most recent additional protocol to the European Convention on Human Rights, which was opened for signature on 2 October 2013. The Protocol enables the highest courts and tribunals of the States Parties to the Convention to request an advisory opinion from the European Court of Human Rights on questions of principle relating to the interpretation of the rights and freedoms of the Convention in the context of cases pending before them. It enters into force three months after ten ratifications. As of 1 January 2016, six states had ratified the Protocol and an additional 10 States had signed the Protocol.[1]

The introduction of an advisory jurisdiction of the ECtHR in specific cases in national proceedings is one of a range of reform measures adopted since 2000 to enhance the long-term effectiveness of the control mechanism of the Convention.[2] It was put firmly on the agenda in the Brighton Declaration in April 2012, as a means to

> strengthen the interaction between the Court and national authorities to introduce a further power of the Court, which States Parties could optionally accept, to deliver advisory opinions upon request on the interpretation of the Convention in the context of a specific case at domestic level, without prejudice to the non-binding character of the opinions for the other States Parties.[3]

1 Protocol No. 16 to the Convention for the Protection of Human Rights and Fundamental Freedoms, CETS No. 214.

2 On 4 November 2000 the Committee of Ministers adopted in Rome the Declaration, The European Convention on Human Rights at 50: What Future for the Protection of Human Rights in Europe? <www.coe.int/t/dghl/standardsetting/cddh/reformechr/DH_GDR/Declaration-Rome_en.pdf> accessed 1 August 2015. This can be considered to be a starting point for the adoption of number of the numerous reform measures adopted by the Committee in the following decade.

3 High Level Conference on the Future of the European Court of Human Rights, Brighton Declaration (19 and 20 April 2012) <www.echr.coe.int/Documents/2012_Brighton_FinalDeclaration_ENG.pdf> accessed 1 August 2015, para. 12d.

This procedural innovation is closely connected to the objectives of Protocol No. 15 in strengthening the principle of subsidiarity and the domestic implementation of the obligations deriving from the Convention, emphasising that human rights must be protected first and foremost at national level.[4] In this spirit, the Preamble of Protocol No. 16 declares that the extension of the Court's competence to give advisory opinions is intended to 'further enhance the interaction between the Court and national authorities and thereby reinforce implementation of the Convention, in accordance with the principle of subsidiarity'. The new procedure has been described by Dean Spielmann, President of the Strasbourg Court, as a means to open a formal and direct channel for dialogue between the national and European judges with the potential to improve implementation of the Convention.[5]

Protocol No. 16 provides for a new type of advisory jurisdiction of the ECtHR, fundamentally different from the already existing advisory jurisdiction stipulated in Articles 47–49 of the Convention. In some aspects it is similar to the preliminary reference procedure to the Court of Justice of the EU and the advisory opinion procedure to the EFTA Court available to national courts in States Parties to the EEA Agreement. Nevertheless there are major differences between these procedures, and the main ones will be compared here to some extent.

This chapter will seek to answer some, though certainly not all, of the questions which Protocol No. 16 raises. An assessment will be made as to whether the Protocol may affect the positioning of the centre of gravity of European human rights protection. The focus will be on the Protocol's objectives and the question of whether the advisory procedure is likely to contribute to more effective domestic implementation of human rights, eventually reducing the case flow to Strasbourg, or whether it is more of a symbolic step, a politically motivated measure to underline the role of national institutions at times of tension between Strasbourg and national courts. The impact of the inevitably overlapping contentious and advisory jurisdictions of the Court will be addressed, as well as the viewpoint of national procedural law, particularly how it may affect the rights of parties in civil or criminal proceedings pending in proceedings in the national court which requests an advisory opinion.

4 The emphasis on the subsidiarity principle coincides with the objectives of previous initiatives, notably Protocol No. 14, amending the Control system of the Convention (CETS No. 194), as explained in its Explanatory Report, paras 12 and 15, and High Level Conference on the Future of the European Court of Human Rights, Interlaken Declaration (19 February 2010). <www.coe.int/t/dghl/cooperation/capacitybuilding/Source/interlaken_declaration_en.pdf> accessed 1 August 2015, Action Plan, para. B.4.

5 Dean Spielmann, 'Judgments of the European Court of Human Rights Effects and Implementation' (Keynote Speech at Conference at the Paulinerkirche Göttingen Georg-August-University, Göttingen, 20 September 2013), <www.echr.coe.int/Documents/Speech_20130920_Spielmann_Gottingen_ENG.pdf> accessed 1 August 2012, 4.

2 Existing advisory jurisdictions and the aims of Protocol No. 16

2.1 Article 47 of ECHR and reasons underlying its limited scope

The ECtHR has had an advisory jurisdiction since the adoption of Protocol No. 2 of 1963, which conferred upon the Court the competence to give advisory opinions at the request of the Committee of Ministers.[6] Provisions on this procedure are now to be found in Articles 47–49 of the ECHR, which define the conditions and procedure for requesting such opinion. These conditions are quite restrictive and the scope of the contents of such opinion is very limited. According to Article 47, only *the Committee of Ministers* may request advisory opinions on legal question concerning the interpretation of the Court. In addition, such opinions *shall not deal with any question relating to the content or scope of the rights and freedoms* enshrined in the Convention and its protocols *or any other question* which the Court or the Committee might have to consider in consequence of *any such proceedings as could be instituted* in accordance with the Convention. This limited scope, as explained in the preparatory texts of Protocol No. 2, reflects the concern that an international tribunal's advisory jurisdiction should avoid overlapping with its contentious jurisdiction, in order to avoid double adjudication in the same case.[7] In view of the narrowly defined scope of the jurisdiction it is not surprising that this procedure has turned out to be of very little practical significance and to date only two such opinions have been issued, in 2008 and 2010, involving legal questions concerning the functioning of the procedures to be followed to elect new judges to the Court.[8]

In this respect the Court's advisory jurisdiction under Article 47 of the Convention can be distinguished from similar jurisdictions of some other international

6 Protocol No. 2 to the Convention, CETS No. 44. The Protocol entered into force on 21 September 1970.

7 Kanstantsin Dzehtsiarou and Noreen O'Meara, 'Advisory Jurisdiction and the European Court of Human Rights: A Magic Bullet for Dialogue and Docket-Control?' (2014) 34(3), *Legal Studies*, 444–468. This article provides a detailed description of the background and underlying objectives of Protocol No. 2 to the Convention. See also *Travaux Préparatoires Relating to Protocol No 2 to the Convention for the Protection of Human Rights and Fundamental Freedoms* (Council of Europe, 1966) <www.echr.coe.int/LibraryDocs/Travaux/ECHRTravaux-P2-EN2907903.pdf> accessed 1 August 2014; with minutes of the meetings, draft texts and discussion of the drafters.

8 Advisory Opinion of 12 February 2008, 2/000 and Advisory Opinion (No. 2) of 22 January 2010, 3/000. The first request from the Committee of Ministers for an advisory opinion on the basis of Article 47 was rejected by the Court in its Decision of 2 June 2004 (1/000) on the competence of the Court to give an advisory opinion. There the Court presented detailed argumentation regarding its competence in this respect, referring to the examples taken in the *travaux préparatoires* of Protocol No. 2 indicating that it concerned primarily procedural points such as the election of judges, the duties of the Secretary General of the Council of Europe under the Convention and the procedure of the Committee of Ministers in exercising its role in the execution of judgments. Accordingly, this prevented the Court from giving opinions on questions concerning the admissibility of complaints, which would only be addressed in contentious proceedings under the Convention, see paras 28 and 35.

and regional courts.[9] Such advisory jurisdictions are usually broader and provide for the delivery of an opinion on the interpretation of treaty provisions in an abstract manner, without precluding the possibility that the same issue can later be brought up in contentious proceedings. The most relevant example is the Inter-American Court of Human Rights, which is authorised under Article 64 of the American Convention on Human Rights of 1969 to provide a Member State of the Organization of American States (OAS) with opinions regarding the compatibility of any of its domestic laws with the Convention. In addition, the Member States of the OAS may consult the Court regarding the interpretation of the Convention. It has been argued that the rationale for advisory opinions becomes less relevant once an international court has the opportunity to set standards through its contentious cases. This has been proved by the experience of the Inter-American Court where the accumulation of contentious case law has resulted in a parallel decline in the number of advisory opinions delivered.[10]

2.2 Background, constitutional elements and models for the new advisory jurisdiction

The idea of establishing a preliminary ruling system or advisory jurisdiction in concrete cases before the ECtHR has been under discussion for more than two decades.[11] But the rationale behind such a procedure is different in nature from the present advisory jurisdiction in Articles 47–49 ECHR as well as the advisory jurisdiction of the Inter-American Court of Human Rights discussed above. Instead of being primarily a tool for assisting State Parties in interpreting and implementing the treaty obligations and encouraging states to behave in a certain manner, a mechanism of preliminary rulings or advisory opinions from an international court in concrete cases pending in domestic proceedings aims at a harmonised interpretation of obligations by the Member States and resembles the role of constitutional courts found in many European states. It is inspired by national judicial systems, such as those in Germany and Italy, where general courts are authorised, and sometimes obliged, to seek preliminary rulings with regard to issues brought up in actions involving constitutional questions.[12]

9 It should be mentioned that according to Article 29 of the Council of Europe Convention on Human Rights and Biomedicine of 4 April 1997, CETS No. 164, the ECtHR may give, without direct reference to any specific proceedings pending in a court, advisory opinions on legal questions concerning the interpretation of the Biomedicine Convention at the request of the government of a State Party or a Committee established under the Convention. As yet such a request has not been submitted to the Court.

10 Dzehtsiarou and O'Meara (n. 7) 449–450. On the use of advisory jurisdiction in international courts with respect to human rights, see also Julie Calidonio Schmid, 'Advisory Opinions on Human Rights: Moving beyond a Pyrrhic Victory' (2006) 16 *Duke Journal of Comparative and International Law* 417.

11 See e.g. Stefan Mar Stefansson, 'Preliminary Rulings in Human Rights Cases' (1992–1993) 61–62 *Nordic Journal of International Law* 151.

12 Ibid. 152.

This model has been transferred successfully to the European level in the supranational order which governs the relationship between EU institutions and national institutions and the relationship between the Court of Justice of the European Union (CJEU) and national courts. In the constitutional system which has evolved in the EU, the preliminary ruling procedure, now codified in Article 267 TFEU, has been an essential factor in securing harmonised implementation and homogeneity in the application of EU law in the Member States. The procedure has played a central role in the integration of the legal systems of the EU Member States and the development of the EU legal systems as it presently stands.[13] But the important fact must be stressed that, as the constitutional courts of EU Member States have acknowledged, the structural features of the EU's supranational order are unique. This entails, firstly, that the autonomy of the CJEU is constituted by the transfer of sovereign powers, i.e. internal competences of the Member States; secondly, the direct effect of the norms of this legal order and their immediate normative validity in the national legal orders; and as a third element, its primacy over national law.[14]

Another procedure, less commonly referred to in discussion about the advisory jurisdiction under Protocol No. 16, is the advisory jurisdiction of the EFTA Court. The EFTA Court functions in accordance with the Agreement on the European Economic Area (EEA) between the EU Member States and the EFTA Member States, Norway, Iceland and Lichtenstein, and the Agreement between the EFTA States on the Establishment of a Surveillance Authority and a Court of Justice (both adopted in 1993).[15] Its jurisdiction is similar in some aspects to that of the CJEU. However, there is the fundamental difference between these two in that the EEA cooperation is neither founded on a supranational order nor on the transfer of state power to the EEA institutions as is the case of the EU. It does not acknowledge the principles of direct effect and primacy of EEA law, which can partly be explained by the fact that two EFTA states, Iceland and Norway, adhere to a dualistic approach towards the relationship between international law and national law.[16] This entails that the EFTA Court combines elements of a traditional international court with functions similar to those of the CJEU.

Under Article 34 on the Agreement on the EFTA Court, it has jurisdiction to give advisory opinions on the interpretation of the EEA Agreement. Where such a question is raised before any court or tribunal in an EFTA State, that court or

13 Janneke Gerards, 'Advisory Opinions, Preliminary Rulings and the New Protocol No. 16 to the European Convention of Human Rights' (2014) 21 *Maastricht Journal of European and Comparative Law* 640.

14 Rainer Arnold, 'The Federal Constitutional Court of Germany in the Context of the European Integration', in Patricia Popelier, Catherine Van de Heyning and Piet Van Nuffel (eds), *Human Rights Protection in the European Legal Order: The Interaction between the European and the National Courts* (Intersentia, 2011) 241–242.

15 See the EEA Agreement and its Annexes and Protocols at <www.efta.int/legal-texts/eea> and the Statute of the EFTA Court at <www.eftacourt.int/the-court/procedure/statute> accessed 1 August 2015.

16 M. Elvira Méndez-Pinedo, *EC and EEA Law. A Comparative Study of the Effectiveness of European Law* (Europa Law Publishing, 2009) 28–29.

tribunal may, if it considers it necessary to enable it to give judgment in a concrete case pending before it, request the EFTA Court to give such opinion. This mechanism is modelled on Article 267 of TFEU, but is in many ways narrower in scope. Firstly, the national courts in EFTA states are not obliged under EEA law to seek an advisory opinion and furthermore the opinions of the EFTA Court are not legally binding upon the national court requesting them when it adjudicates the case. However, practice reveals that they are usually followed by national courts and it has been argued that they are no weaker that the preliminary rulings rendered by the CJEU.[17]

Accordingly, and in light of the fact that the ECtHR is in principle a traditional international tribunal, the new procedure under Protocol No. 16 resembles more the advisory jurisdiction of the EFTA Court, even though it is also inspired by the CJEU preliminary ruling procedure.[18]

2.3 The objectives of Protocol No. 16: a first step in what direction?

The idea to create a new mechanism gained impetus in the context of the reform measures taken to ensure the effectiveness of the implementation of the ECHR at national level, as a reaction to the increasing flow of applications to Strasbourg. An influential contribution to the reform process was the Report of the Group of Wise Persons to the Committee of Ministers issued in 2006 which presented a number of proposals on the reform of the Court. It paid close attention to the relations between the ECtHR and the national courts, where the role of the states' highest courts in applying the Convention was considered of paramount importance and the possibility of institutionalising these links was studied. Even though, in the view of the Group, the EU preliminary ruling mechanism would be unsuitable for transposition in the Council of Europe, it suggested it would be useful to introduce a system under which national courts could apply to the ECtHR for advisory opinions on legal questions related to the interpretation of the Convention. The main advantage was considered to be that this would foster dialogue between courts and enhance the Court's 'constitutional role'. However, the new advisory jurisdiction should be subject to strict conditions, and to prevent proliferation of such requests, they would be submitted by a constitutional court or national court of last instance only, would always be optional and the opinions given by the ECtHR would not be binding.[19] In the Izmir declaration of 2011,

17 Ibid. 37–41. This is not without exceptions and the non-binding effect has repeatedly been referred to in the case law of the Norwegian and Icelandic Supreme Courts. See e.g. Halvard Haukeland Frederiksen and Gjermund Mathisen, *EØS-rett* (2nd edn, Fagbokforlaget, 2014) 202.

18 See the detailed comparison between the procedures and legal effects of the EU preliminary reference procedure and the procedure in Protocol No. 16 in Paul Gragl, '(Judicial) Love Is Not a One-Way Street: The EU Preliminary Reference Procedure as a Model for ECtHR Advisory Opinions under Draft Protocol No. 16' (2013) 38 *European Law Review* 229.

19 Report of the Group of Wise Persons to the Committee of Ministers (979bis meeting, CM (2006) 203, 15 November 2006) <https://wcd.coe.int/ViewDoc.jsp?id=1063779> accessed 1 August 2015, paras 76–86 and 135.

the idea of an advisory opinion procedure was suggested as a possible measure in the reforms of the Court to diminish the number of applications received.[20]

The ECtHR was initially not enthusiastic about this idea. Even though it was welcomed in principle, such a procedure could obviously entail more work for the Court and other practical solutions to address the Court's workload were recommended.[21] In preparation of the agenda for the Brighton Conference, and at the drafting stage of Protocol No. 16, the Court presented a more detailed assessment on the issue in two opinions of February 2012 and May 2013.[22] From these documents, it can be seen that opinion within the Court was divided, although the majority eventually became convinced of the added value of the Protocol. It acknowledged that, although there was a risk that it might initially generate more work, the longer-term objective would clearly be to ensure that more cases were dealt with satisfactorily at national level.[23]

The objectives of the advisory opinion procedure are set forth in paragraph 3 of the Protocol's Preamble and further elaborated in the Explanatory Report. The extension of the Court's competence to give advisory opinions is intended to further enhance the interaction between the Court and national authorities and thereby reinforce implementation of the Convention, in accordance with the principle of subsidiarity. It is hoped to result in national courts showing more awareness of the Convention and applying it in a correct manner.[24] In this context the objective is to institutionalise the dialogue between the ECtHR and national courts and emphasise the cooperative nature of the issue. Obviously the initiative in this direction must come from the highest courts of the States Parties, which are expected to show a high degree of willingness to implement non-binding advisory opinions, when they have chosen to refer questions in the first place.[25] This could eventually result in fewer applications to Strasbourg, not least if the principles set forth in an advisory opinion have impacts on a number of individuals and 'clone

20 High Level Conference on the Future of the European Court of Human Rights, Izmir Declaration (26–27 April 2011) <https://wcd.coe.int/ViewDoc.jsp?id=1781937> accessed 1 August 2014, part D.

21 Opinion of the Court on the Wise Persons' Report (as adopted by the Plenary Court on 2 April 2007) <www.echr.coe.int/Documents/2007_Wise_Person_Opinion_ENG.pdf> accessed 1 August 2015, 3.

22 Reflection paper on the proposal to extend the Court's advisory jurisdiction (ref. no. 3853038, 20 February 2012), <www.echr.coe.int/Documents/2013_Courts_advisory_jurisdiction_ENG.pdf> accessed 1 August 2014 and Opinion of the Court on Draft Protocol No. 16 to the Convention extending its competence to give advisory opinions on the interpretation of the Convention (Adopted by the Plenary Court on 6 May 2013) <www.echr.coe.int/Documents/2013_Protocol_16_Court_Opinion_ENG.pdf> accessed 2 December 2014.

23 Ibid, para. 2.

24 Gerards (n. 13) 632.

25 Iain Cameron, 'The Court and the Member States: Procedural Aspects', in Andreas Føllesdal, Birgit Peters and Geir Ulfstein (eds), *Constituting Europe: The European Court of Human Rights in a National, European and Global Context* (Cambridge University Press, 2013) 49.

cases' in the state concerned. The effects could then be similar to those of the pilot judgement procedure, now codified in Rule 61 of the Rules of the Court.[26] The Strasbourg Court has underlined this potential function by stating that the advisory opinions could 'complement the existing pilot-judgment procedure'.[27] However, it could equally apply to cases other than those which reveal structural or systemic problems, but raise questions of principles or of general interest concerning the application of the Convention.[28]

In a wider context, and as Iain Cameron has suggested, one could say that the advisory opinions are in a sense a natural consequence of the ECtHR's assertion that states must take into account judgments affecting other states, and not simply those against themselves.[29] This understanding is supported in the Court's reflection paper of 2012 where it stated that advisory opinion could be of comparable significance to the Court's leading judgments and foster a harmonious interpretation of the minimum standards set by the Convention rights and thus an effective protection of human rights throughout the States Parties.[30]

Despite the noble aims of the advisory jurisdiction and its potentials there are a number of question marks, on procedural aspect, the principles involved related to this new jurisdiction and on the direction in which the Court is heading. As pointed out by Luzius Wildhaber, the former President of the Court, and Steven Greer, the official debate on the objectives and the advantages of Protocol No. 16 and other recent reform initiatives has been dominated by Strasbourg officials, diplomats and NGOs and is to some extent characterised both by unwillingness to discuss thoroughly what the primary functions of the Court could and should be, and by confusion. In contrast, the academic or judicial debate has been more preoccupied with identifying the core contemporary functions of the Strasbourg process and diagnosing the central problems, and also with identifying coherent and integrated frameworks within which detailed reform measures could be conceived and implemented.[31]

As yet, considering how recently Protocol No. 16 was adopted, the legal literature is relatively limited. What has been written so far seems to reflect a rather sceptical

26 This would be of particular relevance if the request from a national court for an advisory opinion relates to a systemic domestic problem, which can be solved by the court on the basis of an advisory opinion received from the ECtHR. The ideal feedback, just as in the pilot judgment procedure, would be if the state concerned would endeavour to change its laws or policies in order to address similar cases and avoid new violations. On the objectives and functioning of the pilot procedure, see further Chapter 7, this volume.

27 Reflection paper on the proposal to extend the Court's advisory jurisdiction (n. 22), para. 5.

28 Ibid. para. 14.

29 Cameron (n. 25) 49.

30 Reflection paper on the proposal to extend the Court's advisory jurisdiction (n. 22), para. 5.

31 Steven Greer and Luzius Wildhaber, 'Revisiting the Debate about "Constitutionalising" the European Court of Human Rights' (2012) 12 *Human Rights Law Review* 655, 659 and 662.

approach about the future impact of this new function of the Court. It has been indicated that advisory opinions would represent the *first step* towards a further institutionalisation of the links and contacts between the domestic courts and the ECtHR, without envisaging what the next step in this direction should be.[32] Matti Pellonpää, the former judge from Finland at the ECtHR, has described it as a *careful step*, intended only as a supplementary jurisdiction, while at the same time expressing concerns over the complications it may bring about.[33] Janneke Gerards has argued that it is far from certain that the procedure will enable the achievement of the intended objectives, particularly when a comparison is drawn with the preliminary ruling procedure as it has been developed in EU law.[34] Others, such as Dzehtsiarou and O'Meara, have argued that the mechanism carries a number of significant drawbacks, notably that it risks adding to the Court's workload.[35] Some authors appear to more optimistic emphasising the added value of the Protocol, that it indeed 'creates a platform for a productive and fruitful dialogue between the highest national courts and the ECtHR because it can formalize their relations and guide their interaction, which until now, have taken place implicitly by way of exhaustion of domestic remedies'.[36] However, the most severe criticism against Protocol No. 16 is undoubtedly set forth in the opinion of the CJEU No. 2/13 of 18 December 2014, which reflects a negative approach towards the new advisory procedure, and even predicts that the Protocol poses a potential threat to the autonomy of EU law by undermining the preliminary ruling procedure provided for in Article 267 TFEU. These critical approaches will be addressed further below. In the following section special characteristics of the procedure will be assessed, with attention given to factors that may undermine its application and effectiveness.

3 Characteristics of the procedure and the essence of advisory opinions

3.1 The optional jurisdiction and organisational flexibility

The procedure provided for in Protocol No. 16 is an innovation in comparison to previous protocols to the ECHR in many aspects. When its provisions are examined, what stands out is the unusual flexibility of organisational issues and procedure and how loosely the rules related to a request for an advisory opinion and its

32 Gragl (n. 18) 233.

33 Matti Pellonpää, 'Dialog mellom Den europeiske menneskerettdomstol og nasjonale domstoler' (Forhandlingerne ved det 40. nordiske Juristmøte i Oslo 21–22 August 2014) <http://nordiskjurist.org/wp-content/uploads/2013/08/40nordiskejurist_referat.pdf> accessed 1 August 2015, Bind I, 324.

34 Gerards (n. 13) 650.

35 Dzehtsiarou and O'Meara (n. 7) 468.

36 Christos Giannopoulos, 'Considerations on Protocol No. 16: Can the New Advisory Competence of the European Court of Human Rights Breathe New Life into the European Convention on Human Rights?' (2015) 16 *German Law Journal* 337, 349.

process are prescribed in the Protocol text itself. Obviously the Court will elaborate the procedure further in the Rules of Court when the Protocol enters into force, but this will not change these main characteristics.

A key feature of the Protocol is that it is optional for States Parties to accept this new type of jurisdiction in the Convention's control system. Previous procedural amendments related to the Court's jurisdiction have, as a rule, required the ratification of all States Parties.[37] From the outset it was suggested, however, that the jurisdiction should be optional for States Parties, without any precise reasons being given for this, though these probably included concern over an added workload and the view that the new jurisdiction was not intended to be among the Court's principal functions.[38] Not least, it was foreseen that a consensus among States Parties about the procedure would be unlikely, in addition to the fact that the new procedure is not an essential reform measure for the Court. Actually, the more widespread view is that it may be more likely to add to the Court's caseload than to reduce it; this will be addressed below.[39] The Court itself explains that even though protocols making procedural amendments have, as a rule, not been optional, it could be advisable to keep this particular system optional for those States Parties that consider the advisory jurisdiction of the Court to be useful for assisting them in achieving better compliance with the standards set by the Convention.[40] Fragmenting procedural measures in the control system of the Convention on the basis that some States Parties may find such procedures useful, and others not, is a peculiar step. It might be a point of concern because of its future implications as a step in the direction of moving away from the principle that procedure for all Member States before the ECtHR should be harmonised.

Important elements of the procedure set out in Article 1 of Protocol No. 16 underline the flexibility of some organisational issues but at the same time this may create some inconsistencies.[41] Firstly, the Article provides that only the *highest national courts and tribunals* nominated by the State Party concerned can request opinions. In this respect each State Party has discretion as to how define highest national courts. This permits the potential inclusion of those courts or tribunals that, although inferior to the constitutional or supreme court in the state, are nevertheless of special relevance on account of being the 'highest' for a particular

37 Protocol No. 9 to the Convention, CETS No. 140 should be mentioned even though it did not strictly involve jurisdictional issues. It was adopted on 6 November 1990 and enabled persons, non-governmental organisations or group of individuals having lodged the complaint with the Commission to bring a case before the Court. It was optional and came into force following ratification of ten states in 1994, but due to the reform of the Court and the entry into force of Protocol No. 11 in 1998 it was of little practical significance.

38 Report of the Group of Wise Persons to the Committee of Ministers (n. 19), paras 82 and 85.

39 Greer and Wildhaber (n. 31) 659.

40 Reflection paper on the proposal to extend the Court's advisory jurisdiction (n. 22), para. 47.

41 Pellonpää (n. 33) 324.

category of case.[42] Secondly, subject to this condition, a *freedom of choice* is granted to States Parties as to which court fulfilling the criteria will be nominated. In addition, under Article 2, States Parties may change such nominations at any later date, by adding or removing courts and tribunals from such a list. This level of flexibility could present inconsistency between states with regard to which courts are nominated. The outcome depends on the discretion of the national authorities on which highest courts will be nominated which will eventually affect the scope of application of the Protocol in each Member State. The Protocol is however clear on the point that lower courts are excluded, because the currently existing 'dialogue' is now taking place between the ECtHR and highest national courts.[43]

Most importantly, the nominated national courts and tribunals are *allowed*, but not obliged, to request an advisory opinion. Accordingly, the power to decide whether this jurisdiction is utilised rests solely with the court concerned, and the decision-making power is also understood to enable the requesting court to withdraw its request, presumably at any time.[44] This is an essential element of the procedure, and one of the fundamental differences from the EU preliminary ruling procedure, where Article 267(3) TFEU provides that if a question is raised in a case pending before a court of last resort, that court *shall* bring the matter to the CJEU for a preliminary ruling. This has furthermore been considered as the most important element with regard to the uniform interpretation and application of EU law.[45] In this respect, the procedure in Protocol No. 16 resembles the advisory procedure in force at the EFTA Court, as the courts of the EFTA States are not obliged under the EEA Agreement to seek an advisory opinion.

3.2 The contents of advisory opinions and formulation of questions of principle

When it comes to the contents of the opinion and circumstances under which it can be sought, Article 1, paragraph 1 requires that the request for an opinion must involve *questions of principle* relating to the interpretation or application of the rights and freedoms defined in the Convention. In addition, paragraph 2 states that this can only be done in the context of a case pending before a domestic court. This aims to avoid requests for an abstract opinion which is not to be applied in a specific pending case.[46] One can expect that in laying down a principle, the Court would apply methodology already used in its judgments. In its attempts to establish clearer uniform standards of interpretation of the Convention for domestic courts, the Court tends to begin its assessment of the legal issues in a case by sketching out the applicable principles which apply generally to the area.[47]

42 Explanatory Report to Protocol No. 16 <http://conventions.coe.int/Treaty/en/reports/html/214.htm> accessed 1 August 2015, para. 8.
43 Gerards (n. 13) 632.
44 Explanatory Report to Protocol No. 16 (n. 42), para. 7.
45 Gragl (n. 18) 234.
46 Explanatory Report to Protocol No. 16 (n. 42), para. 10.
47 Cameron (n. 25) 49.

The idea that the opinion shall only concern questions of principle in a given case has both advantages and disadvantages. On the one hand, this will respect the national court's margin of appreciation to apply these principles as interpreted by the ECtHR when adjudicating the case.[48] But, on the other hand, issuing an opinion on principles related to interpretation may be too open and subject to vagueness as to how to apply it in the factual circumstances in the concrete case. As will be discussed later, the way would be open for a dissatisfied party in the domestic proceedings to challenge the conclusion by submitting an application to Strasbourg. So, the question is: what additional value would there be in the advisory opinion under such circumstances with respect to the individual case? In this respect it has been suggested that the content and preciseness of an opinion from the ECtHR could be different from preliminary rulings from the CJEU and the EFTA Court, as the latter could be more precise as to the facts of the case, and as an example provide interpretation of a concrete provision of an EU directive of a technical nature.[49] However, it has also been argued that this difference will be less important in practice in light of the fact that just like the ECtHR, the CJEU distinguishes between the interpretation of EU law on one hand and the application of that interpretation in the concrete case on the other. Accordingly, in many cases the CJEU leaves it to the national courts to apply such principles, standards and criteria to the facts of the case at hand.[50] The dividing line between the two is not always entirely clear and it differs in how detailed the guidance from CJEU is.[51]

Another issue relates to the formulation of a request from a national court to the ECtHR to give an opinion on a matter of principle. Apparently, discretion is granted to the domestic courts to suggest which principles are involved. The national court concerned must give reasons for its request and provide the relevant legal and factual background of the pending case under to Article 1, paragraph 3.[52] Meanwhile, the Protocol and its Explanatory Report are silent on the Court's authority to reformulate the question or even point out new principles not suggested by the national court. Curiously, in the draft Explanatory Report there was a sentence in brackets stating that the Court would remain free to reformulate the

48 Matti Pellonpää has argued that an advisory opinion from the ECtHR, given beforehand in the pending domestic proceedings, is more likely to undermine genuine dialogue between Strasbourg and national courts. On the basis of the subsidiarity principle the national courts should do the balancing of interest, subject to a later revision in Strasbourg (Pellonpää (n. 33) 323).

49 Ibid. 322.

50 Gerards (n. 13) 644.

51 On the content and preciseness of preliminary rulings in EU law, see e.g. Takis Tridimas, 'Constitutional Review of Member State Action: The Virtues and Vices of an Incomplete Jurisdiction, (2011) 9 *International Journal of Constitutional Law* 737–756.

52 Further clarification on how to provide relevant legal and factual background is provided in the Explanatory Report to Protocol No. 16 (n. 42), para. 12. This should *inter alia* include, if possible and appropriate, a statement of the domestic court's views on the question, including any analysis it may itself have made of the question.

questions, which was deleted in the final version and it remains open how this deletion should be interpreted.[53]

3.3 The admissibility of requests for advisory opinions

Under Article 2, paragraph 2 of Protocol No. 16, advisory opinions will be delivered exclusively by the Grand Chamber of the Court. When a national court has submitted such a request, a panel of five judges must first decide whether it is admissible or not under Article 2, paragraph 1. This system is similar to that provided for in Article 43 of the Convention regarding the referral of cases to the Grand Chamber. Here the Panel has some discretion. But if it refuses to accept the request, it must give reasons for its opinion and a kind of admissibility decision has to be issued. This requirement has been controversial, as the ECtHR expressed the opinion that it should not be obliged to give reasons for refusal.[54] This suggestion was not followed in the final text. In the explanatory notes on this point it is argued that unlike the procedure under Article 43, the reasoning for the Panel's refusal is seen as a *part of the dialogue* between the Court and national judicial systems, including through clarification of the Court's interpretation of what is meant by questions of principle related to the interpretation of application of the Convention's rights and freedoms.[55]

The reference to a *dialogue* here about what constitutes a principle is not explained or supported with further arguments. It is indeed difficult to assess what conclusions a national court could draw from a decision by the Panel to the effect that its request for an advisory opinion is to be rejected, since this does not involve questions of principle. This will all depend on the preciseness of such reasoning. It is not unlikely that the Court will interpret the criteria strictly, when it is borne in mind that wide access to advisory opinions could increase the workload significantly, even though the Court's workload as such cannot constitute a ground for rejection.[56] Such a decision would have to be published with other decisions by the Court so as to clarify the Court's position in defining what may constitute questions of principle in requests for advisory opinions.

3.4 Who will take part in the advisory opinion procedure?

When a request has been accepted by the Panel, Article 3 of Protocol No. 16 grants the Council of Europe's Commissioner for Human Rights and the State Party concerned the right to submit written comments and take part in any hearing. Meanwhile, the way lies open for the Court to invite others, such as the parties

53 See Draft Explanatory Report to Protocol No. 16 (DH-GDR(2012)020, 2 November 2012) <www.coe.int/t/dghl/standardsetting/cddh/DH_GDR/DH-GDR%282012%29020_Draft%20Explanatory%20Report_Protocol%20no%20%2016_ECHR%20%283%29.pdf> accessed 1 August 2015, para. 9.
54 Opinion of the Court on Draft Protocol No. 16 (n. 22), para. 9.
55 Explanatory Report to Protocol No. 16 (n. 42), para. 15.
56 Dzehtsiarou and O'Meara (n. 7) 19.

to the case in the domestic proceedings, to submit written comments or take part in any hearing. This can be done if the Court considers it to be in the interest of the proper administration of justice. In the Explanatory Report it is noted that it is indeed expected that the parties to the case in the context of which the advisory opinion was requested would be invited to take part in the proceedings.[57]

A difficult balance must be maintained in this respect. As Dzehtsiarou and O'Meara suggest, this procedure would indeed become less demanding in terms of time and resources, and more efficient, providing it were not adversarial. However, this argument is both normatively and procedurally problematic. If one or both parties in the domestic proceedings have no input to contribute to the advisory opinion proceedings, it will undermine the legitimacy of the exercise. Should the parties in the domestic proceedings on the other hand be automatically allowed to submit their observations the advisory opinion procedure would become time-consuming and the borderline with an adversarial procedure in contentious cases would become blurred.[58] Nevertheless, the interests of the parties in the domestic proceedings and their right to take part in the advisory proceedings, should have been given more weight, instead of giving the ECtHR the discretion to decide from one case to another whether proper administration of justice requires that the parties should be invited to submit their observation.

3.5 The priority of the procedure

Obviously, waiting for an advisory opinion from the ECtHR could delay the conclusion of the case in the domestic court, and there is nothing in the text of the Protocol to promote or guarantee speed of handling in Strasbourg. When it is borne in mind that the Grand Chamber's capacity to adjudicate in substantive cases is limited (it delivers about 30 judgments annually), this gives cause for concern.

The issue is addressed in the Explanatory Report, where it is stated that the prioritisation to be given to proceedings under this Protocol would be a matter for the Court, as it is with respect to all other proceedings. That being said, the nature of the questions on which it would be appropriate for the Court to give its advisory opinion suggests that such proceedings would have high priority. Undue delay in advisory opinion proceedings before the Court would also cause delay in proceedings in the case pending before the requesting court or tribunal and should therefore be avoided.[59] Otherwise there is a potential risk for the parties in the domestic proceedings that their right to fair trial within a reasonable time as guaranteed in Article 6 of the ECHR will be violated.

57 Explanatory Report to Protocol No. 16 (n. 42), para. 20.
58 Dzehtsiarou and O'Meara (n. 7) 18.
59 Explanatory Report to Protocol No. 16 (n. 42), para. 17.

3.6 Reasoned opinion and separate opinions

The Court is to give reasons for is advisory opinion, as stipulated in Article 4 of the Protocol. Obviously it is essential, as one of the main objectives is to guide the national requesting court, that the Court expresses clear argumentation when presenting the principles applicable to the concrete case. What undermines this, however, is that any judge sitting on the case is to be entitled to deliver a separate opinion. Such separate opinions on applicable principles are likely to weaken the force of guidance given to the national court adjudicating the case. In this respect the advisory opinion procedure is fundamentally different from that of the preliminary ruling system of the CJEU which does not allow separate opinions.

4 Assessment of the impact of advisory opinions on domestic implementation and case flow to ECtHR

Article 5 of the Protocol stipulates that advisory opinions shall not be binding. It therefore depends entirely on the domestic court concerned to determine the effect of the advisory opinion on the domestic proceedings. It is possible, as Cameron has suggested, that the national court would feel 'ownership' of the issue and, it is hoped, would show a high degree of willingness to implement the opinion even though it were non-binding, since it decided to refer the question for an opinion in the first place.[60] Others have expressed more pessimistic views and pointed out that the attitude of national authorities towards the Strasbourg Court and the Convention more generally is often rather critical. The idea that national courts should participate in an 'institutional dialogue' is alien to courts in many states and quite distant from the core role of the judiciary. Such a partnership between the ECtHR and the national courts therefore seems hardly realistic.[61]

But, as discussed above, this may depend a lot on the nature of the principle clarified in the opinion. Accordingly, how to apply the general principle defined in the opinion to the factual circumstances of the case can easily give rise to disagreement in the national court. The fact that opinions lack the binding character of a judgment in itself undermines the idea that seeking the opinion of the ECtHR in a case pending before domestic courts could be an effective tool in resolving the domestic case.[62] It is hardly likely to strengthen the implementation of rights at national level if the national courts do not in fact follow a controversial advisory opinion of the Strasbourg Court, the meaning of which may in turn also be subject to interpretation. This could easily be the case if the Court's opinion is divided, with dissenting opinions accompanying it.

In the wider context, the advisory opinion mechanism means that the domestic courts of all Member States can implement the general principles which the Court

60 Cameron (n. 25) 48.

61 Gerards (n. 13) 646.

62 It should be noted that a number of judges in the Court pleaded in favour of making the opinions binding. See Reflection paper on the proposal to extend the Court's advisory jurisdiction (n. 22), paras 43 and 44.

lays down in relation to a concrete question in its advisory opinion to any domestic court. Accordingly, the effects could be similar to the impact of general principles laid down in the Court's judgments. This could possibly strengthen the subsidiarity element underlining the responsibility of the States Parties to guarantee the application and implementation of the Convention. Guidance from the Court in this respect would help to avoid controversies between domestic courts and Strasbourg and reduce the likelihood that the case would be taken to Strasbourg. As the Court expressed it, this new advisory jurisdiction could foster a harmonious interpretation of the minimum standards set by the Convention rights. The ultimate goal of the procedure would be that the principle addressed in an advisory opinion would be implemented in all Member States.

In its reflection paper, the Court pointed out some types of cases which could be appropriate for advisory opinions. Among the examples taken was the Grand Chamber judgment in the case of *MSS* v. *Belgium and Greece*, No. 30696/09 of 21 January 2011. The case concerned the compatibility with the Convention of the expulsion of an asylum seeker to Greece in application of the Dublin II Regulation, which raised a question of principle relevant to many States Parties to the Convention in which the legal situation was identical.[63] This is indeed an example of a situation where a new jurisdiction could eventually result in a reduced number of complaints sent to Strasbourg.

But this brings us back to the same point as before: parties in proceedings who are dissatisfied with a conclusion reached by a domestic court which implements a principle presented in an advisory opinion cannot be prevented from submitting their cases to Strasbourg. In such circumstances, new questions arise with respect to the possibility of overlapping jurisdictions of the Court in contentious and advisory cases, which will be discussed in section 5.

The Explanatory Report to Protocol No. 16 states that advisory opinions shall form part of the case law of the Court, alongside its judgments and decisions. They would not have any direct effect on later applications, but the interpretation of the Convention contained therein would have the same effect as the interpretative elements of the Court's judgments and decisions.[64] This would require that advisory opinions be published in order to ensure that they would be accessible in all the Member States.

5 The overlapping contentious and advisory jurisdictions of the ECtHR

As previously discussed the idea behind the limited scope of advisory opinions requested by the Committee of Ministers according to Article 47 was to avoid double adjudication in the same case. When the scope of jurisdiction under Protocol No. 16 is assessed it appears that some overlap between the Court's contentious and advisory jurisdiction becomes inevitable.[65] This raises new questions. It should

63 Ibid. para. 30.
64 Explanatory Report to Protocol No. 16 (n. 42), para. 26.
65 Dzehtsiarou and O'Meara (n. 7) 4.

be recalled that the adoption of the Protocol is strongly motivated by the need to underline the general impact of the Court's interpretation rather than its role in adjudicating the substance of individual cases. Already, the ECtHR performs two functions: it is mainly an adjudicatory court but it has also developed its functions more into defining the underlying principles and criteria for applying them in concrete cases. When (and if) the Protocol comes into force, this second ('constitutional') function of the ECtHR will be emphasised, and an overlap between jurisdictions will evolve. Two possible situations can be envisaged in this respect. First, there is one in which a party in domestic proceedings on which an advisory opinion has been sought decides nevertheless to take the case to Strasbourg. The Explanatory Report addresses this issue by stating that if the advisory opinion of the Court *has effectively been followed*, it is expected that such elements of the application that relate to the issues addressed in the advisory opinion would be declared inadmissible or struck out.[66] Apparently, this is intended to be a working rule of the Court rather than being codified as an admissibility criterion.

The second issue is the general relationship between procedures in contentious cases and advisory opinions, especially if the legal issue raised in the request could be more suitably dealt with in an individual application. One can foresee a potential situation in which an application under Article 34 of the ECHR is formally pending before the Strasbourg Court when a national court requests an advisory opinion in an identical case. The draft Explanatory Report initially stated that under such circumstances the individual application procedure should be given priority.[67] However, this was deleted from the final version of the Explanatory Report, so it is left in the hands of the Court to decide which policy shall apply. Gragl has pointed out as a possible drawback in this scenario that only the judgment in the regular Article 34 ECHR procedure would be binding, whereas Strasbourg's legal expertise in advisory opinions would provide guidance on how to adjudicate a concrete case but it would still be optional for the domestic court whether it acts in compliance with it. This might lead to an 'incoherent implementation within the legal orders of the high contracting parties, as the same or comparable cases could lead, on the one hand, to binding judgments (via individual applications), and, on the other hand, to non-binding advisory opinions'.[68] Even though this situation could be theoretically possible, it is unlikely to influence the implementation seriously. Nevertheless, it reveals one unfortunate aspect resulting from the overlapping jurisdictions.

6 Impact on parties in the domestic proceedings pending in the requesting court

One remaining question which Protocol No. 16 raises relates to the consequences of mixing the procedure in concrete cases before a domestic court with the

66 Explanatory Report to Protocol No. 16 (n. 42), para. 26.
67 See Draft Explanatory Report to Protocol No. 16 (n. 53), para. 17.
68 Gragl (n. 18) 242.

advisory opinion procedure in Strasbourg. From the viewpoint of the party in the domestic proceedings, whether this is a private individual or a legal person, the status is left somewhat vague. This is understandable to some extent since it must be up to the State Party to enact its national procedural law and to define further the position of the parties in the domestic case.

One can foresee a situation where a party opposes the decision by the national court where his case is pending to seek an advisory opinion from Strasbourg. Having regard to the fact that the national court has discretion under the Protocol to decide whether or not to request an advisory opinion, it is an open question whether national law provides a party in such proceedings any procedural remedies on this point. In civil proceedings, the procedural law of most State Parties is based on the principle of control by the litigating parties over the scope of a civil action even though it may vary from one state to another how this is regulated. From this principle it follows that at least one of the parties in a case must be contending for his part, directly or indirectly, that the provisions of the ECHR may have an influence to some extent upon the outcome of the case in order for that question to be raised for consideration. The question whether a national court or tribunal would decide of its own accord to utilise this procedure if no argument to such effect is advanced by the parties involved needs to be addressed in national law. The national law could possibly elaborate further whether it will be required that a party to a case requests reference for an advisory opinion or whether the domestic court can request advisory opinion *ex officio*. It should be noted at the same time that procedural rules will only have this effect in civil lawsuits and not in criminal cases, over which the parties do not have similar control.

While the advisory procedure is pending in Strasbourg, the domestic proceedings would be suspended: as otherwise the purpose of the procedure will not be achieved. Delays in the Strasbourg advisory proceedings can therefore have direct consequences in delaying the proceedings in the domestic court for a considerable period of time. This may jeopardise the individual's right to a hearing within a reasonable time before a domestic court, which is guaranteed under Article 6 of the ECHR. This creates conflict. The general aim of Protocol No. 16, to create a dialogue between the ECtHR and national courts to enhance harmonisation and strengthen the image of the Strasbourg Court as a constitutional court, is perhaps too costly, compromising individual procedural guarantees. It must not be forgotten that the interests of the individual may have greater weight than the benefits of legal harmonisation.[69] Therefore the parties in the domestic proceedings should have a say as to whether an advisory opinion is sought.

7 CJEU's critical approach – a final blow to Protocol No. 16?

The advisory opinion procedure under Protocol No. 16 became subject to a special scrutiny in the opinion of the CJEU No. 2/13 of 18 December 2014 regarding the draft agreement on the accession of the European Union to the ECHR. One

69 Stefansson (n. 11) 158.

could say that this came as a surprise and for valid reasons. Firstly, in the light of the fact that the Protocol did not exist when the draft agreement was adopted on 5 April 2013, and understandably, therefore, no references or explanations are to be found regarding the Protocol in the draft agreement or its Explanatory Report. Secondly, and more importantly, there is no legal link between the possible accession of the EU to the ECHR and the existence of Protocol No. 16. They were from the outset intended to exist independently; accordingly, the Protocol had no direct bearing on the accession agreement and vice versa. In the light of this fact, neither the text of Protocol No. 16 nor its Explanatory Report refers to the relationship between the mechanism established by the Protocol and the preliminary ruling procedure provided for in Article 267 TFEU, in relation to the foreseeable accession of the EU to the ECHR.

In spite of this lack of connection between the two documents, a serious criticism against Protocol No. 16 was set forth in the opinion of the CJEU. Indeed, the Court took note of the fact that the Protocol was finalised after the adoption of the draft agreement in the autumn of 2013. However, it referred to the fact that since the ECHR would form an integral part of EU law, the mechanism established by Protocol No. 16 could, notably where the issue concerns rights guaranteed by the EU Charter of Fundamental Right corresponding to those secured by the ECHR, affect the autonomy and effectiveness of the preliminary ruling procedure provided for in Article 267 TFEU. In particular, it could not be ruled out that a request for an advisory opinion made pursuant to Protocol No. 16 by a court or tribunal of a Member State that had acceded to that protocol could trigger the procedure for the prior involvement of the Court of Justice provided for in Article 267 TFEU, thus creating a risk that the preliminary ruling procedure, the keystone of the judicial system established by the Treaties, might be circumvented. By failing to make any provision in respect of the relationship between the mechanism established by Protocol No. 16 and the preliminary ruling procedure provided for in Article 267 TFEU, the CJEU was of the view that the agreement was liable to affect adversely the autonomy and effectiveness of the latter procedure, and accordingly affect the specific characteristics of EU law and its autonomy.[70]

This argumentation and CJEU's negative approach towards Protocol No. 16 has been criticised for being both unfounded and unreasonable.[71] Indeed, the opinion itself illustrates a reasonable clarification given by Advocate General J. Kokott regarding the situation of coexisting procedures under Article 267 TFEU and Protocol No. 16. The possible effects of Protocol No. 16 on the powers of the CJEU were briefly discussed with the participants in the procedure before CJEU on the draft accession agreement on the basis of questions posed by

70 CJEU, Opinion 2/13, EU Accession to the ECHR, paras 196–200.

71 Paul Gragl, 'The Reasonableness of Jealousy: Opinion 2/13 and EU Accession to the ECHR' (1 February 2015), forthcoming in W. Benedek and others (eds), *European Yearbook on Human Rights* (Neuer Wissenschaftlicher Verlag, 2015), available at <http://ssrn.com/abstract=2563455> accessed 1 August 2015, 10.

the members of the Court. Advocate Kokott identified the Court's concern that the highest Member State courts could then be tempted to refer questions regarding the interpretation of the ECHR to Strasbourg rather than to Luxembourg. In response, she made the crucial point that such a temptation to prefer the ECtHR over the CJEU would not be a consequence of accession, since even before accession, Member States which have ratified Protocol No. 16 could turn to the ECtHR with questions concerning the interpretation of ECHR provisions which were identical in substance to the Charter. Moreover, she argued that this problem could be easily resolved on the basis of Article 267(3) TFEU which *obligates* the Member States' courts of last instance to request a preliminary ruling from the CJEU if in doubt with respect to the correct interpretation and application of EU law. Article 267(3) TFEU would always take precedence over national law and thus also over any posterior international agreement, such as Protocol No. 16, that has been ratified by the Member States. Thereby proper functioning and effectiveness of the preliminary ruling procedure would be ensured.[72]

Among those who have criticised the Court's narrow and rigid approach towards Protocol No. 16 is Paul Gragl, who also stresses the different objectives and nature of the two procedures. He points out that in contrast to the mandatory element of Article 267(3) TFEU, the advisory procedure under Protocol No. 16 will be entirely voluntary and that such advisory opinions would not be binding on the requesting court.[73] In this respect as generally regarding the CJEU's opinion on the accession issue, Gragl claims that it 'leaves a bitter taste and a fair share of pessimism among all those who are interested in human rights and their effective protection and enforcement'. In short, Opinion 2/13 confirms the impression that the CJEU is a 'selfish court', and its general approach on the permissibility of involving other international courts in settling disputes in relation to EU law 'casts a shadow on the feasibility of the accession project'.[74] Opinion 2/13 will at the best delay the EU accession to the ECHR for years, but more likely the accession will never occur. The consequences are more extensive, as it appears that Protocol No. 16 has also been shot down by the CJEU. Accordingly, the firm position of the Court against the new advisory procedure of the ECtHR, is highly likely to have a great impact to reduce the willingness of EU states to ratify Protocol No. 16 in the future.

8 Conclusion

This chapter has expressed some scepticism that the advisory jurisdiction under Protocol No. 16 will achieve the objectives of enhancing the domestic implementation of human rights, reducing the case flow to Strasbourg and strengthening the constitutional role of the ECtHR.

72 CJEU, Opinion 2/13, EU Accession to the ECHR, View of Advocate General Kokott of 13 June 2014, paras 139–141.

73 Gragl (n. 71) 10.

74 Ibid. 15.

When assessing the potential impact of Protocol No. 16, the political reality in the Member States of the ECHR is an essential factor. Their political willingness to enhance the Court's constitutional role by ratifying the Protocol is, after all, the main condition for the future of the new jurisdiction. The fact that the Court has slowly and gradually assumed the role of a constitutional court for Europe, without having been defined as such through the democratic processes of the States Parties, has raised questions regarding its legitimacy, the role of the national constitutional legislature and judiciary and ultimately the sovereignty of Member States.[75] Referring to the constitutional role of the ECtHR is controversial as it creates clashes with principles of national constitutional law in many Member States, and the idea of a constitutional role for the Court is certainly not likely to be supported by all of them.[76] One should also bear in mind that the concept and functions of a national constitutional court are not inherent in the legal systems of many Member States to the Convention; one could mention the group of the five Nordic states as examples.

A prerequisite for making the new advisory procedure under Protocol No. 16 work is that the national highest court or tribunal must be genuinely interested in hearing the opinion of the ECtHR. This should not be taken for granted, especially in states with generally well-functioning national systems for the protection of human rights. Furthermore, as has been argued, States Parties to the Protocol must implement procedural requirements in their national legislation in relation to requests for an advisory opinion. The duties of national courts towards parties in the proceedings remain to be regulated by national rules in connection with the ratification of the Protocol.

To conclude, it would be unrealistic to expect that Protocol No. 16 will have a significant impact on the implementation of the Convention in the States Parties to the ECHR, though it may be of value in exceptional circumstances, at best in a situation where systemic problems in a Member State could be solved at an early stage under the guidance of the ECtHR. Clearly, if the highest national court of a Member State is genuinely willing to seek the opinion of the ECtHR on a principle regarding interpretation of the ECHR, and applies the principles correctly to the case at hand, this would undoubtedly contribute to the development of shifting centres of gravity in human rights protection. However, this would not prevent the party in domestic proceedings to file an application in Strasbourg.

The Protocol has been described as representing a step towards a further institutionalisation of the links and contacts between the domestic courts and the ECtHR. In the light of the arguments set forth in this chapter, the author's view is that this step is first and foremost a symbolic one, however, blurring the lines between substantive and advisory jurisdictions. This also reflects the reluctance of

75 Andreas Føllesdal, Birgit Peters and Geir Ulfstein, 'Introduction', in Andreas Føllesdal, Birgit Peters and Geir Ulfstein (eds), *Constituting Europe. The European Court of Human Rights in a National, European and Global Context* (Cambridge University Press, 2013) 6.

76 Generally, as regards the idea that ECtHR practice has constitutional implications, see Chapter 4, this volume.

Member States to present a clear vision on how to define role of the Court vis-à-vis the domestic courts. If the intention were to redefine the role of the Court so as to have it function genuinely as a constitutional court in the traditional meaning of that concept this would require a political commitment on behalf of the States Parties to the ECHR to creating a new institution of a fundamentally different nature from that of the ECtHR as it is today. This would require States Parties to go all the way, including the transferral of their judicial powers to Strasbourg and the acknowledgement of the direct effect of its decisions in their national legal orders and their primacy over national law. It is difficult to foresee whether the political willingness to create a properly functioning enforcement mechanism of that type in Strasbourg will increase in the near future. Moreover, after the CJEU delivered its Opinion 2/2013 expressing its highly sceptical view on Protocol No. 16, a European consensus on the issue and willingness to ratify the Protocol seems to be more distant than ever.

7 Flying or landing? The pilot judgment procedure in the changing European human rights architecture

Antoine Buyse

1 Introduction

Polyana Valcheva, a member of the Bar in Bulgaria, was hit by the metaphorical boomerang twice. In 2004 she tipped a local prosecutor about possible documentary fraud by her former de facto spouse. In the course of the enquiry the investigating authorities found indications that Ms Valcheva herself had forged a document in order for her former partner to obtain a retirement pension. Criminal proceedings were started against both of them. Her tip about someone else led to her own prosecution. Finally, in 2010, she was acquitted. That same year she complained in Strasbourg about the excessive length of the proceedings, under Article 6 ECHR. In the summer of 2013 the European Court of Human Rights declared her complaint inadmissible.[1]

The reason is telling. In 2011 the Court had issued a pilot judgment, *Dimitrov and Hamanov*, on the systemic problem of overly long criminal proceedings in Bulgaria.[2] In that pilot judgment the Court held that the problem with such proceedings was not only 'recurrent and persistent' but also affected a potentially large number of people for whom there was need for redress at the national level.[3] In addition, the Court noted, it had found violations in over 80 cases about the same problem in the past decade and had over 200 of such cases still on the docket. Although the Court refrained from giving specific indications on how to solve the problem, as Bulgaria was already under scrutiny of the Council of Europe's Committee of Ministers on this, it did indicate that Bulgaria should put in place remedies not just for current but also for past excesses in this respect and enumerated a number of requirements such remedies should meet. Notably, the Court reiterated that

> the introduction of effective domestic remedies in this domain would be particularly important in view of the subsidiarity principle, so that individuals are

1 *Polyana Ivanova Valcheva and Enyo Nikolov Abrashev* v. *Bulgaria* App. Nos 6194/11 and 34887/11 (adm dec, ECtHR, 18 June 2013).

2 *Dimitrov and Hamanov* v. *Bulgaria* App. Nos 48059/06 and 2708/09 (ECtHR, 10 May 2011).

3 Ibid. para. 109.

> not systematically forced to refer to the Court in Strasbourg complaints that could otherwise, and in the Court's opinion more appropriately, have been addressed in the first place within the national legal system.[4]

When the Court had to decide in 2013 on Polyana, it reviewed a new remedial system set in place in Bulgaria to address the issue and concluded that it could be seen as effective, in spite of the lack of a long-term practice of implementing it. She was in effect asked to go back to the national system and try the domestic remedy first: trying to bring her case to a resolution at the European level thus failed – the second boomerang for her.

This episode in the Court's case law is illustrative of a practice developed over the past decade known as the pilot judgment procedure. It is a specific way of dealing with applications reaching the Court in Strasbourg in addressing systemic or structural human rights problems by way of giving states indications on what to try and solve these. It could be said to potentially shift the gravity of European human rights protection towards the Court, as it takes on a more intrusive supervisory role, adjudicating not just the symptoms of a problem but also looking into the root causes. By contrast, it could *also* be said to shift the centre of gravity more firmly back to the states, in line with the principle of subsidiarity. After all, by indicating parameters of how a solution of a structural problem should look like, the Court puts the bulk of decision-making in individual cases in the hands of the domestic authorities, while retaining its role as supervisor of the Convention's rights and freedoms. The pilot judgment procedure has also led to shifts in the division of labour between the Court and the Committee of Ministers and it may lead to shifts of gravity within the domestic legal order. Finally, a possible future accession of the European Union[5] may lead to a new shift, if the Court would apply its pilot judgment procedure to structural defects in the Union's legal order.

This chapter will delve into the pilot judgment procedure and the shifts in gravity of human rights protection it may result in. First, I will briefly go into the origins and the goals of the pilot judgments procedure. Second, I will investigate the conditions in which a pilot judgment can or should be applied. Third, the gravity shifts which may result from its application will be addressed.

2 Origins and goals

The pilot judgment procedure originates in two connected problems: systemic problems of human rights violations within the States Parties to the European Convention and ensuing large numbers of applications concerning these issues coming to the European Court of Human Rights in Strasbourg. In an ideal feedback loop this issue would not occur, as once a violation would be found by the Court in one case, the state concerned would endeavour to remedy the problem

4 Ibid. para. 122.

5 Which now seems a prospect relegated to the very distant future, with the Court of Justice of the European Union's Advisory Opinion 2/13.

not only for the individual applicant of the case, but if necessary also change its laws or policies in order to address similar cases and avoid new violations. This would then prevent new applications on the same issue being lodged with the Court. However, in practice, states have very often either been unable or unwilling to implement the necessary changes. In addition, effective remedies to offer at least some relief to victims at the national level do not always exist. As a result, systemic human rights violations of various kinds, ranging from unclear restitution schemes to unduly delayed judicial procedures, have plagued Europe in spite of the presence of a long-established human rights protection system. To be sure, the problem that to a certain extent may have occurred in any event, was compounded by the accession of a large number of new state parties after the end of the Cold War in the 1990s. Many of these states struggled with the extensive process of change from communist dictatorship to capitalist democracy. On top of this, some regions such as the Balkans and the Caucasus were plagued by violent conflict.

All of the above changed the rôle of the Court. No longer could it limit itself to fine-tuning the parameters of relatively well-functioning states and to taking the time to deal with a relatively small amount of cases.[6] Indeed, one of the key reasons to make the Court a permanent, full-time institution as of 1998 was partly caused by a large increase in applications – and thus underlying human rights problems – reaching the Court. The number of human rights complaints was larger than what the Court could effectively deal with. In 1998, the backlog of cases was around 7,000.[7] These numbers would increase exponentially in the following years. The problem of the backlog quickly became an existential threat to the Court and attempts to reform the Court to deal more effectively with it has become a recurring theme in the years since. The rise in pending applications was only reverted from 2011 onwards, when it reached a peak of 161,000. The bulk of the admissible cases among those were repetitive cases, relating to recurring human rights violations.[8] In the discussions leading up to one of the key reform protocols to address the problem, Protocol No. 14 adopted in 2004, the pilot judgment procedure was born. The representatives of the state parties were of the opinion, contrary to the Court's own wishes, that it was not necessary to include the new idea formally in Protocol 14. Rather, the Steering Committee on Human Rights of the Committee of Ministers of the Council of Europe, argued that a new approach could be adopted within the existing rules.[9] This stance may have been triggered by expediency: the process of ratification and entry into force of a new

6 Wojciech Sadurski, 'Partnering with Strasbourg: Constitutionalization of the European Court of Human Rights, the Accession of Central and Eastern European States to the Council of Europe, and the Idea of Pilot Judgments', *Sydney Law School Legal Studies Research Paper* No. 08/135 (2008), at: <ssrn.com/abstract=1295652>.

7 European Court of Human Rights, *Annual Report 2005*, 24, at: <echr.coe.int>.

8 European Court of Human Rights, *Annual Report 2014*, foreword.

9 Costas Paraskeva, 'Returning the Protection of Human Rights to Where They Belong: At Home' (2008) 12 *International Journal of Human Rights* 415, 434.

protocol could take years[10] and new and creative solutions were called for right away.

Thus, the Committee of Ministers issued a resolution in 2004 on judgments revealing systemic problems with the implementation of the Convention.[11] The Court was invited to

> identify, in its judgments finding a violation of the Convention, what it considers to be an underlying systemic problem and the source of this problem, in particular when it is likely to give rise to numerous applications, so as to assist states in finding the appropriate solution and the Committee of Ministers in supervising the execution of judgments.[12]

The resolution indicated that this would both help to guarantee the effectiveness of Strasbourg's human rights protection system – by preventing it from becoming bogged down in an overflow of applications – and that it would enable state parties to receive guidance on both the identification and tackling of systemic human rights problems.

In spite of discussion, even within the Court itself, about the lack of a clear legal basis,[13] the Court began using the procedure right away. The 'pilot case' of the pilot procedure itself was *Broniowski* v. *Poland*, a case focused on the lack of sufficient compensation for Poles who had been forcibly displaced at the end of the Second World War.[14]

3 What is a pilot judgment procedure?

From the perspective of shifting gravities the pilot judgment procedure entails an increased role for the Court in the triangle Court (judicial decision-making) – Committee of Ministers (supervision of execution of judgments) – state (implementation of judgments). After all, the Court is called upon to take a more active role in both the assessment of an issue and in directions for its resolution. It also specifically is meant to go beyond the mere specifics of a single selected case. The direction the Court may suggest is more explicitly relevant for other similar cases than in its ordinary judgments. And state parties are more explicitly required than in such ordinary cases to make wider policy or legislative changes. Considering this

10 Indeed, Protocol 14 only entered into force as late as 2010.

11 Committee of Ministers, resolution Res(2004)3 on judgments revealing an underlying systemic problem, 12 May 2004.

12 Ibid.

13 See e.g. Lech Garlicki, 'Broniowski and After: On the Dual Nature of "Pilot Judgments"', in Lucius Caflisch and others (eds), *Human Rights – Strasbourg Views. Liber Amicorum Luzius Wildhaber* (Engel Verlag, 2007) 177, at 182–191.

14 *Broniowski* v. *Poland* App. No. 31443/96 (ECtHR, 22 June 2004). The decisions on the admissibility and on the friendly settlement reached were made on 19 December 2002 and 28 September 2005 respectively.

enhanced role for the Court it is all the more important to have a clear understanding of what a pilot judgment is and when it should be applied. The then President of the Court, Luzius Wildhaber, seems to have been a proponent of a sparing approach of the procedure. Taking his cue from the *Broniowski* case, he later identified no fewer than eight specific characteristics which turn a Strasbourg case into a pilot judgment. One of the underlying reasons might have been to preclude the Court from overstepping its boundaries and losing the goodwill of the state parties. The more strings one attaches to the application of a pilot judgment, the less one may be seen as overly activist. These eight characteristics are the following: (1) the Grand Chamber of the Court finds a violation of the Convention affecting a whole category of people in a similar situation; (2) the Court concludes that, as a result, this violation has brought or will bring many similar applications to Strasbourg; (3) the Court gives general instructions to the state concerned in order to address the issue; (4) such state measures should also retroactively apply to deal with comparable situations, e.g. when new remedies are offered; (5) the Court 'freezes' or adjourns similar pending cases; (6) the operative part of the judgment explicitly indicates the need for general measures, so as to increase the authority and effect of the pilot elements of the judgment; (7) just satisfaction in the particular case is deferred until the state has taken measures of implementation; (8) and, finally, the key Council of Europe institutions are informed of developments in the pilot case.[15] These institutions include the Committee of Ministers, the Parliamentary Assembly and the Human Rights Commissioner. The latter characteristic is illustrative of the fact that any potential shift in gravity goes hand in hand with enhanced cooperation between the institutions involved. The introduction of the pilot judgment is therefore far from a judicial coup by the Court – after all it was introduced at the prompting of the states themselves. Rather, it should be seen as a method of closer cooperation in the triangle mentioned above in order to solve systemic issues at the national level *and* preventing the meltdown of the European supervisory system.

The eight characteristics have not become the defining boundaries of the pilot judgment procedures. Rather the Court's practice shows a high number of variations upon a common theme. These could, as I have argued elsewhere,[16] be seen as a continuum: on the one extreme are those cases that fulfil all eight of Wildhaber's ideal-type requirements. On the other extreme there are those cases in which the Court has, also before 2004, established that there is a systematic problem or that a specific measure by a state is called for. These, in themselves, do not turn a case into a pilot judgment. Rather, it is the combination of these two factors that does:

15 Luzius Wildhaber, 'Pilot Judgments in Cases of Structural or Systemic Problems on the National Level', in Rüdiger Wolfrum and Ulrike Deutsch (eds), *The European Court of Human Rights Overwhelmed by Applications: Problems and Possible Solutions* (Springer, 2009) 69, 71.

16 Antoine Buyse, 'The Pilot Judgment Procedure at the European Court of Human Rights: Possibilities and Challenges' (2009) 57 *Nomiko Vima* 1913.

first, identification of a systemic problem and, second, explicit guidance from the Court to the state concerned.[17]

In the first few years of practice many variations occurred. To mention just a few examples: in the 2005 judgment of *Lukenda* v. *Slovenia*,[18] on overly lengthy judicial procedures, the Court identified a systemic problem resulting from failing legislation and inefficient administration of justice. It did not, however, freeze comparable pending cases. These cases continued to be decided upon by the Court until the very moment that Slovenia put in place an effective domestic system in 2007.[19] Sometimes, pilot judgments were issued by sections of the Court, rather than by the Grand Chamber, such as in *Xenides-Arestis* v. *Turkey*.[20] In other instances, the Court did not at the time of the judgment itself dub a judgment as 'pilot' but rather did so after the fact: in 2006, in *İçyer*, on displacement in Eastern Turkey, the Court held that Turkey had put in place a relevant new domestic mechanism and declared the application inadmissible.[21] In the decision it referred to the original judgment in which it identified the problem, *Doğan and others* from 2004,[22] as the relevant pilot judgment on the issue – retroactively, as *Doğan* had not been called a pilot judgment previously. In the Italian case of *Scordino* the Court did identify systemic problems on several counts and asked Italy to address to issue within six months, but it did not mention this in the operative part of the judgment.[23]

These variations may benevolently be seen as a test phase in which the Court tested in which ways the pilot judgment procedure could work. However, these variations themselves caused criticism. Judge Zagrebelsky indicated in his dissenting opinion in the *Lukenda* case that for reasons of consistency of case law in such an important procedure, only the Grand Chamber should issue pilot judgments. In addition, the variations were not always to the liking of both states and applicants. Both have an interest in some kind of legal certainty as to when and how the Court would apply such a procedure. Especially for applicants whose cases are adjourned because they are in a comparable situation as the applicant in the pilot case, a lot is at stake. For them, justice delayed may feel as justice denied.

These practical concerns about the flexible application of pilot judgment linked up to concerns about the lack of legal basis. The Court was initially pragmatic in its response to these uncertainties. In a reversal of its initial position in 2004, it was of the opinion in 2007 that practical experience on the pilot judgments

17 See also: Erik Fribergh, 'Pilot Judgments from the Court's Perspective', in Council of Europe, *Towards Stronger Implementation of the European Convention on Human Rights. Proceedings of the Colloquy Organised under the Swedish Chairmanship of the Committee of Ministers of the Council of Europe* (Council of Europe, 2008) 86, 91.

18 *Lukenda* v. *Slovenia* App. No. 23032/02 (ECtHR, 6 October 2005).

19 *Korenjak* v. *Slovenia* App. No. 463/03 (ECtHR, 15 May 2007).

20 *Xenides-Arestis* v. *Turkey* (merits) App. No. 46347/99 (ECtHR, 22 December 2005).

21 *İçyer* v. *Turkey* App. No. 18888/02 (adm dec, ECtHR, 12 January 2006).

22 *Doğan and Others* v. *Turkey* App. Nos 8803–8811/02 and others (ECtHR, 29 June 2004).

23 *Scordino* v. *Italy* App. No. 36813/97 (ECtHR, 29 March 2006).

procedure's efficacy was necessary before thinking about a change of the Convention itself.[24] The Court based its pilot judgments on an existing Convention provision, Article 46 ECHR. This article provides in its first paragraph that state parties are bound to abide by the final judgments of the Court in cases in which they are parties. Before the entry into force of Protocol 14 and thus during the first years of pilot judgment practice, Article 46 only had one second paragraph indicating that judgments were to be transmitted to the Committee of Ministers which would supervise the execution of judgments. Thus, the Court had to specify in its case law that the provision did provide, in its interpretation, a legal basis for giving more specific indications to state parties. It had done so as early as 2000 in the Italian *Scozzari and Giunta* case,[25] and repeated it in the first pilot judgment, *Broniowski*: Article 46 included an obligation which went beyond the paying of just satisfaction under Article 41. It included a state's legal duty to 'select, subject to supervision by the Committee of Ministers, the general and/or, if appropriate, individual measures to be adopted in their domestic legal order to put an end to the violation found by the Court and to redress so far as possible the effects'.[26] The Court held that the state was free to choose the means of implementation, but added that this was subject to monitoring by the Committee of Ministers and 'provided that such means are compatible with the conclusions set out in the Court's judgment'.[27] In doing so, the Court gave itself jurisprudential foundation to further develop the pilot judgments on.

After a number of years, the Court solidified the legal basis and enhanced legal certainty by including the pilot judgment procedure in its Rules of Court in 2011.[28] One may surmise that two developments triggered this. First, the Court had by then gained experience in the pros and cons of the possible variations in the procedure.[29] Second, Protocol 14 had, after a very slow ratification process, finally entered into force in 2010. The Protocol, among other matters, extended Article 46 ECHR on some crucial elements of the division of tasks between the Committee of Ministers and the Court – all the more important for pilot judgments. The new version of the provision gives the Committee the option to ask the Court for an interpretation of a judgment if the execution of that judgment is hindered by a problem of interpretation. In addition, it gives the Committee the opportunity, if a state party refuses to implement a judgment, to ask the Court for a formal pronouncement on whether this is indeed the case. Finally, if the Court finds a violation of a state's duty under paragraph 1 of the Article to abide by its

24 European Court of Human Rights, *Opinion of the Court on the Wise Persons' Report* (2 April 2007) 5, at: <echr.coe.int>.
25 *Scozzari and Giunta* v. *Italy* App. Nos 39221/98 and 41963/98 (ECtHR, 13 July 2000) para. 249.
26 *Broniowski* (n. 14), para. 192.
27 Ibid.
28 To be found at: <echr.coe.int>.
29 On the practice of the pilot judgment procedure, see extensively: Philip Leach, Helen Hardman, Svetlana Stephenson and Brad Blitz, *Responding to Systemic Human Rights Violations* (Intersentia, 2010).

final judgments, it shall refer the case to the Committee 'for consideration of the measures to be taken'.[30] What Article 46 does in its new version is to more closely connect the work and tasks of the Court and the Committee to each other. It aims to offer procedures both in cases in which a state is unwilling or unable – due to a lack of clarity in the judgment – to execute a judgment of the Court.

Since 2011, the new rule 61 of the Rules of Court specifies in detail that the Court may start a pilot judgment procedure 'where the facts of an application reveal in the Contracting Party concerned the existence of a structural or systemic problem or other similar dysfunction which has given rise or may give rise to similar applications'. The wider extent of the problem must thus be ascertained. The Court can start the procedure of its own motion or at the request of either the state or the applicant, but will always seek the views of the parties on this. The Court, through this new rule, demands from itself not only to identify the nature of the systemic problem, but also 'the type of remedial measures which the Contracting Party concerned is required to take at the domestic level by virtue of the operative provisions of the judgment'.[31] This may include time limits for implementation.

The new rule also includes procedural guarantees for applicants, as a result of what one could call a learning curve the Court had gone through in the previous years. Not only will they be consulted on the desirability of pilot procedure, such a procedure will also be processed with priority. The Court may still adjourn similar cases, but in such instances the people concerned will be informed of this as well as of developments relevant to their case. And if 'the administration of justice so requires' – read: when the freezing of a case would cause a disproportionate disadvantage or problem for an applicant – the Court may examine an adjourned application. When the violation at hand is very grave, the Court may choose to continue to deal with applications just to 'remind the respondent State on a regular basis of its obligation under the Convention'.[32] Finally, if a friendly settlement is reached in a pilot case, this settlement will include redress to 'other or potential applicants'. Tellingly, the factsheet on pilot judgments on the Court's website now indicates that there is a third objective as compared to the original two (assisting states and keeping the Court's workload manageable): the possibility of speedier redress for individual applicants.[33] If anything, the pilot judgment procedure thus also attempts to create some benefits for applicants – or at least neutralise as far as possible the disadvantages of freezing comparable cases. For some, such as Polyana Valcheva, this may mean having to exhaust newly created domestic remedies.

As can be seen from the above, some but not all of Wildhaber's characteristics of an ideal-type pilot judgment have been preserved. Notably, the Court does not

30 The new paragraphs 3–5 of Article 46 ECHR.

31 Rule 61, para. 3. Thus the factsheet of the Court only includes those judgments and not the judgments in which such issues only feature in the Court's reasoning but not in the operative part.

32 *Varga and Others* v. *Hungary* App. Nos 14097/12 and others (ECtHR, 10 March 2015), para. 116.

33 Factsheet 'Pilot Judgments', version July 2015, to be found at <echr.coe.int>.

need to decide in its formation of a Grand Chamber necessarily. While still preserving a good measure of flexibility, Rule 61 provides more clarity and safeguards for all parties concerned. On top of that, the revised version of Article 46 indicates a clearer division of tasks between the Court and the Committee of Ministers, shaped in the form of closer cooperation. The next section of this chapter will zoom in on the practice of the pilot judgment procedure in the Court's case law.

4 The practising pilot

Like a pilot learning to fly, the development of the pilot judgment procedure has been a process of trial and error and constant fine-tuning, to see what works and what does not. Contrary to pilots, however, the procedure has not been tested in a virtual cockpit, but rather been refined in its application to real cases. The practice of the Court shows that the pilot judgment procedure has been applied in a limited number of situations: basically four categories of cases and two odd ones out. The odd ones out are the British prisoner voting case and the problem of the removal of permanent resident status in Slovenia after the break up of the former Yugoslavia[34] – the former was an unsuccessful example in the sense that the issue has not been resolved, the latter seems to have led to a satisfactory solution.[35] Both were politically sensitive issues and appear to be exceptional. There are, however, four categories of issues in which the Court has issued a number of pilot judgments.[36]

The first category is that of excessive length of national judicial proceedings and the lack of domestic remedies for that problem. This may be the most ironic category in this context, as it is the very problem of lengthy procedures in Strasbourg as a result of the high influx of repetitive cases that prompted the development of the pilot judgment procedure in the first place. These cases related both to civil and criminal proceedings and concerned both long-standing state parties to the Convention (Germany, Greece and Turkey) as well as those who had acceded after the end of the Cold War (Bulgaria, Poland and Hungary). The pattern was similar: the Court indicated, for example in *Finger* v. *Bulgaria*,[37] that deficiencies in the justice system were preventing cases being dealt with within a reasonable time – the requirement under Article 6 ECHR – and indicated that at the very least a domestic remedy for this Convention violation should be put in place so that victims could receive some form of compensation for justice delayed at the national level. It is revealing that even in a pilot judgment like *Finger*, the Court does not take full centre stage but leaves leeway both to the competences of the Committee of Ministers and to the state itself, as is shown here:

34 Respectively, *Greens and M.T.* v. *United Kingdom* App. Nos 60041/08 and 60054/08 (ECtHR, 23 November 2010) and *Kurić and Others* v. *Slovenia* App No. 26828/06 (ECtHR, 26 June 2012).

35 See the just satisfaction judgment in the same case of 12 March 2014.

36 For full and updated overviews, see the Court's own factsheet on pilot judgments.

37 *Finger* v. *Bulgaria* App. No. 37346/05 (ECtHR, 10 May 2011).

> The Contracting States enjoy considerable freedom in the choice of the means calculated to ensure that their judicial systems are in compliance with the requirements of Article 6 of the Convention. Moreover, the unreasonable length of proceedings is a multifaceted problem which may be due to a large number of factors, of both legal and logistical character. Some of those – such as an insufficient number of judges or administrative staff, inadequate court premises, overly complex procedures, procedural loopholes allowing unjustified adjournments, or poor case management – may be internal to the judicial system, whereas others – such as the belated submission of expert reports and failures by the authorities to provide in a timely manner documents needed as evidence – may be extrinsic to that system. The Court will therefore abstain from indicating any specific measures to be taken by the respondent State to tackle the problem. The Committee of Ministers is better placed and equipped to monitor the measures that need to be adopted by Bulgaria in that respect.[38]

Thus, far from being overly activist, the Court is explicitly conscious of its position as an *international* and *judicial* body. It limits itself to requiring a domestic remedy to the identified problem, but leaves the specific solution to address the root cause to the state under the supervision of the Committee of Ministers. And, indeed, once Bulgaria introduced compensatory remedies, the Court declared applications about the issue inadmissible, relegating the cases back to the national level. Basing itself on the scope of the new remedial mechanism and on the means allocated to it to make it effective, the Court held that even if no long-term practical experience with the mechanism existed yet, mere doubt about its efficacy were not enough for applicants not to exhaust the new remedy.[39]

The second category also relates to the national judicial systems: prolonged non-enforcement of court decisions and the lack of remedies for this. The pilot cases in this category thus far all concern states that came into existence after the dissolution of the Soviet Union (Russia, Moldova and Ukraine). These judgments related both to financial claims (judgment debts and honour debts) as well as material claims (for social housing and other public services). The Court's pilot judgments in these cases again show a variety of carrot-and-stick elements. Sometimes the Court stayed the examination of cases and requested the state concerned to introduce domestic remedies. When the state, in this case Ukraine on the issue of remedies for unenforced honour debt judgments, failed to adopt such remedies, the Court decided to resume the examination of the pending similar applications, to put renewed pressure.[40] After an initial indication by the Court, gravity of action thus shifted back to the state and later, when action was not sufficiently

38 Ibid., para. 120.

39 *Anton Antonov Blakchiev and Others* v. *Bulgaria* App. No. 65187/10 (adm dec, ECtHR, 18 June 2013), paras 70–81.

40 *Yuriy Nikolayevich Ivanov* v. *Ukraine* App. No. 40450/04 (ECtHR, 15 October 2009) and ensuing decisions.

taken, the Court took back the initiative. In another case, on enforcement of court decision granting benefits, the Court held that Russia had to set up, in cooperation with the Committee of Ministers (sic!), an effective remedy and had to grant redress to victims in around 600 similar applications pending in Strasbourg within two years.[41] One could speak here of a situation of enhanced supervision while at the same time safeguarding the interests of victims who found themselves in a comparable situation. Overall, the emphasis in this category of cases was on the creation of domestic remedies for the problem: the Court did not tell state parties in detail how to solve the underlying issue. That was a task for the states themselves to take up, if need be in consultation with the Committee of Ministers.

The third category concerns violations of property rights, ranging from failing property restitution or compensation schemes, resulting from the aftermath of Communist expropriations during the Cold War, to repayment problems of foreign currencies saved up during that period in former Yugoslav countries. Thus many, but not all, were closely connected to the transition from communism to democracy. In these instances the Court gave general indications concerning the framework. To Albania, the Court indicated for example that it should not rely purely on financial compensation but also on alternative forms of compensation and to set realistic and binding time limits for each phase of the compensation process. These were aimed at preventing further unnecessary delays. To emphasise this, the Court set a time limit to the state of 18 months to effectively secure the right to compensation.[42]

The fourth and final larger category of cases relates to inhuman and degrading detention conditions. Since this concerns violations of one of the core Convention provisions, Article 3, the Court is more forceful on this issue. All pilot judgments on the issue include precise time-frames of action, between 6 and 18 months, and several include requests to create domestic remedies against complaints of prison overcrowding and bad detention conditions which are not only of a compensatory but also of a preventive nature.[43] Finally, similar applications are usually not adjourned, because the right concerned is so fundamental.[44]

What transpires from this practice is that, even if at first glance the pilot judgment procedure seems to mark a shift of gravity towards the Court, a closer look reveals that this is only true to a limited extent. Yes, the Court does limit a state's freedom to decide what kind of implementation measures are needed, but it does not do so in extreme detail. The framework set by the Court is often relatively general in nature. Many of the issues concern fields, such as the organisation of national justice or socio-economic property issues, in which a wide margin of appreciation

41 *Gerasimov and Others* v. *Russia* App. No. 29920/05 and others (ECtHR, 1 July 2014) and follow-up decisions.

42 *Manushaqe Puto and Others* v. *Albania* App. Nos 604/07 and others (ECtHR, 31 July 2012).

43 E.g. *Neshkov and Others* v. *Bulgaria* App. Nos 36925/10 and others (ECtHR, 27 January 2015).

44 *Ananyev and Others* v. *Russia* App. Nos 42525/07 and 60800/08 (ECtHR, 10 January 2012).

exists. Moreover, the Court in effect often implicitly builds on the principle of subsidiarity by calling for the creation or improvement of remedies at the national level. As judge Zupančič phrased it in an opinion in the pilot judgment *Hutten-Czapska* v. *Poland*, 'Look, you have a serious problem on your hands and we would prefer you to resolve it at home…! If it helps, these are what we think you should take into account as the minimum standards in resolving this problem…'[45]

5 When to apply it?

The practice described above shows that the pilot judgment procedure has become part and parcel of Strasbourg's practice. However, the total number of pilot judgments has not risen above a few dozen so far. This reflects that it is used sparingly, and for good reason. What reasons have been identified on the desirability applying the procedure? We can identify five relevant considerations. Two were highlighted by former judge Garlicki in one of the earlier reflections on the issue.[46]

First, he mentioned that the pilot judgment procedure is to be regarded as a measure of last resort by the Court, when more gentle ways of persuading state parties to take action have not worked. The freezing of comparable cases, which after all is detrimental to the applicants concerned, then becomes more likely to avoid overflowing of the Court's workload. One may surmise that this has become slightly less pertinent with the Court's effective tackling of the backlog of cases.

A second consideration Garlicki put forward is that applying the pilot judgment procedure may be useful to tip the balance. When a stalemate exists between national institutions (e.g. judiciary versus executive) or within them (different parties within the legislative), the Court's verdict may weigh in to tilt the scales towards a more Convention-friendly resolution of an issue. A pilot judgment may then help to shift gravity between a state's domestic actors. The *Hütten-Czapska* judgment is a case in point, where the Court in effect aligned with the national judiciary against the executive, which had been an opponent of using the pilot judgment procedure in the matter of rent (rent-control regulations).

Two other elements have been identified by professor Wojciech Sadurski.[47] The third consideration is, and maybe rather obviously, the prospect of success. In this respect, it should be considered whether domestic judicial or bureaucratic structures are up to the task. Are only legal reforms needed or are complicated policy or even mentality changes also necessary? This consideration may help to explain that the Court focuses often on requiring domestic remedies rather than indicating a precise solution for the underlying problem.

A fourth consideration is the acceptability of quasi-constitutional adjudication by an international court vis-à-vis the state concerned. A pilot judgment with its

45 *Hutten-Czapska* v. *Poland* App. No. 35014/97 (ECtHR, 19 June 2006), partly concurring, partly dissenting opinion of Judge Zupančič.

46 For the first and second considerations, see Garlicki (n. 13).

47 For the third and fourth considerations, see Sadurski (n. 6).

explicitly general character indeed comes close to constitutional decision-making[48] and *qualitate qua* goes beyond the specifics of an individual case. Sadurski has argued that such a role may be more acceptable in the newer democracies of Central and Eastern Europe where the ECHR functions as a tool to anchor the new democratic institutions. He predicted that the procedure would be sparingly used towards more countries that had been state parties to the Convention for a longer time. Although the majority of pilot judgments indeed pertains to the new democracies, practice has shown that this is certainly not exclusively the case.

A fifth consideration relates to the specific human rights issue at hand. Even when a large number of cases coming from a certain state relate to one Convention provision, the factual variety may still be so big, that a common approach is difficult and a representative pilot case may be difficult to find. The Court then has to limit itself to requiring procedural frameworks to be put in place, as the Article 3 pilot cases show.[49]

In applying the new procedure, the Court thus has to make assessments which go beyond its specific judicial role, taking into consideration partly unpredictable factors. This has not prevented it from increasingly using the procedure, in a good number of cases with positive effects.

6 Conclusion

With a procedure that is not laid down in the Convention itself but nevertheless has such far-reaching consequences, support of the state parties is crucial. This support seems to have endured after the initial 2004 Committee of Ministers resolution. The 2012 High Level Brighton Declaration of all state parties, for example, expressed its support for the Court's proactive measures, such as the pilot judgment procedure to tackle its caseload of repetitive cases.[50] This was further enhanced by a call to the states themselves in the same Declaration. The Committee of Ministers was asked to 'pay particular attention to violations disclosing a systemic issue at national level, and should ensure that States Parties quickly and effectively implement pilot judgments'.[51] Pilot judgments thus continue to be of high priority, at least in the rhetoric of states. At a similar high-level conference in Brussels in 2015, representatives of many states reiterated support for the procedure, although concerns about the costs for the countries concerned (by Serbia) and admonitions about keeping more general indications limited to pilot judgments and not using them in ordinary Court judgments (Russia) could also be heard.[52] The latter is

48 On this constitutional character, see Markus Fyrnys, 'Expanding Competences by Judicial Lawmaking: The Pilot Judgment Procedure of the European Court of Human Rights' (2011) 12 *German Law Journal* 1231.

49 See both Buyse (n. 16) and Leach *et al.* (n. 29).

50 High Level Conference on the Future of the European Court of Human Rights, Brighton Declaration, 19–20 April 2012, to be found at: <echr.coe.int>.

51 Ibid.

52 See: *Proceedings of the High-Level Conference on the Implementation of the European Convention on Human Rights, Our Shared Responsibility*, Brussels, 26–27 March 2015, to be found at <coe.int>.

notable, as indeed, from the point of effectiveness of implementation of judgments, the 'quasi-pilot judgments' which reflect only some but not all traits of a pilot judgment procedure seem to have been less productive.[53]

The practice of the Court also shows a reassuring move towards more legal certainty on the pilot procedure, with the codification in Rule 61. In addition, implementation seems reasonable, although one must remember that pilot judgments come into play only when a situation has already vastly deteriorated – the last resort – and the prospects may not be as rosy as the Committee of Ministers noted back in 2013: 'as matters stand today no pilot judgment is unexecuted. The measures specifically prescribed by the Court in the operative provisions have all been taken, even if this has in certain cases taken a long time.'[54]

The pilot judgment has always been in danger of losing in depth (individual justice) what it gains in scope (dealing with larger numbers of situations). The procedural guarantees put down in Rule 61 partly remedy this, but not entirely. Cases can still be frozen. Those applicants whose case is not chosen to be a pilot case, might be asked to go back to the national level to try a newly installed remedy. Apart from detrimental effects for individuals, frozen cases may also in a way let the state off the hook for a while. By contrast, continuing to deal with these comparable cases at some interval – in order not to fall back on an overload of work for the Court – may work as a pedagogic tool, a reminder for the state concerned that the problem needs to be solved. Otherwise, the Court will keep finding violations and keep imposing compensation payments on that state by way of just satisfaction to the victim concerned. But no matter which variation is used, some problems might be so politically sensitive, that no pilot judgment may help to solve them, as the problems with implementing British prisoner voting rights reflect: in *Greens and M.T.*, the Court found that a blanket ban on voting rights for people in prison was a structural problem. It first adjourned and later again started to deal with comparable cases, in an attempt to vary tactics to come to the best solution, but to no avail.[55]

If anything, the pilot judgment procedure can be seen as an additional tool in the Court's toolbox. While it has the potential to shift gravity – giving the Court a more active role in both how a judgment should be implemented and in, at least partially, assessing to what extent the state has abided by those terms – the choice for this shift is in the hands of the Court. It may shift the balance between the Committee of Ministers and the Court, between the Court and state parties and, in 'tipping-point' situations, between domestic state institutions. Moreover, it is

53 Philip Leach, Helen Hardman and Svetlana Stephenson, 'Can the European Court's Pilot Judgment Procedure Help Resolve Systemic Human Rights Violations? *Burdov* and the Failure to Implement Domestic Court Decisions in Russia' (2010) 10 *Human Rights Law Review* 346, 358.

54 Committee of Ministers, *7th Annual Report on Supervision of the Execution of Judgments and Decisions of the European Court of Human Rights* (2013) 10–11, to be found at: <coe.int>.

55 *Greens and M.T.* (n. 34). For other examples, see the Court's factsheet on pilot judgments (n. 33).

the Court which in calling for domestic remedies to be put in place decides to shift gravity towards the national level – even if this means a shift away from the Court, it is still a decision made by the Court itself. While the state parties have originally handed the Court this new tool, the Court decides whether to apply a pilot judgment procedure as well having the final say on its precise modalities. It is thus the Court's ultimate decision whether the pilot defies gravity.

8 The Court of Justice and fundamental rights: if margin of appreciation is the solution, what is the problem?*

Niamh Nic Shuibhne

1 Introduction

Article 51 of the Charter of Fundamental Rights establishes that its provisions 'are addressed to the institutions, bodies, offices and agencies of the Union with due regard for the principle of subsidiarity and to the Member States only when they are implementing Union law'. In the Preamble to the Charter, we find the following statement:

> This Charter reaffirms, with due regard for the powers and tasks of the Union and for the principle of subsidiarity, the rights as they result, in particular, from the constitutional traditions and international obligations common to the Member States, the European Convention for the Protection of Human Rights and Fundamental Freedoms, the Social Charters adopted by the Union and by the Council of Europe and the case-law of the Court of Justice of the European Union and of the European Court of Human Rights.

This extract conveys the plurality of *sources* of fundamental rights applicable within the EU (and within the Member States) as well as the plurality of *interpretations* of those rights that might be relevant – a situation likely to continue as currently regulated for some time to come, noting the chilling effect of Opinion 2/13 on the process of EU accession to the ECHR. But it does not suggest how these sources and interpretations should be managed in concrete situations. Guidance on that aspect of fundamental rights protection can be found in the Charter's general provisions. In particular, Article 52(3) establishes that '[i]n so far as this Charter contains rights which correspond to rights guaranteed by the [ECHR], the meaning and scope of those rights shall be the same as those laid down by the said Convention' – but also noting that '[t]his provision shall not prevent Union law providing more extensive protection'. Article 52(3) thus establishes the Convention as a minimum standard for the meaning and scope of the rights guaranteed by the Charter.

* Sincere thanks to the project editors for their very helpful comments on an earlier draft.

On the relationship between EU and national standards, Article 52(4) provides that '[i]n so far as this Charter recognises fundamental rights as they result from the constitutional traditions common to the Member States, those rights shall be interpreted *in harmony* with those traditions' (emphasis added). Additionally, Article 53 stipulates:

> Nothing in this Charter shall be interpreted as restricting or adversely affecting human rights and fundamental freedoms as recognised, *in their respective fields of application*, by Union law and international law and by international agreements to which the Union or all the Member States are party, including the European Convention for the Protection of Human Rights and Fundamental Freedoms, *and by the Member States' constitutions.* [emphasis added]

The prevailing message here is not self-evident: more specifically, the sense of plurality of sources outlined in the Preamble seems to be undercut by a suggestion of self-containment with respect to the context or locus of their application.

This contribution locates case law and debates on the existence and utility of a margin of appreciation in EU fundamental rights law within these primary law parameters, established by the Charter and by the EU Treaties more generally. In section 2, it is shown that *margin of appreciation* discourse is used explicitly in EU law, but not normally in connection with the protection of fundamental rights. Case law concerned more directly with that objective tends to engage *margin of discretion* language instead.[1] In section 3, judicial interpretations of primary law limits on the *competence* of the Union – and of the Member States – are outlined. Focusing on a set of widely analysed cases in which restrictions placed on free movement rights fall to be justified on the basis of fundamental rights protection, it is then asked in section 4 whether the Court has edged towards a more systematic margin of discretion framework in order to accommodate space for the expression or protection of fundamental rights in distinctive ways at national level. The implications of changes to primary law realised by the Lisbon Treaty are also explored, to determine whether this case law represents limits as *policy* or another facet of competence limitation.

Finally, in section 5, the consequences of applying a more formalised margin of discretion for the wider system of Union law are emphasised. Drawing from elements of the competence-interpreting case law outlined in section 3, this discussion focuses on the splintering of core principles of Union law – its intended *primacy, unity* and *effectiveness* – as a systemic risk that we have to confront.

1 It is worth noting, however, that while the European Court of Human Rights (ECtHR) tends to use 'margin of appreciation' more commonly, it also uses the 'margin of discretion' term (interchangeably); see e.g. *De Souza Ribeiro* v. *France* App. No. 22689/07 (ECHR 2012), para. 85; *Church of Jesus Christ of Latter Day Saints* v. *UK* App. No. 7552/09 (ECtHR, 4 March 2014), para. 33.

2 When is 'margin of appreciation' used (explicitly) in EU law?

In the context of fundamental rights, margin of appreciation is an expression of subsidiarity. It is associated primarily with the jurisprudence of the European Court of Human Rights (ECtHR), providing a mechanism through which that Court devolves decisions that involve the balancing of different interests to national authorities. It has particular relevance when different rights protected by the Convention come into conflict, on the basis that national authorities are better placed to make the relevant assessments. The ECtHR applies a three-step framework when assessing national limitations of most Convention rights: such restrictions must be in accordance with or prescribed by law; the purpose of the restriction must fall within the scope of the legitimate aims prescribed by the relevant provision of the Convention; and the restriction must be necessary in a democratic society.[2] The third criterion indicates the decision-making space in which 'the ECtHR has recognised that states enjoy a margin of appreciation'.[3]

More limited use of the 'margin of appreciation' phrase can be seen in the case law of the Court of Justice. In cases that concern fundamental rights, the expression tends to be used primarily as a point of reference for the principles developed by the ECtHR.[4] More substantively, and more autonomously, the Court of Justice uses margin of appreciation language in two other lines of case law. First, the phrase is often used to confirm the extent to which Union institutions enjoy administrative or legislative autonomy in certain spheres of decision-making. Examples can be found mainly in the case law of the General Court, and mainly in the field of competition law and anti-dumping.[5]

Second, margin of appreciation is also used to indicate a bandwidth of permitted discretion for Member States. From a comparative perspective, this example aligns with the use of the doctrine in the ECHR system in the sense that it reflects similar concern for the principle of subsidiarity. The Court of Justice normally uses the phrase to describe the extent of permitted national discretion in

2 J. A. Sweeney, 'A "Margin of Appreciation" in the Internal Market: Lessons from the European Court of Human Rights' (2007) 34 LIEI 27 at 30.

3 Ibid.

4 E.g. Case C-274/99 P *Connolly* [2001] ECR I-1611, paras 41–49; Case C-540/03 *Parliament* v. *Council (Family Reunification)* [2006] ECR I-5769, paras 54–66; and AG Bot in Case C-300/11 *ZZ*, judgment of 4 June 2013, esp. paras 91–100 of the Opinion. Arguing for more substantive engagement with the case law of the ECtHR, see G. de Búrca, 'After the EU Charter of Fundamental Rights: The Court of Justice as a Human Rights Adjudicator?' (2013) 20 Maast J Eur & Comp L 168.

5 Case T-132/01 *Euroalliages* [2003] ECR II-2359, para. 67: '[w]here assessment of a complex economic situation is involved, the Commission has a broad margin of appreciation when evaluating the Community interest'. Cf. e.g. Case T-201/04 *Microsoft* [2007] ECR II-3601, para. 89: 'while the Community Courts recognise that the Commission has a margin of appreciation in economic or technical matters, that does not mean that they must decline to review the Commission's interpretation of economic or technical data'.

connection with the implementation of directives, but recalling its own jurisdiction to ensure that the limits of that discretion are appropriately linked to the requirements of EU law.[6] For example, in *O and S*, concerning Directive 2003/86 on the right to family reunification, the Court stated:

> It is true that Articles 7 and 24 of the Charter, while emphasising the importance for children of family life, *cannot be interpreted as depriving the Member States of their margin of appreciation* when examining applications for family reunification ... However, in the course of such an examination ... the provisions of that directive must be interpreted and applied in the light of Articles 7 and 24(2) and (3) of the Charter.[7]

Occasionally, margin of appreciation is used in connection with national protection of fundamental rights.[8] But it appears far more frequently for other policy spheres, especially where Member States seek to defend national rules that restrict EU free movement rights. In particular, margin of appreciation language recurs when national restrictions involve an acknowledged degree of sensitivity and/or the absence of a decisive consensus among the Member States[9] – e.g. restrictions

6 E.g. Case C-212/04 *Adeneler* [2006] ECR I-6057, paras 68 and 82. See similarly, AG Sharpston in Case C-427/06 *Bartsch* [2008] ECR I-7245, para. 89 of the Opinion: 'the precise way in which a Member State chooses to make use of the derogation, in Article 6(1) of Directive 2000/78, from the prohibition on age discrimination is, of course, subject to review by the Court against the background of the general principle of equality, and specifically equal treatment irrespective of age. That review ensures that the social and policy choices made by the Member State fall within the terms of the derogation and hence within the margin of appreciation left to the Member State.' Directive 2000/78/EC establishing a general framework for equal treatment in employment and occupation, 2000 OJ L303/16.

7 Joined Cases C-356/11 and C-357/11 *O and S*, judgment of 6 December 2012, paras 79–80 (emphasis added). Directive 2003/86/EC on the right to family reunification, OJ 2003 L251/12.

8 E.g. Case 5/88 *Wachauf* [1989] ECR 2609, para. 22: '[t]he Community regulations in question accordingly leave the competent national authorities a sufficiently wide margin of appreciation to enable them to apply those rules in a manner consistent with the requirements of the protection of fundamental rights'.

9 'The more convergence there is among the legal orders of the Member States, the more the ECJ will tend to follow in their footsteps ... By contrast, where there are important divergences among national legal systems, the ECJ will be careful before adopting an "EU" solution' (K. Lenaerts and J. A. Gutiérrez-Fons, 'The Constitutional Allocation of Powers and General Principles of EU Law, (2010) 47 CML Rev 1629 at 1633–1634). Kokott and Sobotta refer explicitly to the 'value judgements' made in such cases (J. Kokott and C. Sobotta, 'The Charter of Fundamental Rights of the European Union after Lisbon', EUI Working Papers, AEL 2010/6 at 2; at <http://cadmus.eui.eu/bitstream/handle/1814/15208/AEL_WP_2010_06.pdf?sequence=3>).

on gambling and lotteries;[10] maintaining law and order;[11] and access to social benefits.[12] In *Stoß*, a case that concerned restrictions on gambling, Advocate Mengozzi brings many of these elements together:

> [T]he case-law pays attention to the *particular nature* of gaming, a sector in which it is not possible to disregard 'moral, religious or cultural considerations' and which entails 'a high risk of crime or fraud' and which constitutes 'an incitement to spend which may have damaging individual and social consequences'. In view of those factors, *and in default of [EU] harmonisation in the sector*, the Court has held that the Member States have a sufficient margin of appreciation to determine, *according to their own scale of values*, what is required to protect participants and, more generally, to maintain order in society.[13]

Two broader themes emerge from the case law summarised above. First, margin of appreciation language is normally deployed not to remove a situation from the jurisdiction of the Court of Justice: but to do the opposite. In other words, contrary to the conception of the margin of appreciation as a device applied in order *not* to make a decision – seen more typically in ECHR law – margin of appreciation discourse is more commonly used in EU law to confirm the Court's jurisdiction to proceed to a review of the contested national measure.[14] In the case law on gambling restrictions, for example, the Court has emphasised that:

> [R]estrictions on freedom of establishment and on freedom to provide services must satisfy the conditions laid down in the case-law of the Court … the

10 E.g. Case C-67/98 *Zenatti* [1999] ECR I-7289: 'determination of the scope of the protection which a Member State intends providing in its territory in relation to lotteries and other forms of gambling falls within the margin of appreciation which the Court [has] recognised as being enjoyed by the national authorities. It is for those authorities to consider whether, in the context of the aim pursued, it is necessary to prohibit activities of that kind, totally or partially, or only to restrict them and to lay down more or less rigorous procedures for controlling them' (para. 33). See also para. 15.

11 E.g. Case 222/84 *Johnston* [1986] ECR 1651 at 1671: '[a] Member State has a certain margin of appreciation but not an unlimited power removed from all control by the national courts and by the Court of Justice as regards the requirement relating to the maintenance of law and order and serious internal disturbances'.

12 E.g. Case C-103/08 *Gottwald* [2009] ECR I-9117: 'with regard to the degree of connection of the recipient of a benefit with the society of the Member State concerned, the Court has already held that, with regard to benefits that are not covered by Community law … Member States enjoy a wide margin of appreciation in deciding which criteria are to be used when assessing the degree of connection to society' (para. 34).

13 AG Mengozzi in Joined Cases C-316/07 etc. *Stoß* [2010] ECR I-8069, para. 31 of the Opinion (emphasis added, citations omitted).

14 A similar pattern can be seen in the case law of the ECtHR; see further Chapter 10, section 3.2, this volume.

> restrictions must be justified by imperative requirements in the general interest, be suitable for achieving the objective which they pursue and not go beyond what is necessary in order to attain it. They must in any event be applied without discrimination.[15]

Similarly, in *Tas-Hagen and Tas*, on the compatibility with EU law of residence conditions that determined access to benefits for civilian war victims in the Netherlands, the Court confirmed that '[w]ith regard to benefits that are not covered by [EU] law, Member States enjoy a wide margin of appreciation in deciding which criteria are to be used when assessing the degree of connection to society, *while at the same time complying with the limits imposed by [EU] law*'.[16]

However, second, it is also apparent that the *degree* or *intensity* of review applied by the Court tends to be reduced in these circumstances.[17] In free movement law, the Court normally evaluates the proportionality of national measures using a two-stage test: first, an assessment of the measure's appropriateness or suitability for achieving the stated public interest objective(s); second, an assessment of its necessity for that purpose, which usually a 'hard' review of whether the same policy objective could be achieved by using measures that are less restrictive of free movement rights.[18] When the Court finds that Member States enjoy a margin of discretion, this is almost always realised in practical terms through a corresponding adjustment of the intensity of proportionality review. What is not easy to pin down is *when*, the *degree* to which, or *why* less intensive standards might apply. For example, in the *Trailers* case, Italy raised the seemingly straightforward public interest objective of road safety to justify national restrictions placed on the use of certain types of trailers, which the Court had characterised as a restriction of Article 34 TFEU. The Italian policy choice is not really comparable

15 Case C-243/01 *Gambelli* [2003] ECR I-13031, paras 64–65. See also AG Stix-Hackl in Case C-42/02 *Lindman* [2003] ECR I-13519, para. 87 of the Opinion: '[e]ven if, for some Member States, being guaranteed the appropriate margin of appreciation in relation to gambling ... serves economic interests also, that cannot be allowed to obscure the fact that Community law cannot in principle be used as a lever for maintaining restrictions for economic or protectionist reasons'.

16 Case C-192/05 *Tas-Hagen and Tas* [2006] ECR I-10451, para. 36 (emphasis added); see, similarly, Case C-499/06 *Nerkowska* [2008] ECR I-3993, para. 38. The same approach can be seen in the case law of the ECtHR, where it is often stated that the margin 'goes hand in hand with European supervision'; see e.g. *Mouvement raëlien suisse* v. *Switzerland* App. No. 16354/06 (ECHR 2012), para. 48.

17 See, generally, F. de Witte, 'Sex, Drugs & EU Law: The Recognition of Moral and Ethical Diversity in EU Law' (2013) 50 CML Rev 1545.

18 A different standard of review is applied to EU legislative measures; see e.g. Case C-343/09 *Afton Chemical* [2010] ECR I-7027: 'the European Union legislature must be allowed a broad discretion in an area which entails political, economic and social choices on its part, and in which it is called upon to undertake complex assessments. The legality of a measure adopted in that sphere can be affected only if the measure is manifestly inappropriate having regard to the objective which the competent institutions are seeking to pursue' (para. 46).

with the sensitivities normally associated with gambling or access to benefits. Nonetheless, the Court held:

> [I]n the field of road safety a Member State may determine the degree of protection which it wishes to apply in regard to such safety and the way in which that degree of protection is to be achieved. *Since that degree of protection may vary from one Member State to the other*, Member States must be allowed a margin of appreciation and, consequently, the fact that one Member State imposes less strict rules than another Member State does not mean that the latter's rules are disproportionate.[19]

The Court then applied a relatively lenient standard of proportionality review, especially when compared with the conclusions of both AG Léger and AG Bot in the same case.[20] This part of the judgment can be explained at one level as compensating for the broad reading of the scope of Article 34 that had been established in the first place. But it is more difficult to map the application or allocation of discretion along a consciously articulated margin of appreciation framework; a point picked up in more detail in Section 4, in the context of choices made by the Court for reasons of *policy*. Case law that addresses limits applied in fundamental rights case law at the level of *competence* is first outlined below.

3 Fundamental rights in EU law: interpreting the limits on *competence*

The Court of Justice has addressed the compliance of Member State action with EU fundamental rights standards in two key lines of case law. The first set of cases is tied to the principle of conferral, which, according to Article 5(1) TEU, governs the limits of Union competences. As noted in section 1, national measures that *implement* Union law can be tested against EU fundamental rights standards (Article 51 of the Charter). The Court has applied a wide understanding of what 'implementing' Union law actually means, aligning its post-Lisbon approach with pre-Charter case law. Three recent rulings support this claim. First, the Court confirmed in *Åkerberg Fransson* that 'the fundamental rights guaranteed by the Charter must … be complied with where national legislation *falls within the scope of European Union law*'.[21] In *Siragusa*, the Court presented a more detailed analytical framework:

19 Case C-110/05 *Commission* v. *Italy (Trailers)* [2009] ECR I-519, para. 65 (emphasis added).

20 Cf. paras 63–69 of the judgment in *Trailers* (n. 19) with 56–62 of the Opinion of AG Léger and paras 165–172 of the Opinion of AG Bot.

21 Case C-617/10 *Åkerberg Fransson*, judgment of 26 February 2013, para. 21 (emphasis added). The pre-Charter case law cited by the Court includes Case C-260/89 *ERT* [1991] ECR I-2925, para. 42; Case C-299/95 *Kremzow* [1997] ECR I-2629, para. 15; Case C-309/96 *Annibaldi* [2007] ECR I-7493, para. 13; and Case C-94/00 *Roquette Frères* [2002] ECR I-9011, para. 25. See generally, E. Hancox, 'The Meaning of "Implementing" EU Law under Article 51(1) of the Charter: *Åkerberg Fransson*' (2013) 50 CML Rev 1411.

> [T]he concept of 'implementing Union law' ... requires a certain degree of connection above and beyond the matters covered being closely related or one of those matters having an indirect impact on the other ... In order to determine whether national legislation involves the implementation of EU law for the purposes of Article 51 of the Charter, some of the points to be determined are whether that legislation is intended to implement a provision of EU law; the nature of that legislation and whether it pursues objectives other than those covered by EU law, even if it is capable of indirectly affecting EU law; and also whether there are specific rules of EU law on the matter or capable of affecting it ... In particular, the Court has found that fundamental EU rights could not be applied in relation to national legislation because the provisions of EU law in the subject area concerned did not impose any obligation on Member States with regard to the situation at issue in the main proceedings ... It is also important to consider the objective of protecting fundamental rights in EU law, which is to ensure that those rights are not infringed in areas of EU activity, whether through action at EU level or through the implementation of EU law by the Member States.[22]

Conversely, the Court 'has no power to examine the compatibility with the Charter of national legislation lying outside the scope of European Union law'.[23] The Court has linked these limits on its own competence to Article 51(2), which states that 'the Charter does not extend the field of application of European Union law beyond the powers of the Union, and it does not establish any new power or task for the Union, or modify powers and tasks as defined in the Treaties'.[24]

Second, the Court recently confirmed another dimension of its pre-Charter case law in *Pfleger*, reasserting that when Member States seek to justify restrictions of free movement rights, they are implementing Union law and, therefore, such actions can be reviewed for compliance with EU fundamental rights standards.[25] Drawing from its ruling in *Åkerberg Fransson*, the Court held:

> [T]he Court has already observed that it has no power to examine the compatibility with the Charter of national legislation lying outside the scope of EU law. On the other hand, if such legislation falls within the scope of EU law, the Court, when requested to give a preliminary ruling, must provide all the guidance as to interpretation needed in order for the national court to determine whether that legislation is compatible with the fundamental rights the observance of which the Court ensures ... Since the fundamental rights guaranteed by the Charter must therefore be complied with where national

22 Case C-206/13 *Siragusa*, judgment of 6 March 2014, paras 24–31. For extensive discussion, see M. Dougan 'Judicial Review of Member State Action under the General Principles and the Charter: Defining the "Scope of Union Law"' (2015) 52 CML Rev 120.

23 *Åkerberg Fransson* (n. 21), para. 19.

24 Case C-256/11 *Dereci* [2011] ECR I-11315, para. 71.

25 Case C-390/12 *Pfleger*, judgment of 30 April 2014, paras 35–36; confirming e.g. *ERT* (n. 21).

> legislation falls within the scope of EU law, situations cannot exist which are covered in that way by EU law without those fundamental rights being applicable. The applicability of EU law entails applicability of the fundamental rights guaranteed by the Charter.[26]

In this extract, two key points are clear: EU fundamental rights only apply to national measures that fall within the scope of Union law; and the Charter is the primary reference point in terms of sourcing those rights.

Third, the 2013 ruling in the *Melloni* case highlights the complexities of the relationship between Union and Member State standards in practice, even though the objective of ensuring a high level of protection for fundamental rights is the common goal. In *Melloni*, one interpretation of Article 53 of the Charter suggested by the referring court was that the provision 'gives general authorisation to a Member State to apply the standard of protection of fundamental rights guaranteed by its constitution when that standard is higher than that deriving from the Charter and, where necessary, to give it priority over the application of provisions of EU law'.[27] But the Court of Justice responded – in a conspicuous one-line paragraph – that 'such an interpretation ... cannot be accepted'.[28] If Article 53 were applied in that manner, it would, according to the Court, 'undermine the principle of the primacy of EU law inasmuch as it would allow a Member State to disapply EU legal rules which are fully in compliance with the Charter where they infringe the fundamental rights guaranteed by that State's constitution'.[29]

The Court attributed the following purpose to Article 53:

> [W]here an EU legal act calls for national implementing measures, national authorities and courts *remain free to apply national standards of protection* of fundamental rights, *provided that* the level of protection provided for by the Charter, as interpreted by the Court, and the *primacy, unity and effectiveness* of EU law are not thereby compromised.[30]

In contrast to the ruling in *Åkerberg Fransson*, the Court did not refer to the explanations relating to the Charter to flesh out the scope of Article 53. That text does not provide much illumination at first glance; it simply says that '[Article 53] is intended to maintain the level of protection currently afforded within their respective scope by Union law, national law and international law. Owing to its importance, mention is made of the ECHR'.[31] However, the explanations do support the Court's general approach in *Melloni* – essentially, when a national measure does fall within the scope of Union law, then that 'respective scope' trumps the application of national law.

26 Ibid. paras 33–34.
27 Case C-399/11 *Melloni*, judgment of 26 February 2013, para. 56.
28 Ibid. para. 57.
29 Ibid. para. 58.
30 Ibid. para. 60 (emphasis added).
31 2007 OJ C303/17.

On the specific circumstances of the case, the Court emphasised that the harmonisation objective underpinning Framework Decision 2009/299, which sets out the grounds for refusing to execute a European arrest warrant where the person concerned did not appear in person at his trial, is expressly 'to enhance the procedural rights of persons subject to criminal proceedings whilst improving mutual recognition of judicial decisions between Member States'.[32] Member States do not, therefore, have discretion to apply a standard of fundamental rights protection that differs from the standard established by the Charter (as interpreted by the Court). And, crucially, Article 53 of the Charter does not displace that analysis:

> [A]llowing a Member State to avail itself of Article 53 of the Charter to make the surrender of a person convicted in absentia conditional upon the conviction being open to review in the issuing Member State, a possibility not provided for under Framework Decision 2009/299, in order to avoid an adverse effect on the right to a fair trial and the rights of the defence guaranteed by the constitution of the executing Member State, by casting doubt on the uniformity of the standard of protection of fundamental rights as defined in that framework decision, would undermine the principles of mutual trust and recognition which that decision purports to uphold and would, therefore, compromise the efficacy of that framework decision.[33]

In *Åkerberg Fransson*, delivered on the same day as *Melloni*, the inverse Article 53 scenario is outlined:

> [W]here a court of a Member State is called upon to review whether fundamental rights are complied with by a national provision or measure which, in a situation *where action of the Member States is not entirely determined by European Union law*, implements the latter for the purposes of Article 51(1) of the Charter, national authorities and courts *remain free to apply national standards of protection of fundamental rights*, provided that the level of protection provided for by the Charter, as interpreted by the Court, and the

32 *Melloni* (n. 27), para. 51. Article 1 of the Framework Decision provides: '1. The objectives of this Framework Decision are to enhance the procedural rights of persons subject to criminal proceedings, to facilitate judicial cooperation in criminal matters and, in particular, to improve mutual recognition of judicial decisions between Member States. 2. This Framework Decision shall not have the effect of modifying the obligation to respect fundamental rights and fundamental legal principles as enshrined in Article 6 of the [EU Treaty, in the version prior to the Treaty of Lisbon], including the right of defence of persons subject to criminal proceedings, and any obligations incumbent upon judicial authorities in this respect shall remain unaffected' (Council Framework Decision 2009/299/JHA (OJ 2009 L81/24, amending Article 4a(1) of Council Framework Decision 2002/584/JHA on the European arrest warrant and the surrender procedures between Member States (OJ 2002 L190/1)).

33 *Melloni* (n. 27), para. 63.

> primacy, unity and effectiveness of European Union law are not thereby compromised.[34]

Importantly for present purposes, Sarmiento describes the phrasing in *Åkerberg Fransson* – whether EU law either *completely or partially determines* Member State action in a given situation – as 'a concept equivalent to that of *discretion*'.[35]

This brief overview of competence-related case law reveals two broader points. First, it establishes that discretion to choose between different sources of fundamental rights follows the extent to which discretion is or is not prescribed by the relevant EU legal connection point in the case. Questions about competence for the protection of fundamental rights are thus intrinsically linked to the broader system of Union law. But there is one non-discretionary baseline: the Charter is *always* the minimum standard with which Member States must comply when they act within the scope of Union law. In most cases, this 'floor' of protection will in fact be provided by the standards of the ECHR, which also reflects the requirements of Article 52(3) of the Charter.[36]

Second, however, the competence case law highlights fundamental systemic differences between the legal contexts of the Charter and the ECHR. Through the application and evolution of both instruments, an increasingly unified threshold for the protection of fundamental rights is established. Article 53 of the Charter reflects the standard 'floor of protection' principle in Article 53 ECHR vis-à-vis its Contracting Parties.[37] As noted in Section 1, Article 52(3) of the Charter attributes a similar dynamic to the interplay between EU and ECHR law. However, de Boer emphasises the *Melloni*-rooted difference between the two systems when it comes to the interplay between EU and *national* standards: '[w]hereas the [ECHR] can be interpreted as a minimum level of protection, in the EU such an approach would conflict with the demands of primacy, uniformity and effectiveness of EU law'.[38] The translation of doctrines from one system to the other is not, therefore, straightforward.

Against that background, what a more formalised margin of appreciation – an acknowledged pressure release mechanism that negotiates transnational and national understandings of rights – would add to EU fundamental rights protection and to the system of Union law more widely will now be assessed. In section 4.1,

34 *Åkerberg Fransson* (n. 21), para. 29 (emphasis added).

35 D. Sarmiento, 'Who's Afraid of the Charter? The Court of Justice, National Courts and the New Framework of Fundamental Rights Protection in Europe' (2013) 50 CML Rev 1267 at 1289 (emphasis in original).

36 'In so far as this Charter contains rights which correspond to rights guaranteed by the [ECHR], the meaning and scope of those rights shall be the same as those laid down by the said Convention. This provision shall not prevent Union law providing more extensive protection.'

37 'Nothing in this Convention shall be construed as limiting or derogating from any of the human rights and fundamental freedoms which may be ensured under the laws of any High Contracting Party or under any other agreement to which it is a party.'

38 N. de Boer, 'Addressing Rights Divergences under the Charter: *Melloni*' (2013) 50 CML Rev 1083 at 1083.

a second set of fundamental rights cases is explored, i.e. cases where Member States rely on the protection of fundamental rights to justify restrictions of EU free movement rights. It is argued that the application of a margin of discretion in these cases initially indicated the making of a *policy choice* rather than the establishment or following of a *competence limitation.* In contrast to the case law outlined in section 2, where margin of appreciation language was used explicitly, that discourse is absent from the judgments discussed below. But are the *effects* of 'margin of discretion' – i.e. absence of a systematic framework; acknowledgement of jurisdiction to review; softening of proportionality review – the same: as, it was noted at the outset of this chapter, they tend to be in the case law of the ECtHR? Whether constitutional changes have shifted the Court's approach from policy to competence is explored in section 4.2. In section 5, the interconnectedness of the Union legal order is joined to the discussion.

4 Fundamental rights in EU law: from *policy* choice to *competence* limit?

When a Member State defends the restriction of free movement rights by arguing that the contested national measure protects a fundamental right, it presents a challenge to the standard *structure* of free movement law from a normative perspective: is it really appropriate to evaluate derogation and justification arguments based on fundamental rights in the same way as those linked to other public interest concerns? The objection relates to the fact that the structure of free movement law privileges the Treaty freedom as the central or primary right in the first instance. Member State derogation and justification arguments are then addressed, as a second-order question, only after a restriction of the relevant freedom has been confirmed.[39] In practice, however, that standard framework still applies. Therefore, in what follows, case law typically addressed in the search for an EU variant of margin of appreciation will first be outlined briefly,[40] in order to understand whether any adjustments are made *within* the standard process to acknowledge and accommodate the distinctiveness of fundamental rights – is there evidence, for example, of less intensive scrutiny in the analysis of proportionality?

4.1 Applying margin of discretion as a policy choice: Schmidberger *and* Omega

To illustrate the issues at stake, it is useful first to recall that many critics of the Court of Justice's controversial decisions in *Laval* and *Viking* focused on the

39 E.g. C. Brown, comment on *Schmidberger* (2003) 40 CML Rev 1499 at 1508; E. Spaventa, 'Federalisation versus Centralization: Tensions in Fundamental Rights Discourse in the EU', in M. Dougan and S. Currie (eds), *50 Years of the European Treaties: Looking Back and Thinking Forward* (Hart, 2010) 343 at 354–357.

40 For more comprehensive discussion of these cases, see e.g. the essays in S. de Vries, U. Bernitz and S. Weatherill (eds), *The Protection of Fundamental Rights in the EU After Lisbon* (Hart, 2012).

absence of acknowledgment or discussion of the distinctive nature and functions of collective action in the context of labour disputes; and the Court's apparent concern for the market-expansion (economic) rights of the traders over and above the (social) rights dimension of both cases – a dimension that is amplified for present purposes by recalling the constitutional significance of social protection in both Sweden and Finland respectively.[41] The significance conferred on service provision and establishment as the prior claims – a construction that flows, as noted above, from the restriction–derogation structure embedded in the Treaty – was perceived as a failure to recognise the imprint of normative authority that ought to attach to claims based on the protection of fundamental rights. Article 3 (3) TEU as amended by the Lisbon Treaty – i.e. after the decisions in *Laval* and *Viking* – characterises the internal market as 'a highly competitive social market economy, aiming at full employment and social progress'. The problem is that these objectives bring *different* priorities into conflict. Moreover, 'the ambiguity of the relevant legal material ensures that considerable power has been delegated to the Court to choose between competing interpretations: a familiar theme in the history of EU law'.[42]

In contrast, several authors point to the ruling in *Schmidberger* (delivered four years earlier) as a model of good reasoning practice that should be applied when fundamental rights are invoked to defend national restrictions of Treaty freedoms.[43] In that case, a major intra-state transit route in Austria was blocked for approximately 30 hours by an officially approved environmental protest, amounting to a restriction of the free movement of goods and engaging public interest arguments on freedom of assembly and freedom of expression. The judgment

41 Case C-341/05 *Laval un Partneri* [2007] ECR I-11767; Case C-438/05 *International Transport Workers' Federation and Finnish Seamen's Union ('Viking Line')* [2007] ECR I-10779. For analysis, see e.g. A. C. L. Davies, 'One Step Forward, Two Steps Back? *Laval* and *Viking* at the ECJ' (2008) 37 ILJ 126; J. Malmberg and T. Sigeman, 'Industrial Action and EU Economic Freedoms: The Autonomous Collective Bargaining Model Curtailed by the European Court of Justice' (2008) 45 CML Rev 1115; T. Novitz, 'A Human Rights Analysis of the *Viking* and *Laval* Judgments' (2007–2008) 10 CYELS 541; S. Sciarra, '*Viking* and *Laval*: Collective Labour Rights and Market Freedoms in the Enlarged EU' (2007–2008) 10 CYELS 563; P. Syrpis and T. Novitz, 'Economic and Social Rights in Conflict: Political and Judicial Approaches to Their Reconciliation' (2008) 33 EL Rev 411. The fact that the restrictions at issue were not imposed by state bodies brought an added degree of complexity to this case law.

42 S. Weatherill, 'From Economic Rights to Fundamental Rights', in de Vries, Bernitz and Weatherill (eds) (n. 40) 11 at 13.

43 Case C-112/00 *Schmidberger* [2003] ECR I-5659; and see e.g. L. Azoulai, 'The Court of Justice and the Social Market Economy: The Emergence of an Ideal and the Conditions for Its Realization' (2008) 45 CML Rev 1335 at 1349 ('practical method for … reconciliation'); C. O'Brien, 'Social Blind Spots and Monocular Policy Making: The ECJ's Migrant Worker Model' (2009) 46 CML Rev 1107 at 1137 ('integrated interpretation'); S. de Vries, 'The Protection of Fundamental Rights within Europe's Internal Market After Lisbon – An Endeavor for More Harmony', in de Vries, Bernitz and Weatherill (eds) (n. 40), 59 at 94 ('ideal situation').

followed the standard structure of free movement law – restriction; justification based on 'overriding requirements relating to the public interest';[44] proportionality – but the language and method of *balancing* applied by the Court were distinctive. Having established (by referring to the ECHR) that freedom of expression and freedom of assembly are not absolute rights – and that '[c]onsequently, the exercise of those rights may be restricted, provided that the restrictions in fact correspond to objectives of general interest and do not, taking account of the aim of the restrictions, constitute disproportionate and unacceptable interference, impairing the very substance of the rights guaranteed'[45] – the Court continued:

> The *interests involved must be weighed* having regard to all the circumstances of the case in order to determine *whether a fair balance was struck between those interests*. The competent authorities *enjoy a wide margin of discretion* in that regard. *Nevertheless*, it is necessary to determine whether the restrictions placed upon intra-[EU] trade are proportionate in the light of the legitimate objective pursued, namely, in the present case, the protection of fundamental rights.[46]

Economic freedoms and fundamental rights are still 'competing' in the *Schmidberger* judgment; and fundamental rights are still managed at the second (justification) stage of analysis.[47] But the way in which the Court framed the balancing exercise that should be undertaken in such cases – including the allocation of a 'wide margin of discretion' for national authorities – signalled a substantive difference in approach, in terms of both method *and* outcome.

But it is important to remember too that the *level* of protection applied to the rights at issue in *Schmidberger* was not controversial. In other words, authorising a peaceful environmental protest did not raise anything *particular* about Austrian constitutional values. The allocation of national discretion, as well as the determination of its optimal scope, is significantly complicated when Member States raise a *distinctive or specific level of (national) protection* of a fundamental right (rather than a broadly comparable EU standard) to justify the retention of measures or practices that restrict Treaty freedoms. Here, the Court has to engage in the process of '[t]ranslating the peculiarities of national legal orders into EU law'.[48]

44 *Schmidberger* (n. 43), para. 78.

45 Ibid. paras 79–80.

46 Ibid. paras 81–82 (emphasis added). See similarly, Case C-391/09 *Runevič-Vardyn* [2011] ECR I-3787: 'it will be for the national court to decide whether [the refusal to amend the joint surname of the couple in the main proceedings] reflects a fair balance between the interests in issue, that is to say, on the one hand, the right of the applicants in the main proceedings to respect for their private and family life and, on the other hand, the legitimate protection by the Member State concerned of its official national language and its traditions' (para. 91).

47 See similarly, Case C-244/06 *Dynamic Medien* [2008] ECR I-505, confirming that 'the protection of the child is a legitimate interest which, in principle, justifies a restriction on a fundamental freedom guaranteed by the EC Treaty' (para. 42).

48 L. Besselink, case comment on *Sayn-Wittgenstein*, (2012) 49 CML Rev 671 at 680.

The constitutional position on this from the EU perspective was summarised by AG Bot in *Melloni*: 'recourse to provisions of national law, even of a constitutional order, to limit the scope of European Union law would have the effect of impairing the unity and efficacy of that law'.[49] However, the ruling in *Omega* had tempered the conventional approach. The case concerned judicial review of a German police authority decision to prohibit laser games involving the simulation of killing, which in turn impacted on the cross-border provision of related goods and services. The referring court highlighted the fundamental nature of human dignity in the German Constitution.[50] Initially, the Court of Justice stated that it was *not* attaching special significance to the German conception of human dignity:

> [The Union] legal order undeniably strives to ensure respect for human dignity as a general principle of law. There can therefore be no doubt that the objective of protecting human dignity is compatible with [Union] law, *it being immaterial in that respect that, in Germany, the principle of respect for human dignity has a particular status as an independent fundamental right.*[51]

In the next part of the ruling, however, the Court displaced the point extracted above through, first, its characterisation of the German restriction as a legitimate public policy derogation, notwithstanding the very strict parameters normally applied in that respect;[52] and, second, its application of proportionality:

> It is not indispensable ... for the restrictive measure issued by the authorities of a Member State to *correspond to a conception shared by all Member States* as regards the precise way in which the fundamental right or legitimate interest in question is to be protected ... On the contrary ... the need for, and proportionality of, the provisions adopted are not excluded merely because one Member State has chosen a system of protection different from that adopted by another State ... In this case, it should be noted, first, that, according to

49 AG Bot in *Melloni* (n. 27), para. 98 of the Opinion, citing Case 11/70 *Internationale Handelsgesellschaft* [1970] ECR 1125, para. 3; Case C-473/93 *Commission* v. *Luxembourg* [1996] ECR I-3207, para. 38; and Case C-409/06 *Winner Wetten* [2010] ECR I-8015, para. 61. He also emphasised that '[i]t is ... not possible to reason only in terms of a higher or lower level of protection of human rights without taking into account the requirements linked to the action of the European Union and the specific nature of European Union law' (para. 108), a point returned to below.

50 Case C-36/02 *Omega* [2004] ECR I-9609, paras 11–12.

51 Ibid. para. 34 (emphasis added).

52 E.g. Case C-348/96 *Calfa* [1999] ECR I-11, para. 23; Case 231/83 *Cullet* v. *Centre Leclerc* [1985] ECR 305, para. 30. It is also commonly understood that the concept of public policy as a *derogation* from free movement rights is based on *shared* as well as exceptional *ordre public* policy concerns, which makes it difficult to conceptualise as a mechanism for protecting a more distinctive national conception of a particular right or value; see further, J. Morijn, 'Balancing Fundamental Rights and Common Market Freedoms in Union Law: *Schmidberger* and *Omega* in the Light of the European Constitution' (2006) 12 ELJ 15 at 39.

> the referring court, the prohibition on the commercial exploitation of games involving the simulation of acts of violence against persons, in particular the representation of acts of homicide, ***corresponds to the level of protection of human dignity which the national constitution seeks to guarantee*** in the territory of the Federal Republic of Germany. It should also be noted that, by prohibiting only the variant of the laser game the object of which is to fire on human targets and thus 'play at killing' people, the contested order did not go beyond what is necessary in order to attain the objective pursued by the competent national authorities.[53]

In stark contrast, the Court later applied a far less context-sensitive (and thus more typical) version of proportionality review in *Laval*: notwithstanding the distinctiveness of the Swedish conception of the right to collective bargaining; the Court's recognition of that right as a fundamental right protected by EU law; and its confirmation more generally that the Union has 'not only an economic but also a social purpose'.[54] The Court referred to both *Schmidberger* and *Omega* in *Laval* – but to confirm rather than preclude the legitimacy and scope of its judicial review.[55]

The circumstances of *Schmidberger*, *Omega*, *Laval* and *Viking* can be distinguished in some respects: for example, at the level of scale, a single 30-hour closure of one motorway in *Schmidberger*, or closing off one sector of very specific commercial activity in one Member State in *Omega*; compared with clarifying the pan-EU framework for the exercise of economic activity (services and establishment respectively) in *Laval* and *Viking*. The timing of the latter rulings (2007) should also be borne in mind. Judgments that affected the insulation of national markets would have been difficult to reconcile with the fundamental goals of EU enlargement, following so soon after the then-recent 2004 accessions to the Union.[56]

However, it has also been argued that there was clear scope in *Laval* and *Viking* for a more context-sensitive discussion of proportionality, given that these cases involved justification arguments based on fundamental rights too – whether at the level of the context of collective bargaining generally or distinctive national protection more specifically – and by recognising that disruption through strike action is an ***inherent*** element of collective action, meaning that less restrictive measures will ***not*** be as effective for the realisation of the broader social policy goals at stake.[57] Even allowing for the dimensions of scale and political context, then, the

53 *Omega* (n. 50), paras 37–39 (emphasis added).

54 *Laval* (n. 41), para. 110.

55 Ibid. para. 94.

56 See further, Lenaerts and Guttiérrez-Fons (n. 9) 1666–1667.

57 See e.g. the arguments of Davies, Novitz and Sciarra (all n. 41). See also N. Nic Shuibhne, 'Settling Dust? Reflections on the Judgments in *Viking* and *Laval*' (2010) 21 EBLR 581, referring to Case C-222/07 *UTECA* v. *Administración General del Estado* [2009] ECR I-1407, para. 36; C. Barnard, 'A Proportionate Response to Proportionality in the Field of Collective Action' (2012) 37 EL Rev 117.

Court's inconsistent treatment of proportionality – and thus of discretion vis-à-vis Member State defences based on fundamental rights – seemed to be steered by policy rather than legal drivers in this cluster of cases.[58]

4.2 A new constitutional framework?

More recent developments suggest, however, that the outcomes in *Schmidberger* and *Omega* could be recast beyond instances of *exceptional* respect for national discretion, potentially providing the seeds for a more general framework to balance fundamental freedoms and fundamental rights. To date, two examples are significant in this respect: the Lisbon Treaty's strengthening of respect for national identity at the level of primary EU law; and the ruling in *Sayn-Wittgenstein*.[59]

On the first point, Article 4(2) TEU brings an added constitutional dimension to the relevance of national fundamental rights standards within EU law, since it requires that '[t]he Union shall respect the equality of Member States before the Treaties *as well as their national identities, inherent in their fundamental structures, political and constitutional*, inclusive of regional and local self-government'. The fact that EU fundamental rights are inspired by the common constitutional traditions of the Member States is a long-established premise of the case law.[60] That point was also (and continues to be) reflected in Article 6(3) TEU. However, the obligation in Article 4(2) TEU is an expanded version of the more generalised statement in the pre-Lisbon version of Article 6(3), which provided simply that '[t]he Union shall respect the national identities of its Member States'. Does the express reference to *constitutional identity* in the amended text make a substantive – legal – difference?

The Court's ruling in *Sayn-Wittgenstein* came after the Lisbon Treaty – and thus both (Article 53 of) the Charter and Article 4(2) TEU – acquired legal force. The case concerned the decision of an Austrian authority to correct the applicant's surname in the Austrian register of civil status from Fürstin von Sayn-Wittgenstein (indicating a title of nobility) to Sayn-Wittgenstein. The applicant is an Austrian national who resides in Germany; she was adopted as an adult by a German national. The decision to re-register her surname was prompted by:

> a case concerning a situation similar to that of the applicant [which] held that the Law on the abolition of the nobility, which is of constitutional status and

58 The judgment in *Laval* can be distinguished from its sister ruling in *Viking* to some extent, where the Court certainly gave its views on the proportionality of the restriction in question but did leave concrete determination to the referring court. Cf. *Viking* (n. 41), paras 80–89.

59 Case C-208/09 *Sayn-Wittgenstein* [2010] ECR I-3693.

60 This principle was first articulated in Case 4/73 *Nold* [1974] ECR 491: 'fundamental rights form an integral part of the general principles of law, the observance of which it ensures. In safeguarding these rights, the Court is bound to draw inspiration from constitutional traditions common to the Member States, and it cannot therefore uphold measures which are incompatible with fundamental rights recognized and protected by the Constitutions of those States' (para. 13).

> implements the principle of equal treatment in this field, precludes an Austrian citizen from acquiring a surname which includes a former title of nobility by means of adoption by a German national who is permitted to bear that title as a constituent element of his name.[61]

First, the Court of Justice confirmed that

> refusal, by the authorities of a Member State, to recognise all the elements of the surname of a national of that State as determined in another Member State, in which that national resides, and as entered for 15 years in the register of civil status of the first Member State, is a restriction on the freedoms conferred by Article 21 TFEU on every citizen of the Union.[62]

The Court drew from case law establishing that 'a discrepancy in surnames is liable to cause serious inconvenience for those concerned at both professional and private levels', which could impede the exercise of Treaty freedoms.[63]

Second, the Court considered whether the restriction established could be justified on objective public interest grounds. Besselink suggests that '[t]he recognition of diversity did not primarily concern classic fundamental rights, as had been the case in *Omega*, but a constitutional feature regarding the particular political nature of the Austrian State, which is different from some other Member States'.[64] However, when assessing the relevant justification arguments, the Court linked the Law on the abolition of the nobility to Article 20 of the Charter, which 'enshrine[s]' the principle of equal treatment.[65] More generally, there are clear parallels between the circumstances of *Omega* and *Sayn-Wittgenstein*. Both cases concerned a principle protected within the Union legal order (human dignity and equal treatment respectively) that found specific expression in particular national contexts. Once again, a more radical legal revolution tied explicitly to the premise of fundamental rights protection was avoided through the Court's recourse to public policy:

> [T]he concept of public policy as justification for a derogation from a fundamental freedom must be interpreted strictly, so that its scope cannot be determined unilaterally by each Member State without any control by the European Union institutions ... Thus, public policy may be relied on only if there is a genuine and sufficiently serious threat to a fundamental interest of society ... The fact remains, however, that the specific circumstances which may justify recourse to the concept of public policy may vary from one Member State to another and from one era to another. The competent

61 *Sayn-Wittgenstein* (n. 59), para. 25.
62 Ibid. para. 71.
63 Ibid. para. 55, citing Case C-148/02 *Garcia Avello* [2003] ECR I-11613.
64 Besselink (n. 48) 681.
65 *Sayn-Wittgenstein* (n. 59), para. 89.

> national authorities must therefore be allowed a margin of discretion within the limits imposed by the Treaty.[66]

That part of the judgment is a basic reflection of the ruling in *Omega*. But the Court then engaged with interim constitutional developments:

> [I]n accordance with Article 4(2) TEU, the European Union is to respect the national identities of its Member States, which include the status of the State as a Republic … In the present case, *it does not appear disproportionate* for a Member State to seek to attain the objective of protecting the principle of equal treatment by prohibiting any acquisition, possession or use, by its nationals, of titles of nobility or noble elements which may create the impression that the bearer of the name is holder of such a rank. By refusing to recognise the noble elements of a name such as that of the applicant in the main proceedings, the Austrian authorities responsible for civil status matters do not appear to have gone further than is necessary *in order to ensure the attainment of the fundamental constitutional objective pursued by them.*[67]

If this passage provides a basis for attributing national discretion when fundamental freedoms fall to be balanced with fundamental rights forming part of *uncommon* constitutional traditions, two points would appear to be crucial. First, national policy must involve the pursuit of a *fundamental constitutional objective* to facilitate the triggering of Article 4(2). Second, there should be no Union harmonisation of the policy area at issue – meaning that the *Melloni* condition of respect for the primacy, effectiveness and unity of Union law should then, in principle, be more easily met.

Weatherill distinguishes between *Omega* and *Sayn-Wittgenstein* as follows:

> Instead of converting a national constitutional concern into an EU constitutional concern, which was the technique employed in *Omega*, the Court uses Article 4(2) TEU to show concern to respect a specifically *Austrian* concern. One might find a hint here that Article 4(2) is a route to soften free movement law yet further. But more probably this is just a slightly different route to reach the same destination.[68]

However, *Sayn-Wittgenstein* could also represent a formalisation of *Omega*, leading to an extension and generalisation of its objectives. Citing the emerging framework in Article 4(2) TEU would, in turn, shift the role of the Court from the more discretionary sphere of policy choice to the conferral-prescribed question of competence. That framework was not characterised expressly by the Court as a margin of appreciation but its effects are comparable: the Court recognises the

66 Ibid. paras 86–87.
67 Ibid. paras 89–93 (emphasis added).
68 Weatherill (n. 42) 32.

existence of a 'fundamental constitutional objective' at national level; and signals that national authorities are better placed to determine the proportionality of related restrictions on EU free movement rights.

The engagement of Article 4(2) could also address concerns about undue *peculiarising* of the public policy defence noted in section 4.1. Invoking Article 4(2) in *Sayn-Wittgenstein* enabled the Court to put Treaty language around its more furtive protection of national identity through the mechanism of proportionality in *Omega*. Von Bogdandy and Schill point out that 'it is the *very purpose* of Article 4(2) TEU to protect constitutional features that are specific to a Member State'.[69] Importantly, however, they also argue that Article 4(2) applies 'only in *exceptional* cases of conflict between EU law and domestic constitutional law' since 'not every provision of domestic constitutional law forms part of a Member State's constitutional identity'.[70] The orthodox *ordre public* origins of the public policy defence are altered by its incorporation of *difference*; but that shift could be rationalised when the twin elements of protection of a fundamental right and its 'eligibility' for consideration as an element of a state's national identity are present in the scheme of the defence arguments submitted.

However, while the Court of Justice's use of *discretion* shares the ambitions and functions of a margin of appreciation – and much of the substantive method of its application by focusing on the *necessity* of the national restriction – it differs from the underlying expectation of *deference* that we tend to associate intuitively with the application of that doctrine. The fact that the Court reasserted its jurisdiction over national justifications of free movement restrictions in *Pfleger* demonstrates this point. Additionally, a range of approaches to proportionality can be traced in the cases considered in this chapter: a determination that national restrictions were *not* proportionate (*Laval*); a determination that they *were* (*Schmidberger, Omega*[71] and *Sayn-Wittgenstein*); or devolving the determination to the national court, albeit with a strong steer on the preferred outcome (*Viking*). A more structured and systematic approach to all of this would dispel the deeply understandable conclusion that '[t]he present approach towards the levels of intensity seems to be rather haphazard and random'.[72] It will also be important to check whether the Court will continue to invoke and develop the primary law markers used in *Sayn-Wittgenstein* in relevant cases in the future.

However, the centrality of proportionality analysis is also a key feature of Article 4(2) TEU, as outlined by Von Bogdandy and Schill:

69 A. von Bogdandy and S. Schill, 'Overcoming Absolute Primacy: Respect for National Identity under the Lisbon Treaty' (2011) 48 CML Rev 1417 at 1431 (emphasis added).

70 Ibid. (emphasis added).

71 As noted earlier, in one line: 'by prohibiting only the variant of the laser game the object of which is to fire on human targets and thus "play at killing" people, the contested order did not go beyond what is necessary in order to attain the objective pursued by the competent national authorities' (*Omega* (n. 50), para. 39).

72 J. Gerards, 'Pluralism, Deference and the Margin of Appreciation Doctrine' (2011) 17 ELJ 80 at 101.

> The obligation to respect national identity in Article 4(2) TEU does not establish absolute protection for the constitutional values that form part of national identity ... [It] does not accord automatic priority to the constitutional principle of the Member State protected by Article 4(2) TEU, nor does it require domestic constitutional law unconditionally to yield precedence to EU law. Instead, it prevents EU law from interfering in a disproportionate manner with the constitutional identity of Member States. Applying such a proportionality test is warranted because that is what the term 'to respect' generally requires in EU law, above all as used by the Charter of Fundamental Rights.[73]

Application of Article 4(2) TEU does not, in other words, displace the obligation on the Court of Justice to address the inconsistencies in the case law.

It is also imperative to join different strands of the case law together. On that basis, it is difficult to see how a more systematic application of Article 4(2) TEU could *not* have serious repercussions for the *Melloni* criteria of primacy, effectiveness and unity of Union law. The ruling in *Sayn-Wittgenstein* pre-dates the decision in *Melloni.* But rereading the judgment with just one of the *Melloni* criteria in mind – the fact that respect for a national constitutional objective trumped the *effectiveness* of the free movement rights of EU citizens, which are also recognised as fundamental rights in the Charter[74] – underscores the significance of the national discretion recognised in *Sayn-Wittgenstein.*

The ruling in *Melloni* establishes that Article 53 of the Charter does not qualify the primacy of Union law, and that its application must not undermine the effectiveness and unity of Union law. But Article 4(2) TEU – which was not mentioned at all in *Melloni* – brings a different perspective into play, positioning the accommodation of *national* constitutional identity as a *Union* constitutional value. A basic tension then emerges: achieving the right balance between national constitutional diversity as a positive contribution to the protection of fundamental rights, which strengthens the constitutional credentials of the Union legal order in turn, on the one hand; and the risk of excessive splintering of the primacy, unity and effectiveness of Union law – in which the protection of fundamental rights is also respected even if the outcome in an individual case might differ from the national perspective – on the other. In particular, when the outcome of a case results in *lower* protection of rights through the application of EU law than would have occurred had the situation fallen outwith the scope of Union law, something prized is lost. Iglesias Sánchez confirms the function of Article 53 at the formal level as follows:

> Article 53 relates to the level of protection and not to the allocation of responsibilities for this protection: the fact that EU fundamental rights apply

73 Von Bogdandy and Schill (n. 69) 1441.

74 See Article 45(1) of the Charter; see generally, F. de Cecco, 'Fundamental Freedoms, Fundamental Rights, and the Scope of Free Movement Law' (2014) 15 GLJ 383.

> does not necessarily mean a higher level of protection. The question of the scope of application therefore precedes the issue of the level of protection, and the latter cannot be determined unless the 'respective fields of application' have been previously clarified.[75]

Is there a way to win hearts as well as minds[76] for what will be seen as, on one view, compromising the defensible objective of achieving the highest level of protection for fundamental rights that could be applied in each case? To address that question, the broader systemic questions raised by *Melloni* and *Sayn-Wittgenstein* need to be considered in more depth.

5 Implications for the broader system of EU law

It was stated at the outset that legal effect for the Charter means legal effect for the limits as well as the rights that it articulates. Further distinguishing the ECHR and Union legal contexts, it is important also to remember that the allocation of national discretion when protection of fundamental rights intersects with the scope of Union law illuminates broader questions about the system of Union law more completely: about the boundaries between Member State and Union competences, especially the scope and limits of competences that are *shared*; the extent to which national policy choices can or *should* be accommodated by a legal order aiming for an equality of treatment that rejects the utility of state borders; and the plasticity of proportionality review as well as its potential for manipulation – for good or ill – as a policy tool for that reason. The mechanisms for navigating EU–Member State boundaries are blunt – for the most part, a series of principles incrementally represented in the Treaties; the application and interpretation of which further enable a high level of discretion.

While this is an inevitable, and positive, attribute in many respects, reflecting the nature of instruments of primary law generally, the discretion built into the EU system becomes more acute when joined to the prevailing economic and political context. At present, the deep rifts of economic crisis and rising anti-migration sentiment find reflection in waning political and public appetite for the conventional ideology of 'ever closer' integration; amid a growing discourse on cooperation, flexibility and pluralism. Against this perception of context, however, there is also the customary sense that difficult questions are often deliberately bypassed within the political process, in full knowledge that they will therefore fall to be resolved by the EU judiciary – the familiar dynamic of pass the contention. Sarmiento is therefore right to remind us that the Court's placing of the Charter 'at the forefront of European integration' is an 'event that can hardly be a surprise in light of the

75 S. Iglesias Sánchez, 'The Court and the Charter: The Impact of the Entry into Force of the Lisbon Treaty on the ECJ's Approach to Fundamental Rights, (2012) 49 CML Rev 1565 at 1584.

76 M. Dougan, 'The Treaty of Lisbon 2007: Winning Minds, Not Hearts' (2008) 45 CML Rev 617.

prominent status that the Charter was given *by the Member States* once the Lisbon Treaty entered into force'.[77]

Sarmiento also points out that the Council provides a forum in which states can raise the specificity of their constitutional requirements when EU legislation is developed; and that a direct action challenging the lawfulness of enacted EU legislation could be framed as an infringement of the obligation in Article 4(2) TEU.[78] He does not present these options as compensation prizes for states that have to concede a lower standard of protection for fundamental rights than national law would provide in the same situation. Rather, he characterises both options as 'powerful *ex ante* and *ex post* mechanisms safeguarding the integrity of [Member States'] essential constitutional traits',[79] thereby underscoring the need for Member States to take more responsibility for their own shaping of the scope of Union law: it is often their *own* overreliance on the judicial process that needs to be checked more than the fact that the Court answered – as it must – the questions put before it.

In *Melloni*, AG Bot argued that a primacy-centred interpretation of Article 53 of the Charter does 'not overlook the fact that the European Union is required, as Article 4(2) TEU provides, to respect the national identity of the Member States, "inherent in their fundamental structures, political and constitutional"'.[80] But he also cautioned that

> [A] concept demanding protection for a fundamental right *must not be confused with an attack on the national identity or, more specifically, the constitutional identity of a Member State*. The present case does indeed concern a fundamental right protected by the Spanish Constitution, the importance of which cannot be underestimated, but that does not mean that the application of Article 4(2) TEU must be envisaged here.[81]

However, a particularly interesting idea comes from an earlier passage of the Opinion, where, building on the premise that context must shape the interpretation and application of fundamental rights protection, AG Bot argues:

77 Sarmiento (n. 35) 1268 (emphasis added). See similarly, Lenaerts and Gutiérrez-Fons (n. 9) 1656; Gerards (n. 72) 94–97.
78 Sarmiento (n. 35) 1292.
79 Ibid. at 1298.
80 AG Bot in *Melloni* (n. 27), para. 138 of the Opinion.
81 Ibid. para. 142 of the Opinion (emphasis added); in paras 140–145, he expands on his view that national identity concerns were not infringed in the circumstances of the present case. He also argued that the 'in their respective fields of application' phrase of Article 53 encapsulates the autonomy of Union as well as of national and ECHR law, and referred to the political reinforcement of primacy effected more generally through the attachment of Declaration 17 to the Lisbon Treaty (see para. 100 of the Opinion). This view is supported by the drafting history of the provision; see de Boer (n. 38) at 1092–1093. It should be recalled, however, that the original intention was to include the principle of primacy in the main text of the Treaty; see Article I-6 of the 2004 draft Treaty establishing a Constitution for Europe (OJ 2004 C310/13).

> The fundamental rights to be protected and the level of protection to be afforded to them reflect *the choices of a society* as regards the proper balance to be achieved between the interests of individuals and those of the community to which they belong. That determination is *closely linked to assessments which are specific to the legal order concerned*, relating particularly to the social, cultural and historical context of that order, and *cannot therefore be transposed automatically to other contexts.* To interpret Article 53 of the Charter as allowing Member States to apply, in the field of application of European Union law, their constitutional rule guaranteeing a higher level of protection for the fundamental right in question, would therefore be tantamount to disregarding the fact that the exercise of determining the level of protection for fundamental rights to be achieved cannot be separated from the context in which it is carried out. Accordingly, even though the objective is to tend towards a high level of protection for fundamental rights, the specific nature of European Union law means that the level of protection deriving from the interpretation of a national constitution cannot be automatically transposed to the European Union level nor can it be relied upon as an argument in the context of the application of European Union law.[82]

Here, the Advocate General takes arguments commonly used to support greater discretion at *national* level and turns them around: positing the *Union* as a community of shared values that aims to respect and apply *shared* standards of protection for fundamental rights. In this way, he brings an added normative dimension to the primacy–effectiveness–unity formula.

In the specific circumstances of *Melloni*, AG Bot sought to balance the requirements of fundamental rights protection with the politically agreed aims and objectives of the Union's area of freedom, security and justice. In turn, as noted in section 3, the Court emphasised that the harmonisation objective underpinning Framework Decision 2009/299 is *precisely* 'to enhance the procedural rights of persons subject to criminal proceedings whilst improving mutual recognition of judicial decisions between Member States', referring to Article 1 of the Decision.[83] Lenaerts and Gutiérrez-Fons have argued similarly that, in *Laval*, the Posted Workers Directive 'was decisive in determining the level of discretion enjoyed by the Member States'.[84] They also contrast the market-shielding protectionism apparent in *Laval* and *Viking* when compared to *Omega*.

The decisions in *Schmidberger, Omega* and *Sayn-Wittgenstein* reflect a different approach: one that still takes the realisation of free movement rights – as one of the Union's core shared values – as a starting point. The requirement to structure the analysis in that way can be linked to the *Melloni* criteria of the primacy, effectiveness and unity of Union law. However, the individual circumstances of each case are

82 AG Bot in *Melloni* (n. 27), paras 109–111 of the Opinion (emphasis added).

83 *Melloni* (n. 27), para. 51.

84 Lenaerts and Gutiérrez-Fons (n. 9) 1665. Directive 96/71/EC concerning the posting of workers in the framework of the provision of services, 1997 OJ L18/1.

reflected through the application of proportionality. Looking across the balance of that case law, it is clear that the also-shared values of respect for fundamental rights and respect for national (constitutional) identity reduce the *level* of proportionality analysis applied. So it would be naive to conclude that *no* impact on the effectiveness, in particular, of Union law results from the case law recalibration that gives effect to a margin of discretion in these cases. But that impact is potentially balanced by the requirement to preserve the *unity* of Union law – the primary law of which, recalling the point made earlier, requires that all kinds of objectives and values must be protected even though it does not delineate a clear system within which these objectives and values should be balanced in concrete cases.

Commenting on *Melloni*, Besselink suggests that the *unity* of Union law may represent a meaningful 'renovation of the more classic expressions "uniformity" or "uniform effect". Semantically, the difference might be significant, since "the unity of EU law" is not immediately at stake if there is no "uniformity".'[85] He cites *Omega* as an example of this; but cautions that 'we should not overestimate the Court's ability and willingness to deal in a more mature and differentiated manner with issues of uniformity and unity', noting that 'the Court itself within two paragraphs switches back from the "unity" of EU law in paragraph 60, to the "uniformity" of EU law in paragraph 63 – which is the language of 1970 (*Internationale Handelsgesellschaft*)'. However, he too points out that the secondary legislation/harmonisation context of *Melloni* differs from the primary free movement rights circumstances of *Omega*. In the latter type of case then – the focus of the present discussion – the distinction between unity and uniformity could well be legally significant.

The issues discussed above also raise a practical question about the sustainability of the more rigid *uniformity* approach to EU law in a Union of 28 states. That commitment is in many respects a tenacious veneer that masks a whole range of disagreements among and across the Member States, and a whole range of differences brought about by varied national practices in reality. For example, even in implementing the fundamental status of Member State nationals through the requirements of Union citizenship, multiple pockets of divergence in the transposition, application and interpretation of Union rules persist across the Member States.[86] At one level, the reality of national difference in a legal order of this scale and complexity is inevitable. All that the Court of Justice can do is reiterate the commitment to uniformity as an offshoot of equal treatment – something that it *must* continue to do since, first, the Court has a responsibility to communicate the constitutional ideal; second, as noted, the Member States have tended to add objectives and values to primary Union law without signalling a relative normative

85 L. Besselink, 'Constitutional Conflict and Fundamental Rights Protection in Europe: The Parameters after *Melloni*' (2014) 39 EL Rev 531.

86 See further, N. Nic Shuibhne and J. Shaw, 'General Report – Union Citizenship: Development, Impact and Challenges', in U. Neergaard, C. Jacqueson and N. Holst-Christensen (eds), *The XXVI FIDE Congress in Copenhagen 2014: Congress Publications Vol. 2* (DJOEF Publishing, 2014) 65–227; and the national reports published in the same volume.

ordering; and, third, it is likely that unpicking one element of the primacy construct in an overt way will, sooner or later, irrevocably destabilise the Union legal order more generally. Nothing that the Member States have done in the sequential Treaty amendment processes suggests a sufficiently shared, widespread or calculated intention to do that, whatever the tenor of political debate might be within individual Member States, at any given time, or on specific policy questions.

The corollary of retaining idealism – and oversight – at the constitutional level is that the Court of Justice has to trust national institutions to make reasonable and balanced judgments on a case-by-case basis; and to trust that the Commission will step in should systematic breaches of that trust ensue.[87] The manifestation of this trust is not just about encouraging a pluralist inter-court dialogue, something advocated within several branches of EU scholarship.[88] Rather, it preserves the formally hierarchical relationship between the Court of Justice and national courts, but acknowledges that trust – *mutual* trust, to recall the Court's own words in *Melloni*[89] – works both ways. It does involve a critical *element* of dialogue, through the preliminary reference procedure in particular; and these processes do flourish in the cooperative ethos of pluralism. But it cannot be ignored that the Court of Justice continues to fix – and has the authority to fix – red legal lines in order to fulfil its duty under Article 19 TEU. The Member States can depart from that interpretation, but only through amendment of the Treaties. Such an understanding of EU law does not advocate a simplistic version of primacy in an *absolute* sense; but it does focus on the different roles of legal and political actors in settling the system's constitution. Again, the contrast with the ECHR system is apparent, as summarised by Cameron:

> [T]he ECtHR accepts in principle that it should defer to national balancing exercises, but only when these have been performed in accordance with principles laid down by the ECtHR. Thus, it always has the option of examining the balance struck and the process of striking it … [201] It is even less likely that the [Court of Justice], the guardian of a proto-federal system, will be willing to accept a simple 'rationality check' function, and the sort of divergences an international court can and should accept.[90]

87 See Case C-129/00 *Commission* v. *Italy* [2003] ECR I-14637, finding, in the context of the interpretation of EU law by national courts, that '[a] Member State's failure to fulfil obligations may, in principle, be established under Article [258 TFEU] whatever the agency of that State whose action or inaction is the cause of the failure to fulfil its obligations, even in the case of a constitutionally independent institution' (para. 29).

88 On this point, see Sarmiento (n. 35) 1302; Gerards (n. 72) 80–85; Von Bogdandy and Schill (n. 69) 1419.

89 *Melloni* (n. 27), para. 63.

90 I. Cameron, 'Competing Rights?', in de Vries, Bernitz and Weatherill (eds) (n. 40) 181 at 200–201.

Understanding the Court's responsibility here as one of preserving the *unity* rather than the uniformity of Union law at the systemic level could well reflect the nuanced constitutional alterations brought about through the Lisbon Treaty process.

The points of difficulty are that, first, an Article 4(2)-coloured understanding of the EU constitution that balances national discretion with the primacy, effectiveness and unity of Union law may require more explicit working out of a non-negotiable *core* of Union law, i.e. the red lines that signal where discretion or divergence will not be tolerated. How is that to be determined without the making of value judgements that are not necessarily supported by the non-delineated structure of the Treaties? Lenaerts and Gutiérrez-Fons argue that '[a] *moderate* discourse on constitutional pluralism introduces a welcome element of balance into the development of general principles of EU law. However, the ECJ must still guarantee a core nucleus of shared values vital to the *integrity* of the EU legal order'.[91] But they also note that '[t]he question that then arises is how to define the outer limits of this nucleus'.[92] Sarmiento uses the examples of *Kadi* and *Ruiz Zambrano* to illustrate that the nascent construction of a constitutional core of EU law is already underway.[93] If the idea is to have a meaningful future, especially in an understanding of *loosened uniformity* as the *unity* of Union law, the boundaries of the core beyond the very particular, and exceptional, situations in those two cases would need to be carefully considered. Additionally, determining the core of Union law has to be a shared enterprise: shared between the different Union institutions; but also between the Union and the Member States, including through the process of Treaty shaping.

6 Conclusion

This contribution has argued that the Court of Justice has not embraced margin of appreciation discourse more explicitly in case law that balances protection of fundamental rights with other Union objectives; perhaps to avoid mistaken conflation with the development and application of that doctrine in ECHR law. However, especially where Member States raise justification arguments based on the protection of fundamental rights to defend restrictions of EU free movement rights, the Court does, on balance, allocate a margin of discretion to national authorities to determine the proportionality of those restrictions. That framework evolved through case law over time; it now includes specific reference to the requirement to respect national (constitutional) identity in Article 4(2) TEU. However, in order to reconcile this case law with case law on the interpretation of the Charter of Fundamental Rights, and especially Article 53 of the Charter, it may be necessary to nuance the application and understanding of the primacy,

91 Lenaerts and Gutiérrez-Fons (n. 9) 1664.
92 Ibid.
93 Sarmiento (n. 35) 1295.

effectiveness and unity of Union law, and to begin to ascribe legal significance to the idea of the *unity* rather than *uniformity* of Union law in particular.

At a more systemic level, these issues and the implications of addressing them more overtly highlight the Union's unsettled purposes as well as its several possible futures in a somewhat hazardous way. Union law rests on an edifice of interconnected principles. The constitution described by the Treaties does not confer a general responsibility on the Union for the monitoring of fundamental rights protection within the Member States. Instead, the requirements of fundamental rights protection are mainstreamed across the various tasks and objectives of the Union. The Charter accommodates a minimum threshold idea within it, especially for the relationship between EU and ECHR law. But, as *Melloni* demonstrates, the level of protection to be applied in situations that fall within the scope of Union law has to be determined within the complex balance of powers between the Union and the Member States more generally, on a premise that protection of fundamental rights is one of a series of shared objectives and values.

Overall, there is, therefore, a wide disconnect between the scale of the issues at stake here, and the more discrete 'solution' of introducing a formalised margin of appreciation into EU law. Sweeney characterises the margin of appreciation as 'allow[ing] the impulses of European commonality and national particularism visibly to interact but never fully to defeat each other'.[94] But the rules of that encounter must come from the broader system of EU law – and must be compatible with it.

94 Sweeney (n. 2) 41.

9 From flexible to variable standards of judicial review: the responsible domestic courts doctrine at the European Court of Human Rights*

Başak Çalı

1 Introduction

The relationship between the highest domestic courts and the European Court of Human Rights (ECtHR) has been subject to much pan-European debate in the past decade.[1] A great deal of criticism of the ECtHR has relied on the assumption that it has attempted to micro-manage domestic high courts that are perfectly capable of carrying out Strasbourg-proof rights interpretation themselves. This criticism has typically come from strong apex courts in the pan-European area with a long-standing tradition of interpreting the human rights and fundamental freedoms enshrined in the European Convention on Human Rights and Fundamental Freedoms (ECHR). While the judges of the ECtHR have on occasion addressed such criticisms by their domestic counterparts,[2] the ECtHR has also taken up the

* This chapter was originally presented at the conference Shifting Centres of Gravity in European Human Rights Protection, Reykjavík, Iceland, 6–7 March 2014 and subsequently at the annual conference European Society of International Law, Vienna, 4–5 September 2014. I would like to thank conference participants at both events and in particular, Oddný Mjöll Arnardóttir, Antoine Buyse, Rory O'Connell, Philip Leach and Yuval Shany for comments, and Cem Tecimer for research assistance. The chapter builds on my earlier work on emerging standards of judicial review at the ECtHR, in particular, 'Domestic Courts and the European Court of Human Rights: Towards Developing Standards of Weak International Judicial Review?', *Opinio Juris*, January 2013 <http://opiniojuris.org/2013/01/11/domestic-courts-and-the-european-court-of-human-rights-towards-developing-standards-of-weak-international-judicial-review>.

1 Richard S. Kay, 'The European Convention on Human Rights and the Control of Private Law' (2005) 5 EHRLR 466; Jochen A. Frowein, 'The Transformation of Constitutional Law through the European Convention on Human Rights' (2008) 41 Israel L Rev 489; Laurence R. Helfer, 'Redesigning the European Court of Human Rights: Embeddedness as the Deep Structural Principle of the European Human Rights Regime' (2008) 19 EJIL 125; Leonard Hoffmann, 'The Universality of Human Rights' (2009) 125 LQR 416; Brenda Hale, 'Common Law and Convention Law: The Limits to Interpretation' (2011) 16 EHRLR 534.

2 See *Dialogue between Judges 2012: How can we ensure greater involvement of national courts in the Convention System?* (European Court of Human Rights Publications 2012) <http://www.echr.coe.int/Documents/Dialogue_2012_ENG.pdf> accessed 27 June 2014. See also Nicolas Bratza, 'The Relationship between the UK Courts and the Strasbourg Court' (2011) 5 EHRLR 505.

challenge of this criticism doctrinally. This chapter focuses on this doctrinal response.

Specifically, in this chapter I argue that the ECtHR has started to shift its existing flexible standard of judicial review towards a variable standard of juridical review. The latter manifests itself in a fine-grained doctrinal refinement, which I dub as the 'responsible courts doctrine'.[3] The flexible standard of judicial review of the ECtHR has been marked by a case-by-case review with a special emphasis on the dynamic interpretation of the Convention by the ECtHR. In contrast, the variable standard of judicial review focuses on how domestic courts take into account the case law of the ECtHR and points to the stability of case law standards of the ECtHR. Under this nascent responsible courts doctrine, the ECtHR allows domestic courts a larger discretionary interpretative space with regard to making rights violation determinations, provided that domestic courts take ECtHR case law seriously. The responsible courts doctrine at its core signals that the ECtHR is willing to carry out either a lenient or strict form of judicial review, depending on the conduct of the domestic courts. This stands in contrast to the flexible judicial review focusing on the attributes of the case as a whole.

The responsible courts doctrine is nascent and contested as a standard of review. Its relationship to other forms of deference to domestic authorities under the umbrella of margin of appreciation and deference to the Court of Justice of the European Union (CJEU) under the 'equivalent protection doctrine'[4] is also under-determined. A series of dissenting opinions from judges in cases where the doctrine has been employed or failed to be employed further points to deeper divisions on the ECtHR bench over whether the doctrine supports or hinders the effective application of the ECHR as a pan-European instrument.[5] There is, therefore, a lot at stake in carefully identifying the emergence and contours of this review standard and assessing whether this is a transient approach largely developed to improve relationships with well-established unhappy domestic courts, or a more principled doctrinal development indicating a more permanent shift in approach to supranational judicial review standards of domestic courts by the ECtHR.

In what follows, I start with definitional questions regarding standards of judicial review and highlight the importance of legal cultural background in the development of judicial review standards. I then turn to the characteristics of the standards of judicial review within the traditional jurisprudence of the ECtHR. In particular, I show that the *sui generis* characteristics of the ECtHR as a supranational human

3 In characterising the doctrine in this way, I am inspired by the 'Responsible Governments Doctrine' espoused by the World Trade Organization Appellate Body, in particular in its decision WTO, *EC Measures Concerning Meat and Meat Products (Hormones) – Complaint by Canada – Report of the Appellate Body* (16 January 1998) WT/DS26/AB/R and WT/DS48/AB/R.

4 See *Bosphorus Hava Yollari Turizm* v. *Ireland* (2006) 42 EHRR 1, paras 155–156.

5 See dissenting opinions in *Palomo Sanchez and Others* v. *Spain* (2012) 54 EHRR 24; *Aksu* v. *Turkey* (2013) 56 EHRR 4; and more recently, *Erla Hlynsdottir (No. 3)* v. *Iceland*, App. No. 54145/10 (ECtHR, 2 June 2015), para. 59 and the Concurring Opinion of Judge Sajo.

rights court have resulted in the Court developing a flexible approach to articulating standards of judicial review. This has been due to the emphasis on the 'case-by-case' and 'right-by-right' analyses that have dominated much of its earlier case law development, alongside the *diverse* uses of the margin of appreciation doctrine.[6] Next, I review the development of and trigger conditions for the responsible courts doctrine in Strasbourg case law with reference to a number of paradigmatic cases attesting to this doctrine. I then compare this doctrine with the existing judicial review standards used by Strasbourg and discuss the opportunities and pitfalls inherent in the model of deference to responsible domestic courts. In conclusion, I turn to the legal policy implications of this nascent doctrine, in particular, in the light of the debates over EU accession to the Convention.

2 Standards of judicial review and comparative constitutional law: a framework

Standards of judicial review is an established domain of comparative inquiry into constitutional and supreme courts.[7] In domestic law contexts, there are two distinct theoretical lines of inquiry into standards of judicial review. The first is the relationship between judicial review and legislative and executive powers.[8] American constitutional law scholarship has asserted that in this domain the central question regarding standards of judicial review is the strength of the judicial review powers of domestic constitutional courts in relation to other branches of government. Gardbaum and Tushnet, in particular, have advanced the idea that judicial review is a matter of degree in terms of the extent to which the judiciary interferes in the decision-making domains of the legislative and the executive. Judicial review is strongest when courts spell out the terms of compliance in detail, leaving no leeway to implementing actors, and furthermore have the power to enforce these stipulations. In contrast, judicial review is regarded as weak when courts do not have the authority to stipulate specific remedies, but instead provide overall

6 For a comprehensive analysis of how margin shifts according to rights, see Howard Charles Yourow, *The Margin of Appreciation Doctrine in the Dynamics of European Human Rights Jurisprudence* (Kluwer, 1996). For a view that argues that the European Court of Human Rights is precedent bound, see Luzius Wildhaber, 'Precedent in the European Court of Human Rights', in Paul Mahoney (ed.), *Protection des droits de l'homme: la perspective européenne, mélanges à la mémoire de Rolv Ryssdal* (Heymann, 2000) 1529–1545.

7 C. Neal Tate, 'Comparative Judicial Review and Public Policy: Concepts and Overview', in Donald Jackson and C. Neal Tate (eds), *Comparative Judicial Review and Public Policy* (Greenwood Press, 1992); Stephen Gardbaum, 'The New Commonwealth Model of Constitutionalism' (2001) 49 Am J Comp L 707, 743; Mark V. Tushnet, 'New Forms of Judicial Review and the Persistence of Rights- and Democracy-Based Worries' (2003) 38 Wake Forest L Rev 813, 820; Mark V. Tushnet, *Weak Courts, Strong Rights: Judicial Review and Social Welfare Rights in Comparative Constitutional Law* (Princeton University Press, 2008).

8 Gardbaum (n. 8) 743; Tushnet, 'New Forms of Judicial Review' (n. 8) 820; Tushnet, *Weak Courts, Strong Rights* (n. 8).

guidance to legislatures or to the executive regarding which form of action would be most appropriate. Domestic judiciaries can thus be ranked according to their strength of judicial review, with different types of review offering different advantages and disadvantages for the implementation of domestic judgments.

The second line of inquiry, which is the central concern of this chapter, focuses on the relationship between courts with review powers and lower courts and the rationale for exercising review powers by the former over the latter. Here, the core issue at stake is the nature and intensity of review.[9] The nature of review concerns the purpose of review and the aims that a review court seeks to achieve by conducting the review. The intensity of review follows from the purpose assigned to the review. It concerns the degree to which a review court assigns autonomy to the lower court over the adjudication process. In turn, the review standards can be characterised as more or less lenient or strict.

As Pound has observed, the nature of review turns to whether a review court defines its function as (a) correction of error or (b) declaration of legal principle.[10] The former places greater emphasis on the quality of the adjudication of a single case and, therefore, may be characterised as backward-looking. The latter, in contrast, is concerned with forward-looking systemic standard setting.

The strictest form of review of court judgments for corrections of error is full review where a review court is interested in how facts are determined, assessed and analysed and how the law is applied to the case at hand. This in effect amounts to a full retrial of a case, leaving no space for discretion for a lower court in the adjudication process as a whole. Correction of error can also be carried out in less strict forms. Review courts may defer to the lower court as to the determination of facts, but carry out a full review of the evidence and law as applied to the facts of the case without any deference to the findings of the lower courts.[11] An alternative to this is the *clear abuse standard*:[12] a highly deferential lenient review, indicating that as long as there is not a manifest error, the review court will not change its view of the domestic court's assessment of facts. Review courts may also carry out an *abuse of discretion* review of an assessment of facts and law, in which they would assess whether a domestic court had overstepped its jurisdiction in deciding on a case.[13] How an appellate court moves between these different standards fundamentally turns to how their role and functions are defined in the legal system as a whole.

9 I take this definition from Jan Bohanes and Nicolas Lockhart, 'Standard of Review in WTO Law', in Daniel Bethlehem and others (eds), *The Oxford Handbook of International Trade Law* (Oxford University Press, 2009) 378–433, 379. See also William W Burke-White and Andreas von Staden, 'Private Litigation in a Public Law Sphere: The Standard of Review in Investor-State Arbitrations' (2010) 35 Yale J Int'l L 283.

10 R. Pound, *Appellate Procedure in Civil Cases* (Little Brown and Company, 1941) 3.

11 In the US context, for example, this is termed as *de novo* review. Cf. *Whatley* v. *CNA Ins. Co.*, 189 F.3d 1310, 1313 (11th Cir., 1999); *Rompilla* v. *Beard*, 545 US 374 (2005).

12 For application of this in the US context, see *Concrete Pipe and Prods.* v. *Construction Laborers Pension Trust*, 508 US 602, 623 (1993).

13 See *Cooter & Gell* v. *Hartmarx Corp.*, 496 US 384, 400 (1990).

Constitutional courts in domestic contexts are often regarded as courts that focus on reviewing the decisions of lower courts for the purposes of declaration of a legal principle, and not of corrections of error.[14] Constitutional courts are there to assess whether the way in which the case has been decided meets an independent standard of constitutionality imposed on the correct interpretation of laws (hereinafter law-based review). Law-based review focuses on *de novo* review only of the constitutional compatibility of the decisions of lower courts and has an indirect instrumental interest in the assessment of facts and correction of error. The latter may be by-products of law-based review based on the types of remedies a constitutional court is allowed to deliver in a single case.

The distinction between law-based review and correction of error review of a particular case is often blurred in practice. This is because law-based review may affect the outcome of adjudication, even though this is not the purpose of review. The distinction, however, has important doctrinal purchase. It offers a general logic of why the judgments of review courts in cases with similar facts may differ in terms of their compatibility with law-based review.

Courts that carry out law-based review also have an interest in drawing up specific standards with respect to the intensity of their review. Law-based review courts adopt lenient standards of review in legal orders that are less hierarchically ordered. This can be particularly observed in civil law systems where there are multiple apex courts with no clear hierarchical relationship among them. Lenient forms of law-based review then are mindful of the normative–interpretative powers of other actors within the legal system. In contrast, in legal systems where normative hierarchy of interpretation is paramount, the highest review courts are less likely to leave interpretative space for the interpretation of the norms by other courts.

These general observations concerning the types, nature and the intensity of review point to the importance of legal culture in a given domestic context. The standards of review that develop within a legal system cannot be divorced from the shared legal culture of which the standards of legal review form part. The purpose of review and the subsequent justification of the intensity of review that follows vary across specific legal cultures.[15]

3 Effective and dynamic interpretation, margin of appreciation and the flexible ECtHR standards of review

There is no doubt that in a general sense the ECtHR aims to carry out a Convention-based review (akin to law-based review) and views the retrial of a case

14 Sylvia Snowiss, *Judicial Review and the Law of the Constitution* (Yale University Press, 1990); Michel Rosenfeld and András Sajó (eds), *The Oxford Handbook of Comparative Constitutional Law* (Oxford University Press, 2012).

15 On the differences in the interpretation of constitutional review standards in Europe, see Federico Fabbrini, 'Reasonableness as a Test for Judicial Review of Legislation in the French Constitutional Council' (2009) 4(1) *Journal of Comparative Law* 39.

or correction of error review as an exceptional state of affairs in supranational human rights adjudication.[16] That is, the basis of the review of the domestic court decisions by the ECtHR has always relied on the interpretation of the standards set out in the ECHR and the compatibility of domestic court decisions with these standards. Furthermore, the ECtHR has explicitly rejected views that it is a fourth-instance court.[17] The intensity of the Convention review, however, offers us a more complex picture and there are calls from the Strasbourg bench both for lenient and strict forms of Convention review.[18]

It is well known that how the ECtHR has traditionally interpreted the Convention is deeply entrenched in the principles of effective and dynamic interpretation of the rights enshrined in the Convention.[19] Effective interpretation requires the Court to have due regard of the consequences of the interpretation of the rights for the real (not illusory) enjoyment of rights by the applicant that brings the case before the Court.[20] The dynamic interpretation of rights, on the other hand, requires the Court to be responsive to the constantly changing political, economic, social and moral developments in the *espace juridique* of the Council of Europe, and more recently beyond.[21]

These two aspects of effective and dynamic interpretation, taken together, have built in what I call a 'surprise element' to the case law of the ECtHR. As the sole interpreter of the Convention, the Court, on a case-by-case basis, has sought to develop legal principles for human rights law adjudication that were distinct from domestic rights interpretations.[22] This is not to suggest that the ECtHR has not

16 Exceptions have been justified, in situations in which the Court (and the Commission) have carried out fact-finding missions and declared domestic courts unable to deliver a domestic remedy, see *Kurt* v. *Turkey* (1998) 27 EHRR 373; *Timurtas* v. *Turkey* (2000) 33 EHRR 121; *Akdeniz and Others* v. *Turkey* App. No. 23954/94 (ECtHR, 31 May 2001); *Ipek* v. *Turkey* App. No. 25760/94 (ECtHR, 17 February 2004). See also Philip Leach, Costas Paraskeva and Gordana Uzelac, 'Human Rights Fact-finding: the European Court of Human Rights at a Crossroads' (2010) 28(1) NQHR 41.

17 The rejection of the status as 'fourth instance' has been frequently discussed, in particular when the ECtHR reviews allegations of the violation of right to fair trial by domestic courts. See *Rowe and Davis* v. *United Kingdom* (2000) 30 EHRR 1.

18 See Joint Partly Dissenting opinion of Judges Jungwiert, Vajic, Gyulumyan, Jaeger, Myjer, Berro-Lefevre and Vucinic in *Orsus and Others* v. *Croatia* (2010) 52 EHRR 7; and the dissenting opinion of Judge Lopez Guerra, Joined by Judges Jungwiert, Jaeger, Villiger and Poalelungi in *Axel Springer AG* v. *Germany* (2012) 55 EHRR 218.

19 See generally, Jonas Christoffersen and Mikael Rask Madsen (eds), *The European Court of Human Rights between Law and Politics* (Oxford University Press, 2011); Andreas Føllesdal, Birgit Peters and Geir Ulfstein (eds), *Constituting Europe: The European Court of Human Rights in a National, European and Global Context* (Cambridge University Press, 2013). On the common interpretative cannons of regional human rights courts, see Başak Çalı, 'Specialised Rules of Treaty Interpretation: Human Rights', in Duncan B. Hollis (ed.), *The Oxford Guide to Treaties* (Oxford University Press, 2012) 525–550.

20 *Airey* v. *UK* (1979–1980) 2 EHRR 305.

21 *Baykara* v. *Turkey* (2009) 48 EHRR 54; *Bayatyan* v. *Armenia* (2012) 54 EHRR 15.

22 *Christine Goodwin* v. *UK* (2002) 35 EHRR 18.

aimed to develop persuasive precedents.[23] The ECtHR, however, has insisted that the international interpretation of human rights provisions must remain transient, fluid and open to revision in the face of the facts of an individual case as part of the Strasbourg Court's self-defined mission of improving human rights standards. In *Christine Goodwin* v. *UK* the ECtHR sets out the relationship between predictability and effectiveness as follows:

> While the Court is not formally bound to follow its previous judgments, it is in the interests of legal certainty, foreseeability and equality before the law that it should not depart, without good reason, from precedents laid down in previous cases ... However, since the Convention is first and foremost a system for the protection of human rights, the Court must have regard to the changing conditions within the respondent State and within Contracting States generally and respond, for example, to any evolving convergence as to the standards to be achieved ... It is of crucial importance that the Convention is interpreted and applied in a manner which renders its rights practical and effective, not theoretical and illusory. A failure by the Court to maintain a dynamic and evolutive approach would indeed risk rendering it a bar to reform or improvement.[24]

This historic and transformative mission of the ECtHR has traditionally set the ECtHR apart from ordinary courts bound by legislation and constitutional courts bound by their own social contract. The perception of the ECtHR as a court that can challenge domestic courts and legislatures has also contributed much to its popularity.[25] The fluidness of the interpretation of the Convention principles, however, has also attested to the difficulty of placing the ECtHR within the conventional categories domestic standards of judicial review, which by their very nature, rely on more stable domestic legal frameworks and corresponding legal adjudicatory culture.

In fact, the intrinsic relationship between identifying and assigning meaning to relevant facts and interpretation of the Convention has been openly acknowledged by the ECtHR jurisprudence. This can best be seen in the early doctrinal formulation by the ECtHR of its relationship with domestic courts. The ECtHR has traditionally demanded that all domestic courts, to the best of their ability, formulate 'relevant' or 'sufficient' reasons when assessing whether they have made a genuine effort to decide whether a right was engaged or violated.[26] 'Relevant and sufficient reasons' are heuristic tools for review of domestic court decisions. But

23 M. Balcerzak, 'The Doctrine of Precedent in the International Court of Justice and the European Court of Human Rights' (2004–5) 27 *Polish Yearbook of International Law* 131 at 139 and Wildhaber (n. 6).

24 *Christine Goodwin* v. *UK* (n. 22), para. 74.

25 On the ECtHR as a court of the people, see Michael Goldhaber, *A People's History of the European Court of Human Rights* (Rutgers University Press, 2009).

26 *Coster* v. *United Kingdom* (2001) 33 EHRR 479; *Nikula* v. *Finland* (2002) 38 EHRR 45; *Sidabras* v. *Lithuania* (2004) 42 EHRR 6.

whether the reasons are indeed relevant or sufficient in the particular case is ultimately decided by the ECtHR.[27] The 'relevant' and 'sufficient reasons' doctrine has been employed by the ECtHR as both a backward-looking and a forward-looking doctrine. In cases where the Court decides that its previous case law has established a clear guideline as to what these reasons are, the ECtHR is content to refer to this older case law.[28] When the Court decides that the particulars of the case warrants a fresh restatement of the Convention in the light of the principles of effective and dynamic interpretations, the ECtHR is in a position to more substantively assess whether it believes the reasons given, in the light of the facts of the case, are relevant or sufficient or both. The relevant and sufficient reasons, therefore, can lend themselves both to strict review and lenient review, offering the ECtHR flexibility in terms of the standards it may employ based on the kind of case it encounters.

The standard of judicial review of the ECtHR has been further made flexible by the use of the margin of appreciation doctrine. When defined as deference to the state authorities *taking into account their proximity to the* facts and other extra-legal phenomena, such as political circumstances and background historical, social and political conditions on a case-by-case basis,[29] the margin of appreciation doctrine directs the ECtHR not to carry out a strict review of a particular case, but to defer to the state authorities' margin for limiting rights. Margin of appreciation, however, is not a standard of judicial review in and of itself.[30] It merely indicates that the standard of judicial review may vary from case to case, as the margin of appreciation of state authorities is in and of itself a relative criterion to apply a weaker or a more interventionist judicial review.

The flexible character of the Court's review based on effectiveness of the Convention and the living instrument doctrine, is reflected in one of the standard statements of the Court: 'The Court's task in exercising its supervision is not to take the place of the national authorities but rather to review, in the light of the case as a whole, the decisions that they have taken pursuant to their margin of appreciation.'[31] This statement, with its emphasis on 'the case as a whole', the review function of the Court and margins of state authorities, attests to the flexible character of review standards and the difficulty of formulating a stable standard of review in the case law of the Court. The ECtHR positions itself in principle as a court based on a standard-based review, but such standards are formulated in flexible and open-ended terms. The standard of judicial review that the Court uses

27 *Axel Springer AG* v. *Germany* (2012) 55 EHRR 218.
28 *Marper* v. *United Kingdom* (2008) 48 EHRR 50.
29 *Şahin* v. *Turkey* (2007) 44 EHRR 5.
30 Başak Cali, 'Between Legal Cosmopolitanism and a Society of States: The Limits of International Justice at the European Court of Human Rights', in Marie-Benedicte Dembour and Tobias Kelly (eds), *Paths to International Justice: Social and Legal Perspectives* (Cambridge University Press, 2007) 111–133.
31 *Aksu* (n. 5), para. 65. See also *Petrenco* v. *Moldova* App. No. 20928/05 (ECtHR, 30 March 2010); *Petrov* v. *Bulgaria* App. No. 27103/04 (ECtHR, 23 Nov. 2010).

is that of reviewing only the compatibility of the case at hand with the ECHR.[32] The precise review standards, however, cannot be foreseen with full certainty.[33]

4 Responsible courts doctrine: towards a variable standard of judicial review of domestic courts?

The contention of this section is that the ECtHR can no longer afford flexibility and, in turn, is moving to a different form of articulation of its review standards. Specifically, it is turning to a formulation of variable review standards based on the conduct of domestic courts in adjudicating a case. Unlike the flexible standards of its early case law, the ECtHR is proposing a more structured dual track: strict and lenient law-based review of domestic court decisions based on their handling of the ECtHR case law.

This turn to formulation of more structured review standards has been caused by four interrelated developments: the expansion of the Council of Europe membership to diverse judicial audiences, the rise and consolidation of the well-established case law of the ECtHR, diminishing the need for transformative jurisprudence, and the backlash the Court has faced to its effective and dynamic interpretation of human rights case law from some domestic judiciaries. These developments point to a change in the legal culture of European human rights law adjudication in recent decades, calling for a refinement of the flexible review standards and the terms through which the ECtHR defines the purpose and, in turn, intensity of its review.

From the early 1990s onwards, the ECtHR has seen significant expansion of the Convention membership into a post-Soviet, pan-European space[34] and has been transformed into a full-time compulsory Court with a Grand Chamber in 1998.[35] In turn, the ECtHR has experienced a highly diverse and heavy caseload. It has delivered over 18,000 judgments, making it by far the busiest international court.

The expansion of the Convention to a broader community is often associated with the 'caseload problem' turning the ECtHR into an institution that has been under constant review and reform in order to manage the increase in caseload.[36] What is less highlighted is the consolidation of the jurisprudential domain by the

32 *Schenk* v. *Switzerland* (1988) 13 EHRR 242, paras 45–49; *Bernard* v. *France* (2000) 30 EHRR 808, paras 37–41; *G* v. *UK* App. No. 37334/08 (ECtHR, adm dec, 30 August 2011), paras 28–30.

33 *DH and Others* v. *Czech Republic* (2008) 47 EHRR 3.

34 The membership of the Council of Europe expanded from 12 to 47, covering civil and common law countries alongside transition countries that have revamped their legal systems after accepting the compulsory jurisdiction of the Council of Europe.

35 Protocol No. 11 to the Convention for the Protection of Human Rights and Fundamental Freedoms, restructuring the control machinery established thereby, Strasbourg, 11.V.1994.

36 Of course, the ECtHR has also been under the review of the Council of Europe Committee of Ministers who have introduced three rounds of treaty-based reforms in the form of Protocol 14, Protocol 15 and Protocol 16.

very same caseload. The ECtHR, through the repetitive cases manifesting similar fact patterns across different jurisdictions and through Grand Chamber judgments, was able to develop well-established case law across a broad spectrum of Convention provisions. Thereby, it clarified its expectations from domestic judiciaries when applying the Convention to a broad domain of issue areas and normative conflicts. The very broadening of the reach of the Strasbourg case law has also led to a backlash against the ECtHR by some well-established domestic judiciaries. These, in particular, argued that the ECtHR must not erode the interpretative discretion of domestic courts in the interpretation of human rights law and offer them an interpretative space to be the 'co-authors' of human rights law.[37] The standards of review espoused by the ECtHR and the nascent development of the responsible courts doctrine thus need to be located in light of these multiple developments.[38]

The nascent responsible courts doctrine is a culmination of the Court's growing confidence in its existing interpretation of ECHR standards in the form of well-established case law, as well as the growing trust the Court has in domestic courts to responsibly apply these standards. The responsible courts doctrine has seen its clearest formulation in cases where the ECtHR recognises that more than one outcome may be possible and acceptable provided that a domestic court applies the standards developed by the ECtHR appropriately. This is sometimes referred to as a 'corridor of solutions', referring to the possibility of more than one right answer in rights adjudication.[39] It is, therefore, no wonder that cases that exhibit a tension between the enjoyment of more than one right have been the breeding ground for this doctrine. The *Von Hannover (2)* v. *Germany* case is the paradigmatic example of this.[40]

The *Von Hannover (2)* case was the second appearance of Princess Caroline of Monaco before the Strasbourg Court, arguing that the German press had violated her right to privacy. In the first *Van Hannover* case of 2004, Princess Caroline advanced the argument that, given that she does not hold public office or have any public functions, the continuous publication of pictures depicting her private life in the German press violated her right to privacy, and the German courts had failed to protect her. In its first review of the case in 2004, the ECtHR held that, as a matter of principle, when the right to privacy and the right to freedom of

37 Leonard Hoffman, 'The Universality of Human Rights' (Judicial Studies Board Annual Lecture, 19 March 2009) <www.judiciary.gov.uk/wp-content/uploads/2014/12/Hoffmann_2009_JSB_Annual_Lecture_Universality_of_Human_Rights.pdf> accessed 10 August 2015; Brenda Hale, 'Common Law and Convention Law: The Limits to Interpretation' (2011) 16 Eur Hum Rts L Rev 534.

38 The effects of these tensions can also be found in the remedy jurisprudence of the ECtHR. The recent innovations in the remedy regime of the Court, in particular, the pilot judgment procedure, show that the Court's approach to delivering remedies has also become variable. See also Chapter 7, in this volume.

39 *Axel Springer* (n. 27), para. 62.

40 For cases with similar reasoning structures see *Obst* v. *Germany* App. No. 425/03 (ECtHR, 23 September 2010); *Siebenhaar* v. *Germany* App. No. 18136/02 (ECtHR, 3 February 2011); *Schüth* v. *Germany* (2011) 52 EHRR 32.

expression are in competition, domestic courts had to consider the adequate protection of each right. The Strasbourg Court stated that the standard of human rights review developed by the German Constitutional Court in its judgment of 15 December 1999 was a test that a priori favoured freedom of expression and risked under-protecting the right to privacy. The standard afforded protection to a figure in contemporary society 'only if she was in a secluded place out of the public eye to which persons retire with the objectively recognisable aim of being alone and where, confident of being alone, they behave in a manner in which they would not behave in public'.[41] The Strasbourg Court held that 'the criterion of spatial isolation, although apposite in theory, is in reality too vague and difficult for the person concerned to determine in advance'[42] and that, therefore, the standard failed to offer real and practical protection of human rights, a central object and purpose of the whole Convention system. The Court consequently found a violation of the right to privacy based on the argument that the German courts' conduct in reviewing the case was out of step with European human rights law that demanded equal consideration of both rights in cases when rights compete.

In *Von Hannover (2)* the Princess, in the aftermath of the printing of more pictures of her in the German press, returned to the Strasbourg Court alleging that new violations of her right to privacy had taken place. The applicant thought the German courts had paid no heed to the Strasbourg Court's judgment. The Strasbourg Court disagreed with the applicant, deciding that the fact that the German press had been allowed to print pictures of her did not in itself point to a violation of the Convention. What concerned it was whether the German courts had appropriately balanced the rights of privacy and expression in their reasoning for allowing the publication of further pictures and that they did not favour freedom of expression at the expense of the right to privacy in applying principles to the facts of the case. The Court first reiterated the well-known statement of its role as an international court.[43]

> In exercising its supervisory function, the Court's task is not to take the place of the national courts, but rather to review, in the light of the case as a whole, whether the decisions they have taken pursuant to their power of appreciation are compatible with the provisions of the Convention relied on.[44]

More significantly, it went on to reason that '[w]here the balancing exercise has been undertaken by the national authorities in conformity with the criteria laid down in the Court's case-law, the Court would require strong reasons to substitute its view for that of the domestic courts'.[45]

41 *Von Hannover* v. *Germany* (2004) 40 EHRR 1, para. 54.
42 Ibid. para. 75.
43 See also *Rekvényi* v. *Hungary* (2000) 30 EHRR 519, para. 142; *Lindon, Otchakovsky-Laurens and July* v. *France* [GC] (2007) ECHR 2007-XI, para. 45.
44 *Von Hannover* v. *Germany (No. 2)* (2012) 55 EHRR 15, para. 105.
45 Ibid. para. 107.

These statements taken together clearly indicate a departure from the 'relevant and sufficient' reasons doctrine of the ECtHR. Firstly, the ECtHR emphasises 'the power of appreciation' of domestic courts. In so doing, the Court distinguishes domestic courts from other domestic authorities and accords the domestic courts higher status with regard to the appreciation of facts than other domestic institutions. Secondly, the power of appreciation of domestic courts is conditional. The ECtHR empowers domestic courts only when it decides that the domestic courts are interpreting the rights in a Convention-compatible way. Thirdly, the ECtHR explicitly imposes a judicial restraint on itself in carrying out a full review of the case if the domestic court has acted in a responsible way.

As a formal structure, therefore, the responsible courts doctrine operates as follows:

1 The ECtHR declares that the domestic court has dealt convincingly and comprehensively with the Convention as interpreted by the ECtHR in its previous case law.
2 After declaring this finding, the Court asks whether there are 'strong reasons' to differ from the analysis of the facts as offered by the domestic court.
3 If the ECtHR answers the question it posed in step 2 negatively, it defers to the domestic court with regard to whether there is a violation of the Convention rights or not.

5 Responsible courts doctrine: a form of margin of appreciation?

The deference to responsible courts, as formulated above, differs from standards of review that build in a deference to legislative or judicial authorities under the traditional umbrella of margin of appreciation. The significant mark of distinction here is that in the case of the responsible courts doctrine, deference to domestic courts is conditional upon taking and applying the Convention principles seriously. In contrast, the margin of appreciation doctrine, as originally developed, has operated according to an a priori declaration that the authorities enjoy a margin of appreciation by virtue of their qualities that is not dependent on their ability to interpret the Convention standards.[46] In this respect, the responsible courts doctrine is a qualified form of margin of appreciation. The domestic courts earn the margin by showing their loyalty to the Convention standards rather than by their other virtues *qua* domestic courts.

An illustrative example of the difference between responsible courts and the more traditional forms of margin is how the ECtHR constructs the margin of appreciation in relation to the interpretation of Article 6 of the ECHR in non-criminal proceedings. In a string of case law examples, starting with *Roche* v. *United Kingdom*, the ECtHR has developed a doctrine of direct deference to domestic courts in non-criminal Article 6 cases as a standard of review.[47] In its 2012 Grand Chamber judgment in *Boulois* v. *Luxembourg* the ECtHR recognised

46 See *Şahin* (n. 29), paras 109–110.
47 *Roche* v. *United Kingdom* (2006) 42 EHRR 30, paras 116–126.

that the starting point of the interpretation of Article 6 in the sphere of civil rights and obligations must be the provisions of the relevant domestic law and their interpretation by domestic courts.[48] In particular, the ECtHR requires that a civil right, at least on arguable grounds, must be recognised under domestic law, in order to trigger Article 6 protections. Alongside this, the dispute must be genuine and serious; it may relate not only to the actual existence of a right but also to its scope and the manner of its exercise; and the result of the proceedings must be directly decisive for the right in question.[49] The ECtHR here, too, would need 'strong reasons to differ from the conclusions reached by the superior national courts by finding, contrary to their view, that there was arguably a right recognised by domestic law'.[50]

In this way, the ECtHR explicitly recognises the role of superior national courts in deciding the interpretation of the applicability of fair trial rights to non-criminal disputes. Furthermore, by basing its own interpretation on at least the 'arguable' existence of the right in domestic law and interpretation, the ECtHR defers to all domestic courts and not only to the responsible domestic courts in this instance.

In light of the contrast between *Von Hannover (2)* and *Boulois*, we may conclude that the responsible courts doctrine shows important dissimilarities to other uses of the margin of appreciation. The leeway to apply the Convention standards to the facts of a case is only accorded to states that the ECtHR deems as trustworthy and Convention-compliant in the first place.[51] In this regard, *Von Hannover* represents a more nuanced deference doctrine conditional upon the internalisation of Strasbourg principles by domestic courts.

6 The doctrinal weaknesses of the responsible courts doctrine

In the previous section, I described the key qualities of the responsible courts doctrine and its emergence in the competing rights case law of the ECtHR. I have also argued that this doctrine must be distinguished from the 'margin of appreciation' accorded to courts, as it relies on case law being embedded in a court's decision in order to be triggered. The doctrine, however, is not without problems. As with other doctrines of the Court, there is no clear consistency in the usage of the responsible courts doctrine. A survey of dissenting opinions on instances in which this nascent doctrine has been employed points to two different types of issues raised by ECtHR judges. On the one hand, supporters of the responsible courts doctrine are worried that the doctrine is not used consistently. On the other, sceptics of the doctrine are worried that a doctrine of principled deference to

48 *Boulois* (2012) 55 EHRR 32, para. 91; cf. *Roche* (n. 47), paras 119–120.
49 *Boulois* ibid. para. 90.
50 Ibid. para. 91.
51 For a view that regards this doctrine as a mere variant of the margin of appreciation doctrine, see Dean Spielmann, 'Allowing the Right Margin: The European Court of Human Rights and the National Margin of Appreciation Doctrine: Waiver or Subsidiarity of European Review?' (2011–2012) 14 *Cambridge Yearbook European Legal Studies* 381.

domestic courts faces the risk of undermining the effective interpretation of rights and giving undue credit to domestic courts for adequately interpreting Convention rights.

The *Axel Springer* v. *Germany* judgment of the Grand Chamber, and in particular the dissenting opinions of Judges Lopez Guerra, Jungwiert, Jaeger, Villiger and Poalelungi, is an important illustration of the first issue. Decided on the same day as the *Von Hannover (2)* decision, the *Axel Springer* case also involved a tension between the Article 10 rights of a publisher and the Article 8 rights of a well-known public figure. Unlike the *Von Hannover (2)* case, in this instance the publisher was the applicant arguing for his violation of freedom of expression. The Grand Chamber, in this case, reiterated that what matters in competing expression and privacy cases is that the domestic courts have duly considered both rights, taking into account the published information's contribution to a debate of general interest, the previous behaviour and degree of notoriety of the person affected, the content and veracity of the information and the nature of the sanctions and penalties imposed. The Grand Chamber went on to decide that despite the 'margin of appreciation enjoyed by Contracting States', the 'grounds advanced by the respondent State although relevant, are not sufficient to establish that the interference was necessary in a democratic society'.[52]

In their dissenting opinion, five judges queried the standard of review that the ECtHR had employed in this case. In particular, they argued that the finding that the 'Convention rights were not duly considered' by the domestic courts was unfounded.[53] The dissenting judges, following the logic of the responsible courts doctrine espoused in the *Van Hannover* case, further argued that:

> In order to exercise this Court's powers of review without becoming a fourth instance our task in guaranteeing respect for Convention rights in this type of case is essentially to verify whether domestic courts have *duly* balanced the conflicting rights and have taken into account the relevant criteria established in our case-law without any manifest error or omission of any important factor.[54]

The dissenting judges placed more weight on the consideration of Convention standards by domestic courts than on the correct application of the standards to the facts of the case. As stated in the dissenting opinion, unless the application of standards to facts was 'arbitrary, careless, or manifestly unreasonable', the domestic court's decision should not be interfered with by the ECtHR.[55] On the contrary, the majority of judges have referred to the 'relevant, but not sufficient test' in this

52 *Axel Springer* (n. 27) para. 110.

53 *Axel Springer* (n. 27) Dissenting Opinion of Judge López Guerra joined by judges Jungwiert, Jaeger, Villiger and Poalelungi.

54 Ibid. para. 4 (emphasis added).

55 Ibid. para. 6. See also Joint Partly Dissenting opinion of Judges Jungwiert, Vajic, Gyulumyan, Jaeger, Myjer, Berro-Lefevre and Vucinic in *Orsus and Others* v. *Croatia* (2010) 52 EHRR 7.

particular judgment, carrying out a stronger form of review than that set out in the *Von Hannover (2)* judgment.

At the other end of the spectrum, some judges are concerned that the responsible courts doctrine could lead to an undermining of case law standards and inhibit their further development. This was the concern of the dissenting judges in the *Palomo Sanchez* v. *Spain* judgment of the Grand Chamber of the ECtHR.[56] The *Palomo Sanchez* case involved delivery workers who were dismissed from their jobs by an industrial bakery company in Barcelona. The applicants had earlier brought proceedings against the company before Spanish employment tribunals seeking recognition of their status as salaried workers (rather than self-employed or non-salaried delivery workers), in order to be covered by the corresponding social security regime. Representatives of a committee of non-salaried delivery workers within the same company had testified against the applicants in those proceedings. The applicants set up the trade union NAA (Nueva alternativa asamblearia) in 2001 to defend their interests and subsequently published a cartoon in the NAA newsletter showing the company manager and two workers who testified against them in an undignified position. They were dismissed from work as a result of this cartoon.

In this case, the Grand Chamber signalled that it would employ the responsible courts doctrine stating that

> the reasoning of the domestic courts' decisions concerning the limits of freedom of expression in cases involving a person's reputation is sufficient and consistent with the criteria established by the Court's case-law, the Court would require strong reasons to substitute its view for that of the domestic courts.[57]

The Grand Chamber went on to accept that the domestic Spanish court had paid due attention to the criteria of (a) whether the impugned remarks were harmful to others and (b) whether the sanction of dismissal was proportionate to the degree of seriousness of the impugned remarks. In particular, the Grand Chamber decided that the domestic courts duly recognised the importance of freedom of expression and considered these criteria and that the outcome of the reasoning of the domestic courts was not 'manifestly disproportionate'.[58]

Dissenting judges took issue with this qualification and charged the Grand Chamber with refusing to carry out a proper proportionality analysis between the aim of the limitation (to protect the reputation of others) and the means of the limitation (the dismissal of the applicants). According to the dissenting judges, the ECtHR failed to give full effect to the importance of freedom of expression in the field of labour relations and trade union activity. The fact that the ECtHR was interested in whether the situation was manifestly disproportionate meant that the Court approved

56 Joint Dissenting Opinion of Judges Tulkens, David Thor Björgvinsson, Jociene, Popovic and Vucinic in *Palomo Sanchez* (n. 5).

57 *Palomo Sanchez* (n. 5), para. 57.

58 Ibid. para. 77.

> in their entirety and almost word for word, the findings of the domestic courts, which, without taking Article 10 of the Convention into account, took the view that the cartoon and articles in question were offensive and impugned the respectability of the individuals and company concerned.[59]

The dissenting opinions in *Axel Springer* and *Palomo Sanchez* show the difficulties the ECtHR judges have in both deciding the appropriate review standards and whether they should also review how review standards are applied to the facts of the cases by domestic courts. In *Palomo Sanchez* the dissenting judges thought the review standards were wrongly identified through a failure to take into account the importance of freedom of expression for trade unions. In so arguing, they took their cue from the effective interpretation of Convention rights so that they are not merely theoretical or illusory.[60] In *Axel Springer*, the dissenting judges believed that the Grand Chamber had failed in its promise of effectiveness, while it exercised its new deferential standards to responsible courts.

7 Conclusion

At first sight, the responsible courts doctrine appears to be a promising doctrine for mediating the relationship between domestic courts that take the ECtHR case law seriously and the Strasbourg Court. Domestic courts that do want to apply the ECtHR standards do not want to be micro-managed by Strasbourg. The ECtHR itself also does not want to be labelled as a fourth-instance court. It also does not want to share the ultimate interpretative responsibility of the Convention with domestic courts. The responsible courts doctrine is able to speak to all of these concerns by recognising the space for interpretative manoeuvre of domestic courts within a framework of 'weak monism' formed around respect for Convention standards.

When put this way, every judgment of the ECtHR and its *rationes decidendi* participates at least informally in the creation of a supremacy of ECHR standards over domestic law, constitutional law or interpretation. Responsible domestic courts, however, enjoy a power of discretion in the application of standards to facts. This division of labour lies at the heart of the deferral model of the responsible courts doctrine, in trying to define the role of the ECtHR as confined to identifying manifest errors in the employment of the standards. This move represents an advancement of the traditional uses of the margin of appreciation doctrine, which has relied on a dualism between ECtHR standards and the appreciation of domestic laws, facts and situations by domestic authorities.

The responsible courts doctrine occupies a distinct space when compared to the 'equivalent protection' presumption developed by the ECtHR in order to mediate its relationship with the CJEU in the case of *Bosphorus* v. *Ireland*.[61] In this case the

59 *Palomo Sanchez* ibid., Dissenting opinion of Judges Tulkens, David Thór Björgvinsson, Jočienė, Popović and Vučinić, para. 10.

60 Ibid.

61 (n. 4).

ECtHR has not demanded that the CJEU earns its deference through demonstration of how seriously it takes the ECtHR law into account. Instead, it has opined that it will operate with a presumption that the CJEU will do so unless it can be shown that the protection afforded by the CJEU is 'manifestly deficient'.[62] This lenient form of review had the purpose of taking due account of the autonomy of the EU law and the fact that the EU is not a party to the Convention. With the possible accession of the EU to the European Convention system, the responsible courts doctrine may offer a tested resource to reconceive the relationship between the CJEU and the ECtHR, as the latter will have explicit legal duties to respect the Convention standards.

Even if the responsible courts doctrine is a step beyond the margin of appreciation doctrine, and even if it offers a heuristic tool to manage relationship between like-minded courts across the pan-European space, its use is not without problems. The core problem is the stabilisation effect that the doctrine has on the case law of the ECtHR. Unlike the case-by-case approach, the doctrine binds the ECtHR to its past case law and can hamper its dynamism. The emphasis placed on the well-established case law of the ECtHR is a move away from its transformative promise, in particular to those who view the ECtHR as a site to challenge existing interpretations of human rights law, including those emanated by Strasbourg.

From a legal-policy perspective, there are also two risks with the doctrine. Firstly, the doctrine may encourage an internalisation of ECtHR standards as well as a mimicking of ECtHR standards by domestic courts. In the latter, courts may dress rights restrictions in correct language in order to reap the benefits of being perceived to be a responsible court. Secondly, the ECtHR may provoke a new backlash from domestic courts that have not been classified as a responsible domestic court, on the grounds of double standards.

On balance, the ECtHR, through its well-reasoned judgments, has the persuasive tools to manage a variable standard of judicial review through differentiating how domestic courts handle Strasbourg case law, just as it has succeeded in managing the flexible standard of judicial review while it sought to establish human rights standards. The diversity of domestic courts present in the European human rights system and their varying degrees of domestic judicial human rights protection does require the ECtHR to develop more tactful relationships with domestic courts that are in tune with what we may affirm as the European legal culture of human rights. In addition, this new standard of judicial review has the potential to contribute to a rule of law culture by stabilising Strasbourg's expectations from domestic courts. Caution is advised, however, in order not to employ the doctrine unless the ECtHR is absolutely certain about the wisdom of giving up its transformatory jurisprudence.

62 Ibid. para. 156.

10 Speaking the same language? Comparing judicial restraint at the ECtHR and the ECJ*

Oddný Mjöll Arnardóttir and Dóra Guðmundsdóttir

1 Introduction

The main legal tools for navigating the relationship between the European Convention on Human Rights (ECHR, 'the Convention') and national law consist in the principle of subsidiarity and its doctrinal expression through the margin of appreciation.[1] The precise contours of the margin of appreciation, however, remain unclear and the confusion surrounding it is such that its status as a 'doctrine' has been called into question.[2] Many authors also complain that the European Court of Human Rights (ECtHR) does not distinguish between the theoretical basis and different constituent elements of the doctrine clearly enough in its jurisprudence and that this hampers its usefulness.[3] At the same time, the doctrine's significance is on the rise post-Brighton, as evidenced in Protocol 15 to the Convention, and in recent case law.[4] Despite its fuzzy contours, the doctrine has indeed become the most important expression of the idea that there are, and there should be,

* This contribution is published as part of a research project on the margin of appreciation, funded by the Icelandic Research Fund. The authors are grateful to Niamh Nic Shuibhne for her insightful comments on an earlier draft.

1 *Handyside* v. *United Kingdom* (1976) Series A no. 24, para. 48. See also for example Paul Mahoney, 'Judicial Activism and Judicial Restraint in the European Court of Human Rights: Two Sides of the Same Coin' (1990) 11 HRLJ 57, 78; Paolo G. Carozza, 'Subsidiarity as a Structural Principle of International Human Rights Law' (2003) 97 AJIL 38, 61–62; High Level Conference on the Future of the European Court of Human Rights Brighton Declaration, 19–20 April 2012, <www.echr.coe.int/Documents/2012_Brighton_FinalDeclaration_ENG.pdf> accessed 12 November 2014, para. 11.

2 Steven Greer, *The Margin of Appreciation: Interpretation and Discretion under the European Convention on Human Rights* (Council of Europe Publishing, 2000) 32.

3 George Letsas, 'Two Concepts of the Margin of Appreciation' (2006) 26 OJLS 705, 706; Yuval Shany, 'Toward a General Margin of Appreciation Doctrine in International Law?' (2005) 16 EJIL 907, 910; Jan Kratochvíl, 'The Inflation of the Margin of Appreciation by the European Court of Human Rights' (2011) 29 NQHR 324, 354; Greer (n. 2) 32.

4 Brighton Declaration (n. 1) paras 11–12; Protocol No. 15 amending the Convention for the Protection of Human Rights and Fundamental Freedoms (adopted 24 June 2013) CETS No. 213 (inserting reference to the doctrine into the Preamble of the Convention).

some limits to how active a role the ECtHR takes vis-à-vis the democratic prerogatives of the Contracting Parties. The use to which it has been put in practice can certainly sometimes be criticised, but a margin of appreciation doctrine can, and should, be seen as a valid tool with an important role to play in the Convention system. Through its function of governing the scope and intensity of judicial scrutiny in a particular case it is often instrumental in defining where, in the final analysis, the universal minimum standard of protection lies.

The increased emphasis on fundamental human rights protection in the European Union can be said to have culminated in the incorporation of the Charter of Fundamental Rights of the European Union (EUCFR, 'the Charter') into the Treaty framework. Normative convergence between the EU and ECHR systems is clearly aimed for in Article 52(3) of the Charter, which stipulates that in so far as the Charter contains rights that correspond to those protected in the ECHR, their meaning and scope shall be the same.[5] Recently, however, the concern has been raised that since the coming into effect of the EUCFR, the ECJ case law on fundamental rights has become increasingly self-referential, with the effect that the Court is missing the opportunity of developing informed expertise in human rights adjudication through engaging with the more developed standards emanating from other human rights bodies.[6] A strand of the literature has also emphasised the autonomy of the EU legal system vis-à-vis international law, including the ECHR, and the ECJ's rejection of the Draft Agreement on EU accession to the ECHR system seems to lend some support to that perspective.[7] Pluralism as a characteristic of the EU legal order has also become a predominant narrative.[8] Nevertheless, if we apply Eeckhout's characterisation of the EU legal system in the field of fundamental human rights as an integrated system of norms, incorporating the EU, the Member States and the ECHR, we can approach the field from the perspective of a shared jurisdiction between courts in an integrated legal system as

5 See also Joint communication from Presidents Costa and Skouris, 24 January 2011 <http://curia.europa.eu/jcms/upload/docs/application/pdf/2011-02/cedh_cjue_english.pdf> accessed 11 April 2014, para. 1.

6 Gráinne de Búrca, 'After the EU Charter of Fundamental Rights: The Court of Justice as a Human Rights Adjudicator' (2013) 20 MJ 168, 184. See also Jörg Polakiewicz, 'EU Law and the ECHR: Will the European Union's Accession Square the Circle?' [2013] EHRLR 592, 596.

7 See for example Paul Gragl, *The Accession of the European Union to the European Convention on Human Rights* (Hart, 2013) 7–10. The Draft Accession Agreement, rejected by the ECJ in its opinion no 2/13, represented the vision of normative convergence, see Fifth Negotiation Meeting between the CDDH Ad Hoc Negotiation Group and the European Commission on the Accession of the European Union to the European Convention on Human Rights, 'Final report to the CDDH', 47+1(2013) 008rev2 <www.coe.int/t/dlapil/cahdi/Source/Docs2013/47_1_2013_008rev2_EN.pdf> accessed 11 April 2014, Appendix I, Draft Accession Agreement, Preamble.

8 On constitutional pluralism in the EU see generally Damian Chalmers, Gareth Davies and Giorgio Monti, *European Union Law* (Cambridge University Press, 2014) 219–222. See also Janneke Gerards, 'Pluralism, Deference and the Margin of Appreciation Doctrine' (2011) 17 ELJ 80.

opposed to conflict between jurisdictions.[9] On this understanding, the relationship of the respective courts is governed by the principle of '*limited and shared jurisdiction*', which entails that the jurisdiction of each court is mainly limited to its own legal system but, to the extent that the systems are normatively integrated, they share jurisdiction.[10]

Against this background, and as the EU ventures ever further into the sphere of fundamental rights protection, it is understandable that scholars in EU law are gradually beginning to bring the idea of Member States' margin of appreciation to bear upon the case law of the ECJ asking if, and to what extent, a 'margin of appreciation' doctrine is emerging in the EU context.[11] As the doctrine is the established method for exercising judicial restraint in the ECHR system, the EU Member States may also rightly ask whether comparable dynamics apply when the same or similar issues are considered through the lens of EU fundamental rights. The integrated nature of fundamental human rights in Europe and the idea of normative convergence, therefore, call for a clearer understanding of the dynamics of human rights adjudication across both systems. Given the importance of the margin of appreciation doctrine, which gives expression to the reality that most human rights are not absolute and allows nuanced application of human rights norms as appropriate to different local situations, a common understanding of the doctrine seems sorely needed.[12] It is, in a sense, a precondition for understanding normative coherence in human rights protection across Europe.

This contribution aims to facilitate the development of a common understanding of judicial restraint through exploring the question of if and how it is possible to compare its exercise across the two regimes. The focus, however, will not be on detailed comparative analysis of the factors that influence deference or the margin of appreciation at each court in particular types of cases, but on the constitutive elements of *how they approach* judicial restraint. Therefore, the distinction between systemic and normative elements of judicial restraint will be elaborated on for both systems and used as an analytical framework, producing two key findings. The first is that despite differences in presentation, there are some striking similarities in approaches to deference across both systems. The second is that the blending of systemic and normative elements of restraint is a somewhat

9 Piet Eeckhout, 'Human Rights and the Autonomy of EU Law: Pluralism or Integration?' (2013) 66 CLP 169.

10 Ibid. 184–85.

11 James A. Sweeney, 'A "Margin of Appreciation" in the Internal Market: Lessons from the European Court of Human Rights' (2007) 34 LIEI 27; Niamh Nic Shuibhne, 'Margins of Appreciation: National Values, Fundamental Rights and EC Free Movement Law' (2009) 34 E.L. Rev. 230; Gerards (n. 8) 101; Nina-Louisa Arold Lorenz, Xavier Groussot and Gunnar Thor Petursson, *The European Human Rights Culture – A Paradox of Human Rights Protection in Europe?* (Martinus Nijhoff, 2013) 90; Massimo Fichera and Ester Herlin-Karnell, 'The Margin of Appreciation Test and Balancing in the Area of Freedom Security and Justice: A Proportionate Answer for a Europe of Rights?, (2013) 19 EPL 759. See also Chapter 8, this volume.

12 On a similar note, see Fichera and Herlin-Karnell (n. 11) 777.

problematic aspect of the case law of both courts and an area in which they should work towards providing more clarity.

The contribution will start by briefly exploring the preliminary issue of the different purpose and structure of the two regimes (section 2), while also identifying key elements that are nevertheless comparable when it comes to fundamental human rights. Significantly, in section 2.2, it will also be explained how differing levels of harmonisation in EU law set a different context than under the ECHR, which is characterised by a broader mandate and less specific normative guidance. Against that background, in section 3, a much needed comparative disambiguation of the key factors governing the appropriateness and intensity of judicial intervention in both regimes will be provided. After giving an overview of the analytical framework, sections 3.2 and 3.3 are devoted to identifying and elaborating those normative and systemic elements that characterise judicial restraint across both systems, while section 3.4 discusses overlap between the two elements. In conclusion (section 4), it is argued that the findings show that the development of a common language is possible from ingredients that already exist in the case law of both courts. While the findings are not normative in the sense of advocating a particular approach to the further development (or undoing) of the trends identified, they certainly provide some intelligibility to this notoriously complex area and impetus for further study.

2 Comparing the ECHR and the EU fundamental rights regime

Comparing the ECHR and the EU fundamental rights regime is a complex endeavour. The two systems are similar in some respects, for example, by aiming to protect the same core rights,[13] but their purpose and structure differ considerably, which may have various consequences in practice.

2.1 Key features of the two systems

The ECHR system belongs to classical international law and is governed by its principles and theories. The Convention's influence, thus, springs from the Contracting Parties' obligation under international law, including that of their courts when interpreting domestic law, to perform treaty obligations in good faith,[14] and from the binding force of the judgments of the ECtHR for the parties to a case as stipulated in Article 46(1) ECHR. In addition, the Convention has been incorporated into the domestic law of all Council of Europe Member States,[15] which in dualist states was an important step towards securing the influence of the

13 The EUCFR protects further rights, including notably social and economic rights that are not included in the ECHR. The present analysis is for the most part based on provisions that are included in both systems.

14 Vienna Convention on the Law of Treaties (adopted 23 May 1969, entered into force 27 January 1980) 1155 UNTS 331, Article 26.

15 D. J. Harris *et al.*, *Harris, O'Boyle & Warbrick Law of the European Convention on Human Rights* (Oxford University Press, 2009) 23.

Convention domestically. Unlike in EU law, however, there is no doctrine of direct effect or primacy of the Convention over national law.[16]

Within the framework of classical international law, the scope of obligations arising from the ECHR is nevertheless far-reaching, as the Contracting Parties 'shall secure to everyone within their jurisdiction the rights and freedoms defined in [the] Convention' (Article 1 ECHR). The jurisdiction of the ECtHR is equally wide, as Article 19 simply gives it the mandate to 'ensure the observance of the engagements undertaken by the High Contracting Parties', and a jurisdiction that extends to 'all matters concerning the interpretation and application of the Convention' (Article 32(1) ECHR). The ECtHR is also mandated to dispense 'individual' justice. In addition to the rare occasion of interstate cases, the Court may receive applications from any person, non-governmental organisation or group of individuals claiming to be a victim of a violation of Convention rights (Article 34 ECHR). The only real limitation imposed by the Convention on the extensive mandate of the Court is, therefore, to be found in the admissibility criteria stipulated in Article 35 ECHR. Over and above the admissibility criteria, however, the text of the Convention does not impose limitations on the scope or content of the judicial review performed by the ECtHR. Once they are met, and given that a grievance occurs within the jurisdiction of a Contracting Party and can be linked to a protected Convention right (all of which fall to be interpreted by the Court), there will be no limitation on the scope or intensity of the Court's review except as the product of its own judicial restraint.

In contrast, the EU Treaties, including the Charter, have a profound influence on the legal systems of the Member States, going well beyond traditional international law. The system is described as *sui generis*[17] in order to distinguish its characteristics from both an international treaty and a constitutional system. The integration of the supranational and national level into a composite legal order may be captured by reference to the Member State obligation to implement EU law in the national legal orders, going beyond transposition also to include application and enforcement. Within the powers attributed to the institutions of the Union, EU rules, enacted pursuant to the procedures set out in the Treaties, have direct effect within the legal order and primacy over conflicting national legislation. The ECJ has a strong mandate to ensure that 'the law is observed' under the Treaties (Article 19(1) TEU). This includes its mandate to supervise Member State compliance with Treaty obligations[18] and (more importantly in practice) to give interpretative guidance to national courts in preliminary rulings proceedings.[19]

16 Gerards (n. 8) 102.
17 For example Allan Rosas and Lorna Armati, *EU Constitutional Law: An Introduction* (Hart, 2010) chs 2 and 5.
18 Article 258 TFEU.
19 Article 267 TFEU. The highest national courts are for their part under an obligation to refer questions under Article 267(3). Questions of the validity of EU secondary legislation (which may be brought in preliminary rulings proceedings) are always for the ECJ to decide (see also Article 263 TFEU relating to direct actions to contest the validity of secondary legislation).

The Treaties, in their entirety, place considerable limitations on the scope of judicial intervention. The systemic limitations placed on direct review of Member State measures in preliminary rulings proceedings is perhaps the most relevant for our purposes.[20]

The Communities, later Union, did originally not enjoy any attributed powers in relation to fundamental human rights protection. The gradual strengthening of protection, consolidated in the incorporation of the Charter into primary law, has gone hand in hand with an ever broader mandate for the ECJ to guarantee fundamental human rights protection in the Union in all matters that fall within the scope of Union law.[21] Treaty changes have also increased EU legislative competence to protect fundamental human rights.[22] Further, since the Charter was proclaimed, all secondary legislation aims to comply with it[23] and an increasing number of secondary legislation implement particular Charter provisions.

The normative integration of the EU fundamental human rights regime and the national systems, *inter alia* through reference to the foundation of these norms in the 'common constitutional traditions' of the Member States, may in fact lead to 'very little "autonomy"' for each system.[24] The Europeanisation of these common traditions may however be a cause for concern for the Member States in relation to their formal constitutional competences and their 'fundamental boundaries'.[25]

20 National courts apply EU law, as active agents in the enforcement of EU law, or, on a more pluralist reading, as partners in the judicial dialogue. Direct access of individuals to the ECJ is limited and the route for 'individual justice' in the EU therefore continues to be channelled through the national courts. It is an established (if criticised) characteristic of EU law that in direct action cases pursuant to Article 263 TFEU, where (privileged) parties seek annulment of acts of the EU institutions, access of individuals to bring cases directly before the ECJ is limited to narrow situations where they can show direct and individual concern. The Lisbon Treaty amendments of Article 263 TFEU are unlikely to considerably widen direct access of individuals to the ECJ, unless in circumstances where no remedy is available before the national courts, see Paul Craig and Gráinne de Búrca, *EU Law, Text, Cases, and Materials* (Oxford University Press, 2011) 510. See also, critically, Steven Greer and Andrew Williams, 'Human Rights in the Council of Europe and the EU: Towards "Individual", "Constitutional" or "Institutional" Justice?' (2009) 15 ELJ 462, 475.

21 Originally based on the Court's general mandate and the declared respect for fundamental human rights, see now Article 6 TEU, in addition to functional requirements related to establishing supremacy of EU law.

22 Elise Muir, 'The Fundamental Rights Implications of EU Legislation: Some Constitutional Challenges' (2014) 51 CML Rev 219.

23 See for example Communication from the Commission, 'Compliance with the Charter of Fundamental Rights in Commission legislative proposals' (COM (2005) 172 final).

24 Eeckhout (n. 9) 175.

25 Weiler's idea of 'fundamental boundaries' was presented as a metaphor for the principle of enumerated powers or limited competences in a federal state, guaranteeing the autonomy and self-determination of communities against the federal entity, see J. H. H. Weiler, *The Constitution of Europe* (Cambridge University Press, 1999) 103–104. See also Nic Shuibhne (n. 11) 243 and Armin von Bogdandy and Stephan Schill, 'Overcoming Absolute Primacy: Respect for National Identity under the Lisbon Treaty' (2011) 48 CML Rev 1417.

Reflecting Member States' reservations about the risk of centralisation through a binding fundamental human rights instrument at the supranational level,[26] Article 51 EUCFR explicitly pledges to preserve *formally* the 'fundamental boundaries' of the Member States through addressing them only when they 'are implementing Union law' and stating that the Charter 'does not extend the field of application of Union law'. This is, as the literature attests to, the line with which the current case law is preoccupied.[27] Case law to date indicates that while the ECJ interprets Article 51(1) EUCFR broadly so that 'implementing EU law' is equated to the 'scope of EU law' for the purposes of the Charter (including also derogations from Treaty obligations),[28] the Court has nonetheless consistently resisted attempts to extend the field of application of Union law through Charter provisions, thereby drawing formal boundaries between its jurisdiction, in matters within the scope of EU law, and the jurisdiction of national courts in matters that fall outside the scope of EU law.[29]

Accommodating different standards within a limited and shared jurisdiction also takes place with reference to Articles 52(4) and 53 EUCFR, whose provisions similarly reflect respect for the fundamental boundaries of the Member States.[30] Further, the reference to respect for national identities in Article 4(2) TEU can be expected to be invoked as an additional argument and in the context of balancing under proportionality.[31]

Judicial restraint, in the broad meaning applied in this contribution, creates scope for the national authorities to regulate their communities without interference from an international or supranational court. From that perspective the complexity of the integrated EU system of multilevel governance is the first apparent hurdle to

26 Sara Iglesias Sánchez, 'The Court and the Charter: The Impact of the Entry into Force of the Lisbon Treaty on the ECJ's Approach to Fundamental Rights' (2012) 49 CML Rev 1565, 1583; and Gráinne de Búrca, 'The Drafting of the EU Charter of Fundamental Rights' (2000) 25 E.L. Rev. 331.

27 Daniel Sarmiento, 'Who's Afraid of the Charter? The Court of Justice, National Courts and the New Framework of Fundamental Rights protection in Europe' (2013) 50 CML Rev 1267, 1272.

28 The ECJ has in this way rejected any narrowing of established pre-Charter case law, in which situations were considered to fall within scope of EU law when national measures implement EU law, derogate from EU law obligations or display otherwise a sufficient link to EU law, see also Sarmiento (n. 27) 1277 and Iglesias Sánchez (n. 26) 1589. As regards derogations situations, see in particular Case C-390/12 *Pfleger* (Judgment 30 April 2014), paras 35–36.

29 Iglesias Sánchez (n. 26) 1588–1589.

30 Article 52(4) stipulates that 'in so far as [the] Charter recognises fundamental rights as they result from the constitutional traditions common to the Member States, those rights shall be interpreted in harmony with those traditions' and Article 53 requires that the Charter shall not be interpreted 'as restricting or adversely affecting human rights and fundamental freedoms as recognised, in their respective fields of application' by *inter alia* Member States' constitutions or the ECHR.

31 See further Chapter 8, section 4.2, this volume. See also Von Bogdandy and Schill (n. 25) 1441; Nik de Boer, 'Addressing Rights Divergences under the Charter: *Melloni*' (2013) 50 CML Rev 1083, 1097 (note). For a doctrine tailored to Article 4(2) TEU, see Arold Lorenz, Groussot and Petursson (n. 11) 93–101.

hamper a comparative analysis, both from an institutional and a substantive point of view. At the same time, it may well be that it is this very characteristic that calls for a clearer comparative understanding of judicial restraint as a tool to facilitate the nuanced application of human rights norms as appropriate to different situations.

2.2 To what extent is a margin of appreciation appropriate?

The doctrine of the margin of appreciation has evolved in the jurisprudence of the ECtHR as a tool to calibrate the appropriateness or intensity of judicial intervention when questions of human rights violations arise in the national context. The doctrine, therefore, is intended to provide a 'buffer' between the promise of a protective layer of universal human rights on one hand and respect for local democratic processes and legitimate diversity in terms of values and culture on the other.[32] Being the offspring of the ECHR system and its specific characteristics,[33] it is conceived as a consequence of the 'subsidiary nature of the international machinery for collective enforcement established by the Convention'.[34] Another characteristic of the system is the fact that the Convention provides a common minimum baseline of protection with reference to rights that are formulated as abstract principles. There is not much in the way of specification of what these rights actually mean in concrete terms in the language of the Convention itself. This provides special impetus for the Court's interpretative approaches, which have been characterised as those of a 'moral reading' of the Convention as a living instrument,[35] as well as the development of a doctrine of judicial self-restraint as a necessary correlative.

Comparing these aspects between systems we see prima facie two important differences. First, as a result of the *sui generis* integrated legal system, a large part of enforcement of EU law obligations takes place through judicial dialogue, which is formally cooperative, or integrated, rather than subsidiary. This integrated discourse is built into the preliminary rulings mechanism, where the national court is expected, and sometimes obliged, to refer questions of interpretation of EU law to the ECJ, before deciding the case. As opposed to the ECtHR's review of a

32 See for example P. Mahoney, 'Marvellous Richness of Diversity or Invidious Cultural Relativism?' (1998) 19 HRLJ 1.

33 The historical lineage of the margin of appreciation doctrine, however, can be traced back to doctrines of administrative discretion in national law, see for example Yutaka Arai-Takahashi, 'The Margin of Appreciation Doctrine: A Theoretical Analysis of Strasbourg's Variable Geometry', in Andreas Føllesdal, Birgit Peters and Geir Ulfstein (eds), *Constituting Europe: The European Court of Human Rights in a National, European and Global Context* (Cambridge University Press, 2013) 64–65.

34 *Case relating to certain aspects of the laws on the use of languages in education in Belgium* v. *Belgium* (1968) Series A no. 6, pt IA, para. 4. See also *Handyside* v. *the United Kingdom* (1976) Series A no. 24, para. 48.

35 George Letsas, 'Strasbourg's Interpretive Ethic: Lessons for the International Lawyer' (2010) 21 EJIL 509, 512. See also Jean-Paul Costa, 'On the Legitimacy of the European Court of Human Rights' Judgments' (2011) 7 EuConst 173, 177; George Letsas, 'The ECHR as a Living Instrument: Its Meaning and Legitimacy', in Føllesdal, Peters and Ulfstein (eds) (n. 33) 106, 124–125.

national court's final decision, the review of the ECJ is indirect and takes the form of guidance to the national court. However, as Tridimas suggests, the systemic context of the preliminary rulings proceedings has not always prevented 'outcome' cases where the ECJ gives guidance so specific that it can be equated with the full review (interpretation *and* application/balancing) otherwise more characteristic of the ECtHR.[36] Despite the ECJ's formally leaving it to the Member State authorities to balance conflicting interests, it may in a rather detailed fashion require them to apply national law in a way that does not lead to conflict with fundamental human rights.[37] The question is then to what extent a doctrine of judicial restraint may be used to mediate the shared jurisdiction between ECJ and national courts within this context of integrated discourse (see section 3.3).

Second, the EU increasingly provides for more than a minimum baseline of human rights protection, below which Member States may not fall. Instead, through positive harmonisation of Member State standards a certain uniform level of protection is established, which provides at the same time the floor and ceiling of human rights protection in the relevant field. The Court's decision in *Melloni* elucidates the differences between the EU and the ECHR in this respect.[38] Here, the ECJ refused to interpret Article 53 EUCFR as giving a Member State *general authorisation* to apply its own constitutional standard of protection of fundamental rights, when that standard is higher than that protected by harmonised rules which comply with the Charter, if such interpretation undermines the *primacy* of EU law over national law.[39] Quite clearly, then, there is not much scope for deference in situations of this kind. Nevertheless, parallels can be drawn between the systems. In all circumstances, the Charter forms the baseline of protection, when a situation comes within the scope of EU law.[40] As both *Melloni* and *Åkerberg Fransson* make clear, the possibility of applying national norms under Article 53 EUCFR in the sphere of remaining competences of Member States is subject to the condition that '*the level of protection provided for by the Charter*, as interpreted by the Court, and the primacy, unity and effectiveness of European Union law are *not thereby*

36 Takis Tridimas, 'Constitutional Review of Member State Action: The Virtues and Vices of an Incomplete Jurisdiction' (2011) 9 ICON 737, 739. For an example of detailed guidance, see Case C-368/95 *Familiapress* [1997] ECR I-3689.

37 See for example Case C-145/09 *Tsakouridis* [2010] ECR I-11979 and C-356/11 and 357/11 *O and S* v. *Maahanmuuttovirasto* (Judgment 6 December 2012).

38 Case C-399/11 *Stefano Melloni* v. *Ministerio Fiscal* (Judgment 26 February 2013). This well-known case concerned rules relating to the European arrest warrant, harmonised by Council Framework Decision 2002/584/JHA of 13 June 2002 on the European arrest warrant and the surrender procedures between Member States [2002] OJ L 190/1, as amended by Council Framework Decision 2009/299/JHA of 26 February 2009 [2009] OJ L 81/24. The question raised was whether a refusal to execute such a warrant was possible after conviction in absentia.

39 *Melloni* ibid. paras 57–59. The national court asked, first, whether the contested rule was compatible with Articles 47 and 48 of the Charter. The ECJ interpreted the provisions of the Charter in line with ECtHR case law, finding that the right of an accused to appear at a trial was not absolute and could be waived, if done unequivocally, subject to minimum safeguards and not contrary to important public interests (ibid. paras 49–50).

40 See also Chapter 8, section 3, this volume.

compromised'.[41] Different but equally Charter-compliant solutions are thus not ruled out (any more than different choices in national legislation that falls within the scope of the fundamental freedoms),[42] except where harmonised rules, based on particular Treaty provisions limit Member States' discretion in implementation or take priority over national legislation.

Level of harmonisation, carefully crafted through the EU legislative process in terms of form and content alike, therefore governs the extent to which a margin is left for the Member States (i.e. 'the margin for the margin') and additionally steers the Court in its interpretation.[43] There remains nevertheless a normative space for the ECJ in assessing the compatibility of secondary EU legislation with primary law, general principles and the Charter. This applies in instances where secondary legislation implements fundamental human rights norms, or Charter provisions, and where secondary legislation takes Charter rights into account.

3 Towards a common language?

As has been explained, similarities can increasingly be discerned between the EU and ECHR legal systems with respect to directly requiring states to secure fundamental human rights to everyone within their jurisdiction, and when it comes to mediating 'European' rights and legitimate diversity. In the following, we aim to establish the key factors relevant to the appropriateness and intensity of judicial intervention in both regimes. The framework constructed can help to identify when similar approaches apply and, thus, facilitate a clearer understanding of judicial restraint across both systems.

3.1 The distinction between the systemic and the normative

In 2006, George Letsas elucidated his two concepts of the margin of appreciation where the former is 'structural' and relates to the Court's formal status as an international tribunal but the latter is 'substantive' and relates to the limitable character of Convention rights, or their 'non-absoluteness'.[44] Other authors have also endeavoured to explain the different key functions of the doctrine, but there is no clarity or consensus in academic commentary on the precise contours of each

41 *Melloni* (n. 38) para. 60 and C-617/10 *Åklageren* v. *Hans Åkerberg Fransson* (Judgment 26 February 2013), para. 29 (emphasis added).

42 This issue has been discussed extensively, see in particular the literature referred to above (n. 11).

43 Similarly, see Thomas Horsley, 'Reflections on the Role of the Court of Justice as the "Motor" of European Integration: *Legal* Limits to Judicial Lawmaking' (2013) 50 CML Rev 947. Across policy areas falling within the scope of EU law, from the internal market to policy areas as diverse as consumer protection, environmental protection, immigration and asylum, detailed harmonised rules have been enacted, see for example Case C-578/08 *Chakroun* v. *Minister van Buitenlandse Zaken* [2010] ECR I-1839 relating to Directive 2003/86/EC of 22 September 2003 on the right to family reunification [2003] OJ L 251/12 (Family Reunification Directive).

44 Letsas (n. 3) 706 and 714.

of the dual conceptions of the doctrine. This is, perhaps, not surprising as it remains true that the ECtHR itself does not distinguish clearly between two functions or types of margin. Broadly speaking, however, all attempts at elaborating different conceptions of the ECtHR's margin of appreciation doctrine seek clarity through forging some kind of a linkage with the different rationales that support its different elements. These different rationales may overlap in the case law, but can in essence be divided into a systemic or structural one relating to the division of tasks between the national and international levels and a normative or substantive one that relates to the interpretative process of determining the content of rights and legitimate variety in how they are implemented and protected at national level.[45] Following Dean Spielmann's characterisation of the two functions of the doctrine, we will in the following refer to 'systemic' and 'normative' elements to describe these different types of judicial restraint.[46]

In the ECHR context, systemic elements of judicial restraint have been decisively linked to the principle of subsidiarity.[47] As subsidiarity is more commonly viewed as a structural principle which governs how authority (competence) is allocated within a political or legal system, than a normative one, which governs how authority is used once within the sphere of competence, it has only to a lesser extent been referred to in the context of explaining the normative elasticity of Convention norms.[48] Similarly, in the EU context, the doctrinal debate has been focussed on the function of the subsidiarity principle as it is set out in Article 5(3) TEU, as limiting the exercise of EU institutions of their legislative powers.[49] However, applying the principle of subsidiarity to the ECJ as an 'institutional actor', bringing it to bear beyond the EU legislature to the Court's own interpretative function, Horsley has drawn a similar distinction between the systemic and the normative in the EU context.[50] With reference *inter alia* to the division in Article 5(3) and 5(4) TEU between subsidiarity and proportionality, he argues that subsidiarity should guide the ECJ in its interpretation of EU law in areas of shared competences with the Member States, but only in so far as relates to the systemic question of 'whether or not there is a need to exercise competence at

45 R. St. J. Macdonald, 'The Margin of Appreciation', in R. St. J. Macdonald, F. Matscher and H. Petzold (eds), *The European System for the Protection of Human Rights* (Martinus Nijhoff, 1993) 84–85; Howard Charles Yourow, *The Margin of Appreciation Doctrine in the Dynamics of European Human Rights Jurisprudence* (Kluwer, 1996) 195–196; Shany (n. 3) 909–910.

46 Dean Spielmann, 'Whither the Margin of Appreciation' (2014) 67 CLP 49.

47 For example Letsas (n. 3) 721–722; Arai-Takahashi (n. 33) 90.

48 But see Carozza (n. 1) 61–63; Chapter 11, this volume and Letsas (n. 3) 722.

49 Thomas Horsley, 'Subsidiarity and the European Court of Justice: Missing Pieces in the Subsidiarity Jigsaw?' (2012) 50 JCMS 267, 267.

50 Horsley (n. 49) referring to Gráinne de Búrca, 'The Principle of Subsidiarity and the Court of Justice as an Institutional Actor' (1998) 36 J. Com. Mar. St. 217. On subsidiarity as a broad principle in the EU legal order, see also Theodor Schilling, 'A New Dimension of Subsidiarity: Subsidiarity as a Rule and a Principle, (1994) Y.B. Eur. L. 255 and George A. Bermann, 'Taking Subsidiarity Seriously: Federalism in the European Community and the United States' (1994) 94 Colum. L. Rev. 332.

Union level'.[51] As regards the subsequent normative question on the nature of the Court's intervention within that competence, he argues that proportionality is more appropriate as the governing principle.[52] This, again, corresponds to how the normative element of the margin of appreciation doctrine is often seen as almost 'the other side of' the principle of proportionality at the ECtHR.[53]

Using these (emerging) distinctions between systemic and normative elements of judicial restraint as a basis for an analytical framework, we will now turn to a comparative analysis of how they appear in each system. It should be noted, however, that the existing literature is relied upon only to the extent that it is beginning to bring this fundamental distinction to light in different contexts. The details of different author's approaches are, therefore, not part and parcel of our framework. Horsley, for example, chooses single market provisions (fundamental freedoms) as the empirical example to test his normative suggestions relating to the ECJ's self-imposed regard for the principle of subsidiarity. His conclusions have only partial relevance in respect of fundamental human rights.[54] Similarly, while relying on the basic idea of two kinds of margins of appreciation under the ECHR, we will not be relying on the details of any authors' characterisation of how to understand the difference between them. Instead, our framework is simply intended to capture the basic idea that there is to some extent a difference in kind between different approaches to judicial restraint and that this is related to different (systemic and normative) underlying rationales, and to facilitate comparison between systems.[55]

3.2 Systemic restraint

Systemic elements of restraint under the ECHR reflect the formal *division of competences* between the national and international levels. The rationale lies in the special character of the international enforcement system and focuses on institutional or jurisdictional competences as governing factors for the appropriateness of judicial intervention at Strasbourg.[56] This use of the margin of appreciation doctrine (hereinafter 'the systemic margin of appreciation') is, therefore, in a sense of a

51 Horsley (n. 49) 281. Compare however Muir (n. 22) 243, who cautions that the principle of subsidiarity in the Court's work in matters of fundamental rights relates to a different understanding of the principle than that formulated in Article 5(3) TEU and that this understanding is inspired by a broader understanding of the principle. See also Gareth Davies, 'Subsidiarity: The Wrong Idea, in the Wrong Place, at the Wrong Time' (2006) 43 CML Rev 61, 66, cautioning against the principle as ill-suited for the task of drawing the line between EU competences and national autonomy.

52 Horsley (n. 49) 281.

53 Yutaka Arai-Takahashi, *The Margin of Appreciation Doctrine and the Principle of Proportionality in the Jurisprudence of the ECHR* (Intersentia, 2002) 14, also Letsas (n. 3) 706.

54 See Horsley (n. 49) 276–281. It is suggested that it is primarily when determining the 'scope of EU law' for the purposes of application of the Charter that parallels can be drawn with Horsley's analysis, see section 3.2.

55 See also Spielmann (n. 46) 63 on the 'systemic objective of the margin of appreciation' on one hand and its normative function on the other.

56 For example Letsas (n. 3) 721–722; Shany (n. 3) 909.

constitutional nature, by indicating formal deference based on the Court's position in the system of protection and its competence within that system for particular types of assessments. In essence, therefore, the systemic margin delimits *what* the Court does and does not do, or in other words the *scope of its jurisdiction* vis-à-vis the national authorities. If the systemic margin of appreciation is applied, the Court expresses the position that it simply should not (or not fully) perform the task in question. It should be emphasised, however, that due to the wide delimitation of the Court's jurisdiction and competence under the Convention, the systemic aspect of the margin of appreciation doctrine is generally speaking a product of the Court's own judicial self-restraint. The Court, therefore, retains the power to step in when there is evidence of arbitrariness or violation of the basic principles of the rule of law.[57]

The most well-known reliance on a systemic margin of appreciation occurs in the context of cases where the Court categorically declines to undertake the tasks of a national court of third or fourth instance.[58] The 'fourth instance doctrine', which may be seen as part of the larger construct of the margin of appreciation doctrine,[59] expresses the fact that the Court does not have the competence of a higher national courts and has a subsidiary role in relation to them.[60] In cases of this type it is settled jurisprudence, therefore, that the Court's scope of review does not reach the establishment of the facts, including the admission and assessment of evidence before national courts,[61] or the assessment of whether national law has been correctly applied by domestic courts.[62]

57 For example *Maumousseau and Washington* v. *France* App. No. 39388/05 (ECtHR, 6 December 2007) para. 79: 'not its task to substitute its own assessment of the facts and the evidence for that of the Turkish courts regarding the adequacy of such a delicate process or to review the interpretation and application of the provisions of international conventions (in the present case Article 13 of the Hague Convention and Article 12 § 1 of the Convention on the Rights of the Child), other than in cases of an arbitrary decision'.

58 On the 'fourth instance doctrine', see generally European Court of Human Rights, 'Practical Guide on Admissibility Criteria' (2011) <www.dp-rs.si/fileadmin/dp.gov.si/pageuploads/RAZNO/Admissibility_guide_ENG.pdf> accessed 26 November 2014, paras 354–361.

59 Jonas Christoffersen, *Fair Balance: Proportionality, Subsidiarity and Primacy in the European Convention on Human Rights* (Martinus Nijhoff, 2009) 238 for example remarks that both reflect the same aspects of the Court's case law, but that the 'fourth instance' is the preferred term when questions of reviewing errors of fact or law emerge.

60 For example *Ringier Axel Springer Slovakia* v. *Slovakia* App. No. 41262/05 (ECtHR, 26 July 2011), para. 107; *Artemov* v. *Russia* App. No. 14945/03 (ECtHR, 3 April 2014), para. 115.

61 See for example *Shtukaturov* v. *Russia* ECHR 2008 para. 67 and *Marchenko* v. *Ukraine* App. No. 4063/04 (ECtHR, 19 February 2009), para. 48: '[T]he Court notes that the applicant's contention that he had personally not organised and not participated in the action was rejected by the domestic courts of three levels of jurisdiction following adversary proceedings, in the course of which a wide range of evidence, including witness statements, was examined. In the absence of any *prima facie* evidence of procedural unfairness, the Court is not in a position to review this factual conclusion.'

62 See for example *X* v. *Finland* ECHR 2012, para. 216 and *Fedorenko* v. *Ukraine* App. No. 25921/02 (ECtHR, 1 June 2006), para. 27: 'The Court recalls that its

In recent years, however, it seems that there has been a certain increase in reliance on the systemic aspect of the margin of appreciation in other contexts as well, as the Court has become keener on taking a clear stance on the tasks it performs and the tasks it leaves to others. One such example expressing the principle of 'limited and shared jurisdiction' is, of course, to be found in the *Bosphorus Airways* judgment of 2005.[63] The judgment therefore exhibits a limitation on the scope of review of the same kind as otherwise when the systemic margin of appreciation is applied to state action. More recently, the most noteworthy turn towards an increase in the use of the systemic margin of appreciation has occurred in situations where two competing individual interests under Convention rights collide and have to be balanced against each other.[64] While such issues were previously resolved by the Court's own assessments both as regards the *interpretation* of norms and as regards the actual balancing exercise required by their *application* to the facts of the case, and equally couched in terms of the normative margin,[65] the second *Von Hannover* judgment clearly exhibits that they are now beginning to be more clearly characterised by a systemic margin of appreciation which focuses on the *scope of the Court's review* before the Court enters into any substantive proportionality assessment of its own.[66] This development towards the increased formalisation of the margin of appreciation doctrine can be argued to have begun with the *MGN* judgment, where Article 8 and Article 10 had to be balanced against each other. After affirming that the balancing of contradictory individual interests against each other was a difficult matter where the national authorities were in principle 'better placed' than the Court to perform the relevant assessment and should, therefore, enjoy 'a broad margin of appreciation' (in the normative sense), the Court went on to construct a new element of the margin of appreciation in such contexts.[67] It established that if the national court had correctly applied the relevant Convention principles, as elaborated in its case law, and carefully weighed the individual interests in question against each other, the Strasbourg Court 'would require strong reasons to substitute its view for that of the final decision' of the national court.[68] While the Court still pronounces on the *interpretation* of the relevant Convention norms in these cases, the consequence of the new approach is a separate analytical step whereby the Court calibrates the *scope of its review* before deciding whether it also performs the *application* of Convention standards to the facts of the case. The focus of analysis has, thus, shifted from full substantive analysis of all cases towards analysing the quality of the national court's

jurisdiction to verify compliance with the domestic law is limited … and that it is not its task to take the place of the domestic courts. It is primarily for the national authorities, notably the courts, to resolve problems of the interpretation of domestic legislation.'

63 *Bosphorus Hava Yolları Turizm ve Ticaret Anonim Şirketi* v. *Ireland* ECHR 2005-VI, para. 149. See generally the discussion of this judgment in Chapter 3, this volume.

64 See also Spielmann (n. 46) 61–65 and Chapter 9, this volume.

65 For example *Von Hannover* v. *Germany* ECHR 2004-VI.

66 *Von Hannover* v. *Germany (No. 2)* ECHR 2012.

67 *MGN* v. *United Kingdom* App. No. 39401/04 (ECtHR, 18 January 2011), para. 142.

68 Ibid. para. 150.

decision, with the implication of deferral if the national court has conscientiously applied Convention standards.[69] Like before, however, this element of the systemic margin of appreciation is a measure of self-restraint and the Court will step in if manifest deficiencies in the national court's treatment of the issues present themselves.[70]

The approach of dividing the interpretation and application of norms into two steps is of course a characteristic of the EU preliminary rulings proceedings. It is interesting to note, therefore, how this approach seems to be emerging in the recent ECtHR case law on the balancing of competing individual interests under Convention rights. Through giving Contracting States the responsibility for the application of Convention norms, a formal screen is erected behind which they will enjoy more autonomy and control over how Convention norms are implemented nationally. As a general conclusion it can therefore be said that, based on a systemic rationale, this opens up the width of the margin of appreciation when it comes to the application of Convention norms *in concreto*. At the same time, it is clear that another type of judicial restraint may be appropriate to the other step in the judicial process, the interpretation of fundamental human rights norms. Here, a normative margin may be implied as the relevant Court may still through a conscious choice adjust the level of detail with which it provides its interpretative guidance before deferring the application of norms, so interpreted, to the national level.[71]

Issues of competences and their delimitation between the EU institutions (including the ECJ) on the one hand and the EU institutions and Member States on the other overlap to a greater extent in the EU than in the ECHR system.[72] As mentioned, some of the issues dealt with under the systemic element of the margin of appreciation within the ECtHR are an integral part of preliminary rulings proceedings before the ECJ. Facts and rules of evidence are firmly within the jurisdiction of the referring court, both prior to the ECJ giving its interpretative guidance, when the national court formulates the questions and the legal issues,[73] and following the ECJ's interpretation of EU law. Using its interpretative competence, the ECJ however sometimes reformulates the questions posed or

69 See also for example *Palomo Sánchez and Others* v. *Spain* ECHR 2011; *Axel Springer AG* v. *Germany* App. No. 39954/08 (ECtHR, 7 February 2012) (note the dissenting opinion of Judge López Guerra, joined by judges Jungwiert, Jaeger, Villiger and Poalelungi); and *Von Hannover* v. *Germany (No. 2)* (n. 66).

70 See for example *Fáber* v. *Hungary* App. No. 40721/08 (ECtHR, 24 July 2012); *Ristamaki and Korvola* App. No. 66456/09 (ECtHR, 20 October 2013); and *Jalbă* v. *Romania* App. No. 43912/10 (ECtHR, 18 February 2014).

71 As pointed out by Tridimas the ECJ may in 'outcome' cases present the national court with 'an answer so specific that it leaves the referring court no margin for manoeuver and provides it with a ready-made solution to the dispute' (n. 36) 739.

72 See Sacha Prechal, Sybe de Vries and Hanneke van Eijken, 'The Principle of Attributed Powers and the "Scope of EU Law"', in Leonard Besselink, Frans Pennings and Sacha Prechal (eds), *The Eclipse of the Legality Principle in the European Union* (Wolters Kluwer, 2011) 213 and Horsley (n. 43) 391–397.

73 For example *Pfleger* (n. 28) para. 27; *Tsakouridis* (n. 37) para. 35.

modifies or explains the legal context before responding to the referring court.[74] Application of national law also falls within the jurisdiction of the national court, but again the line may be more blurred than in the ECHR context as national law implements EU law and EU law principles require its effective implementation.[75] Particularly in cases where Directives harmonise national law, it is possible to see an increased overlap between systemic deference and normative engagement, depending on the extent of positive harmonisation in each situation. While the ECJ leaves the determination of factual and legal issues to the national court, the normative engagement is reflected by the fact that the national court is still required to interpret national law in conformity with secondary EU legislation and not to rely on an interpretation of secondary EU legislation which would be in conflict with fundamental rights or general principles[76] or would deprive it of its effectiveness.[77]

Determining the 'scope of EU law' is prima facie for the ECJ. If there is doubt as to the situation coming within the scope of EU law, the ECJ may leave that determination to the national court, under an approach that may be compared to the systemic margin under the ECHR. In *Dereci and Others*, for example, it was left to the national court to determine whether residence rights of a third country national came within the scope of EU law, by virtue of his family members' status as Union citizens. The ECJ guided the referring court to examine the issue under Article 7 EUCFR if the situation was found to come within the scope of EU law, but otherwise in light of Article 8 ECHR.[78]

In the EU, judicial competence is broader than legislative competence and has been considered to coincide with the 'scope of EU law'.[79] Building on Horsley's

74 For example *Tsakouridis* (n. 37) para. 26, where the Court reiterated that it may find it necessary, in order to give the national court a useful answer, to consider provisions of EU law which the national court has not referred to. See also *O and S* v. *Maahanmuuttovirasto* (n. 37) para. 60 and Case C-279/09 *Deutsche Energiehandels-und Beratungsgesellschaft mbH* v. *Bundesrepublic Deutschland* [2010] ECR I-13849 (*DEB*), where the ECJ was asked about the compatibility with the principle of effectiveness of national rules relating to litigation costs. The ECJ recast the question as one relating to whether the contested national rules (precluding legal aid to companies) were compatible with Article 47 EUCFR.

75 Case C-176/12 *Association de médiation sociale* v. *Union locale des syndicats CGT and Others* (Judgment 15 January 2014), paras 38–40 and Opinion of Advocate General Cruz Villalón, paras 88–89.

76 See for example Case C-101/01 *Lindqvist* v. *Anklagarkamaren i Jonkoping* [2003] ECR I-12971, para. 87 (proportionality); Case C-403/09 PPU *Detiček* v. *Sgueglia* [2009] ECR I-12193, para. 34.

77 See for example Case C-571/10 *Kamberaj* v. *Instituto per l'Edilizia Sociale della Provincia Autonoma di Bolzano* (Judgment 24 April 2012), para. 78 and *Chakroun* (n. 43), para. 43.

78 Case C-256/11 *Dereci and Others* [2011] ECR I-11315, para. 72. In *Åkerberg Fransson* (n. 41) this determination was also left to the national court while the ECJ confirmed that it falls with its own jurisdiction to interpret the meaning of the applicable Charter provisions (para. 36, cf. para. 29).

79 As both Dashwood and Weatherill have suggested, national action can fall within the scope of EU law in areas where EU institutions do not have competence to legislate. See Alan Dashwood, 'The Limits of European Community Powers' (1996) 21 E.L.

suggestions, here it may be possible to identify a varying degree of systemic restraint, depending on the link with EU competences, and further, depending on the existence and exercise of legislative competences enjoyed by the EU institutions. At this stage, however, only tentative suggestions can be made. While case law to date confirms that the ECJ will not consider the mere existence of legislative competences sufficient to bring matters within the scope of EU law,[80] the exercise of competences by EU institutions may affect the ECJ's scrutiny over Member State measures.[81]

On that construction, cases that concern the implementation of EU obligations, for example through implementation of regulations and directives, provide a stronger impetus for the ECJ to engage in a normative way with the situation in the Member States than in circumstances when the matter comes within the scope of EU law by virtue of negative harmonisation, thereby engaging both general principles and fundamental human rights protection.[82] As an example of the former, showing a strong link with the exercise of EU legislative competences, is the Court's decision in *Volker und Markus Schecke*, where the ECJ engaged normatively with the Charter provisions on the protection of privacy and data protection in interpreting a regulation.[83] In *DEB*, on the other hand, the matter was brought within the scope of EU law by the delayed implementation of a directive and possible liability of the Member State. Here the ECJ left the assessment of compatibility with Article 47 EUCFR of the national rules on legal aid to the national court, albeit with clear guidance as to the outcome.[84]

From case law decided to date, it seems also possible to suggest that where the EU has legislative competences relating to fundamental human rights which are separate from Charter provisions, and where the EU legislature has exercised those competences, the Court shows less systemic restraint than when legislative competences are weaker or where a Charter provision is invoked in isolation.[85] The Directives

Rev. 113 and Stephen Weatherill, 'From Economic Rights to Fundamental Rights', in Sybe de Vries, Ulf Bernitz and Stephen Weatherill (eds), *The Protection of Fundamental Rights in the EU After Lisbon* (Hart, 2013) 17. See also Sarmiento (n. 27) 1272–1287.

80 See for example C-309/96 *Annibaldi* [1997] ECR I-7493. That solution in itself would sit uncomfortably with subsidiarity as a general principle; see generally the suggestions of AG Sharpston in Case C-34/09 *Ruiz Zambrano* [2011] ECR I-1177, paras 163–171, and for the federalising effects of such a construction, paras 172–176. The ECJ has not extended its jurisdiction in this respect in subsequent case law.

81 See also Carozza (n. 1) 55.

82 See Prechal *et al.* (n. 72) 216–217.

83 Joined Cases C-92 and 93/09 *Volker und Markus Schecke* [2010] ECR I-11063. See section 3.3.

84 *DEB* (n. 74), paras 60 and 61. Assessment of access to justice and remedies pursuant to Article 47 EUCFR starts from a position of deference to national authorities under the principle of procedural autonomy of the Member States. The ECJ nevertheless adjusts the intensity of the review depending on the circumstances at hand. See further Koen Lenaerts, 'National Remedies for Private Parties in the Light of the EU Law Principles of Equivalence and Effectiveness' (2011) 46 *Irish Jurist* 13, 16.

85 See generally Muir (n. 22) 223–225.

enacted on the basis of Article 19 TFEU, prohibiting discrimination, are illustrative of this finding. In *Sabine Hennigs*, for example, the ECJ itself undertook the balancing between measures determining pay in collective agreements and the right not to be discriminated against on grounds of age under the Framework Directive on Equal Treatment.[86] The Court declared a broad discretion for the Member States and social partners in matters of social and employment policy and found that the rationale for the rules was legitimate in principle.[87] However, the ECJ applied strict scrutiny to strike down the measure, finding that 'the principle of non-discrimination on grounds of age proclaimed in Article 21 of the Charter and given specific expression in Directive 2000/78, and more particularly Articles 2 and 6(1) of that directive, must be interpreted as precluding a measure laid down by a collective agreement such as that at issue in the main proceedings'.[88] This approach may be contrasted to the Court's approach in cases such as *Dominguez* and *O'Brien* where the ECJ showed more systemic deference in relation to labour law issues engaging Article 31(1) and Article 20 EUCFR respectively.[89] The Charter provisions were not discussed by the ECJ in these cases.

If the above suggestions are correct, we can assume that a 'weaker' link with EU legislative competences leads to more systemic restraint by the ECJ and consequently more leeway for the national court to determine the issue. On this understanding the weakest connection may be found in the so-called derogation cases, where negative harmonisation restricts Member States' regulatory authority, but leaves discretion to implement EU obligations. Fundamental human rights issues may arise in connection with derogations from EU law obligations. Generally, the balancing of Member State *interference* with EU fundamental rights (and the Charter) has not been undertaken consistently by the ECJ in this context and opinion remains divided, both descriptively and normatively, as to the appropriateness of the ECJ's review of concrete fundamental human rights balancing by national authorities in these circumstances.[90] In 2006, Kombos suggested that a

86 Case C-297/10 *Sabine Hennigs* [2011] ECR I-7965, paras 77–78. Directive 2000/78/EC of 27 November 2000 establishing a general framework for equal treatment in employment and occupation [2000] OJ L 303/16.

87 *Sabine Hennigs* (n. 86) para. 65, cf. Article 6(1) of the Framework Directive on Equal Treatment.

88 Ibid. para. 78. See also Case C-88/08 *Hütter* [2009] ECR I-5325, para. 50; Case C-555/07 *Kücükdeveci* [2010] ECR I-365, paras 39–40; Case C-341/08 *Petersen* [2010] ECR I-47, paras 61–62; and Case C-45/09 *Gisela Rosenbladt* [2010] ECR I-9391, para. 51.

89 Case C-282/10 *Dominguez* (Judgment 24 January 2012); Case C-393/10 *O'Brien* v. *Ministry of Justice* (Judgment 1 March 2012).

90 See generally the literature referred to above (n. 11) and, as to the appropriateness of review of human rights issues in the national context, see in particular the extra-judicial opinion of Advocate General Francis Jacobs in Francis G. Jacobs, 'Human Rights in the European Union: The Role of the Court of Justice' (2001) 26 E.L. Rev. 331. Jacobs suggested that fundamental human rights balancing within the Member States was a separate issue from balancing under the fundamental freedoms. See also Koen Lenaerts, 'Exploring the Limits of the EU Charter of Fundamental Rights' (2012) 8 EuConst 375, 383; Armin von Bogdandy *et al.*, 'Reverse Solange – Protecting the

distinction could be drawn between situations where fundamental human rights coexist with the fundamental freedoms without posing a direct conflict, such as in the *ERT* – situation,[91] and situations where fundamental rights have the potential to restrict fundamental freedoms, such as in *Schmidberger* and *Omega*.[92] He argued that the ECJ leaves less systemic deference to the national court in the latter situation than in the former.[93] In derogation cases, where the issue seems better suited for the national court to determine, recent case law indicates such systemic deference – see *Pfleger* – where the ECJ left it to the national court to balance overriding reasons in the public interest against the freedom to provide services in Article 56 TFEU and concluded that the same balancing (undertaken by the national court) was applicable in respect of Articles 15 and 17 EUCFR pursuant to Article 51(2) EUCFR.[94]

Finally, when competing individual interests have to be balanced against each other, such as typically occurs in respect of intellectual property rights, protected in Article 17(2) EUCFR and other rights, such as the right to conduct a business, protected under Article 16 EUCFR, or data protection, protected under Article 8 EUCFR, the Court has left the concrete balancing to the national court. The ECJ has furthermore stressed that the Member States must, when transposing directives in these fields, 'take care to rely on an interpretation of the directives which allows a fair balance to be struck between the various fundamental rights protected by the Community legal order'.[95]

3.3 Normative elements of restraint

In its normative conception, the margin of appreciation doctrine at the ECtHR is used as an aid to the *interpretation* of Convention norms, and/or their *application* to the facts of the case, and functions as the logical counterpart to the Court's

Essence of Fundamental Rights against EU Member States' (2012) 49 CML Rev 489, 494–497.

91 Case C-260/89 *Elliniki Radiophonia Tiléorassi* [1991] ECR I-2925 (*ERT*).

92 Case C-112/00 *Schmidberger* [2003] ECR I-5659; Case C-36/02 *Omega Spielhallen* [2004] ECR I-9609.

93 Costas Kombos, 'Fundamental Rights and Fundamental Freedoms: A Symbiosis on the Basis of Subsidiarity' (2006) 12 EPL 433. *Schmidberger* and *Omega* (n. 92) arguably show less systemic deference than other cases of similar nature. Case C-438/05 *International Transport Workers' Federation* v. *Viking Line* [2007] ECR I-10779 shows systemic deference which may be explained by the national court being better placed to assess the concrete legal question on the relationship between the contested actions and the protection of workers in the concrete circumstances (paras 81–84). Conversely, Case C-341/05 *Laval un Partneri Ltd* v. *Svenska Byggnadsarbetareförbundet* [2007] ECR I-11767 may be read as showing less systemic deference, because of the EU's exercise of legislative competence relating to the protection of posted workers (paras 107–110).

94 *Pfleger* (n. 28), paras 47–52 and para. 60.

95 See C-275/06 *Productores de Musica de Espana (Promusicae) ve Telefonica de Espana* [2008] ECR I-271, para. 68. See also for example Case C-70/10 *Scarlet Extended SA* v. *SABAM* [2011] ECR I-11959.

interpretative approaches.[96] Whether in the abstract terms of interpretation or the concrete terms of balancing and application, this kind of margin (hereinafter 'the normative margin of appreciation') is always linked to the determination of the content and outer limits of a Convention right. A wide normative margin, therefore, has the effect that the right in question allows states a wide range of options as to how they manage their affairs without violating that right. If it is narrow, the outer limits of the right in question are more restrictive and the scope for manoeuvre correspondingly more limited. In this conception, the margin of appreciation, therefore, has a clear ***normative role*** to play by governing ***how*** the Court performs its review, once it finds itself within the scope of review delimited by systemic elements. In terms of distinguishing between the normative and systemic margins, the key criterion is that the normative margin relates to situations where the Court performs its own substantive assessment on the merits of a case and does not defer it as such to the national level, while the standard against which the assessment is made may be either strict or lenient depending on the width of the margin.

When the ECtHR refers to the margin of appreciation in its judgments, it usually does not defer completely to the national level but engages normatively with the substance or merits of the case.[97] The normative function of the margin of appreciation has, therefore, generally been in focus in the literature. The normative margin has a distinct role to play in relation to proportionality assessments,[98] but it is also used in the context of defining the scope of protected rights in more abstract terms,[99] including when questions arise with respect to the existence of positive obligations.[100] As already mentioned, the ECtHR's jurisdiction under Article 32 ECHR extends to 'all matters concerning the ***interpretation and application*** of the Convention' (emphasis added). The default position, therefore, is full review and the Court relies on the normative margin as a tool for calibrating intensity with respect to both jurisdictional elements. However, as already explained in section 3.2, under the new systemic margin for competing private interests the Court may defer application and the actual balancing

96 Mahoney (n. 1).

97 A study of judgments (January 2006–March 2015, reported cases and importance level 1 on HUDOC), where a 'margin of appreciation' is expressly referred to, exhibits that in an overwhelming majority of cases, the margin of appreciation is used in its normative conception linked to the interpretation and application of rights as described in this section. Even where systemic elements of restraint are relied upon, in most cases the Court proceeds nevertheless to own normative assessments, exhibiting only partial deference.

98 For example *Maslov* v. *Austria* ECHR 2008; *Evans* v. *United Kingdom* ECHR 2007-I. See also Kratochvíl (n. 3) 329 and Greer (n. 2) 22.

99 For example *Hatton* v. *United Kingdom* ECHR 2003-VIII, paras 97–103; *Hirst* v. *United Kingdom* ECHR 2005-IX, para. 60. See also Greer (n. 2). The dividing line between the use of the margin of appreciation in relation to concrete balancing under proportionality or in relation to abstract interpretation is not clear-cut, see Kratochvíl (n. 3) 331.

100 For example *Botta* v. *Italy* ECHR 1998-I, para. 33; *Schalk and Kopf* ECHR 2010, para. 105; *Beganovć* v. *Croatia* App. No. 46423/069 (ECtHR, 26 June 2009), para. 80.

of interests under the principle of proportionality to the national courts and limit its review to checking whether they have faithfully applied Convention standards.

Given, first, the formal boundaries between the EU and Member States in interpreting fundamental human rights norms, as reflected in Article 51(1) and 53 EUCFR and, second, the importance of systemic restraint in the exercise of shared jurisdiction, the default position is different before the ECJ. In addition, the scope of review undertaken by the ECJ through the preliminary rulings proceedings under Article 267 TFEU is restricted to interpretation and leaves the task of actual application of fundamental rights norms to the national courts. When assessing Member State action, a normative margin, whether wide or narrow, will in principle only relate to the interpretation of rights. One would therefore assume that the ECJ never presented the referring court with a complete solution to the problematic issue and that all interpretation were performed behind a protective layer of a limited jurisdiction (scope of review), comparable to the decisive reliance on the systemic margin under the ECHR described in section 3.2 above. However, as Tridimas has shown, 'outcome' cases give the national court such a specific answer to a dispute, that it is possible to equate those cases with the more common full substantive review at the ECtHR.[101]

If we situate ourselves within the interpretative dialogue between the ECJ and the national courts, a resonance of the ECHR normative margin of appreciation is discernible. Within these parameters, there are instances where the ECJ performs its own assessment of potential infringements of fundamental human rights in the national context. The Court calibrates the intensity of its review within this interpretation and is therefore in the same way engaged with the determination of the outer limits of the rights protected in the EU legal order through interpretation, including balancing under Article 52(1) EUCFR.

A number of qualifications must nevertheless be considered. First, the ECJ is competent also to consider questions of validity of EU secondary law in preliminary rulings proceedings (Article 267(1)(b) TFEU). When examining the validity of secondary legislation, the ECJ tends to be more assertive than when it examines implementation by the Member States. Here, the question is whether secondary law is in breach of a Charter provision and the ECJ exercises full review.[102] When the validity of secondary legislation is challenged on fundamental human rights grounds, regardless of whether it is in preliminary rulings proceedings or direct action cases under Article 263 TFEU, the ECJ's case law falls on a scale from a wide to a narrow normative margin. In *Volker und Markus Schecke*, for example, a narrow margin seems to have been applied and equally so in

101 Tridimas (n. 36) 739. It is however important for reasons of legitimacy that the final decision is that of the national court, see Anthony Arnull, *The European Union and Its Court of Justice* (Oxford University Press, 2006) 95–96.

102 See for example *Volker und Markus Schecke* (n. 83).

Test-Achats and *Digital Rights Ireland*.[103] Sometimes an intermediate margin may be identified,[104] and in yet other policy areas, a wide margin.[105]

In cases brought before the ECJ under Article 263 TFEU, the Court's assessment does not directly concern the actions or discretion of the Member States. It nevertheless provides a basis for the guidance given to them, and hence for the (subsequent) concrete assessment by the national courts. The ECJ tends to refer to the case law of the ECtHR in its assessment, including also the criteria used by the ECtHR in balancing of competing interests and the margin of appreciation granted as seen for example in *European Parliament* v. *Council*.[106]

The second qualification flows from the specificities of positive harmonisation. The EU institutions balance rights and legitimate Member State interests, as well as conflicting rights, when enacting secondary legislation.[107] Where the ECJ engages normatively with the implementation of regulations and directives in the national context, it takes into account the aim and scope of the harmonised rules, in addition to interpreting the provisions in light of Charter rights. The normative margin accorded to Member States by the ECJ may be wide or narrow, but the assessment and the scope of the margin is invariably also affected by the terms of the secondary legislation (the 'margin for the margin').

Case law relating to the protection of property rights, now expressed in Article 17(1) EUCFR, provides examples of a wide normative margin for both EU institutions and Member States, acting as agents of the EU. A wide margin is reflected in the

103 Case C-236/09 *Test-Achats ASBL and Others* [2011] ECR I-773, para. 32 (maintaining sex as a factor in determining insurance premiums found incompatible with Articles 20 and 21 EUCFR on equal treatment, and therefore invalid); Case C-293/12 *Digital Rights Ireland* (Judgment 8 April 2014), para. 69 (EU institutions found to have exceeded their discretion under Articles 7, 8 and 52(1) EUCFR when enacting Directive 2006/24/EC of 15 March 2006 on the retention of data generated or processed in connection with the provision of publicly available electronic communications services or of public communications networks and amending Directive 2002/58/EC [2006] OJ L 105/54).

104 For example Case C-283/11 *Sky Österreich GmbH* (Judgment 22 January 2013) (a relatively broad margin for the institutions to determine appropriate restrictions on the right to property under Article 17 EUCFR and the freedom to conduct business under Article 16 EUCFR, which had to be balanced against the freedom of expression under Article 11 EUCFR).

105 For example Case C-195/12 *Industrie du bois de Vjelsam & Cie* (Judgment 26 September 2013) (a wide margin to determine appropriate energy production factors with reference to Articles 20 and 21 EUCFR on equal treatment).

106 Case C-540/03 *European Parliament* v. *Council* [2006] ECR I-576. The Directive's provision concerning integration requirements for children over 12 years old were challenged. The ECJ found that the limited margin granted to the Member States in the Directive was in conformity with ECHR standards, and that the relevant provision of the Directive should consequently not be annulled.

107 See further Clemens Ladenburger, 'European Union Institutional Report', in Julia Laffranque (ed.), *The Protection of Fundamental Rights Post-Lisbon: The Interaction between the Charter of Fundamental Rights of the European Union, the European Convention on Human Rights and National Constitutions* (Reports of the XXC FIDE Congress Tallinn, 2012) 192–200.

ECJ's formulation in pre-Charter case law in the following way: restrictions on the exercise of property rights must pursue objectives of general interest and not constitute 'a disproportionate and intolerable interference impairing the very substance of [the] rights'.[108] Harmonisation may, however, narrow the normative margin, such as where German rules on protection of business secrets were found incompatible with harmonised rules on environmental protection. The harmonised rules required the disclosure of the name of the waste producer, thereby narrowing the normative margin accorded to the national authorities.[109] Protection of intellectual property rights, in Article 17(2) EUCFR is, as mentioned above, frequently approached under systemic restraint, where the ECJ leaves it to the national authorities to find a fair balance between conflicting interests, within the margin left to them in the respective Directives.[110] However, the ECJ increasingly engages in a normative assessment in its guidance to the national court and does then vary the intensity of its review depending on the legal and factual circumstances.[111]

Protection of personal data in Article 8 EUCFR is another area characterised by detailed positive harmonisation and legislative balancing of conflicting rights, subject to which the national courts assess the fair balance in the concrete case. Respect for private life, protected in Article 7 EUCFR as distinct from protection of personal data, seems also to fall within the category of cases showing prima facie systemic restraint. The EU has limited competences in matters relating to privacy, resulting in actions of the Member States being brought within the scope of EU law as derogations from the fundamental freedoms. Case law relating to regulation of names, where the matter falls within the scope of EU law by virtue of Article 21 TFEU, shows however the ECJ's normative engagement, establishing an intermediary to a wide normative margin.[112] In *Grunkin-Paul*, for example, German authorities did not recognise the name given to a child in Denmark. The ECJ

108 Joined Cases C-20/00 and 64/00 *Booker Aquacultur Ltd* [2003] ECR I-7411, paras 68 and 92 and Case C-154/04 *Alliance for Natural Health* [2005] ECR I-6451, para. 126. Balancing conflicting interests, also qualifying as fundamental rights, such as protection of human health, may provide additional grounds for a wide margin – see *Alliance for Natural Health* (para. 129), and in respect of the right to conduct a business (Articles 15 and 16 EUCFR), Case C-544/10 *Deutsches Weintor eG* (Judgment 6 September 2012).

109 Case C-1/11 *Interseroh Scrap and Metal Trading GmbH* (Judgment 29 March 2012).

110 See text to (n. 97).

111 For example Case C-70/10 *Scarlet Extended SA* v. *SABAM* [2011] ECR I-11959, where the ECJ found that a fair balance had not been struck between intellectual property rights and the right to conduct a business, and Case C-314/12 *UPC Telekabel Wien GmbH* (Judgment 27 March 2014) where the Court considered national rules on injunctions and found that it did not seem that in the circumstances the injunction infringed the very substance of the freedom of an internet service provider to conduct a business.

112 Article 21 TFEU guarantees Union citizens the right of free movement and residence within the territory of the Union, subject to limitations and conditions set out in the treaties.

found a disproportionate interference with the right of free movement in Article 21 TFEU, interpreted in light of the Charter, but indicated a wider margin in respect of public policy considerations, had such considerations been brought up as a justification for infringement of the right to privacy.[113] In *Runevič-Vardyn* and *Sayn Wittgenstein*, the ECJ, within an approach characterised mainly by systemic restraint, acknowledged a wide normative margin to the Member State to place restrictions on names on the grounds of public policy considerations; the protection of the national language and prohibition of using noble titles in names, respectively.[114]

The right to respect for family life, now protected by Article 7 EUCFR, has historically been subject to a narrow margin for the national authorities in the indirect judicial review performed by the ECJ. Since *Carpenter*, where the ECJ famously established that when applying national immigration law in the context of the freedom to provide services, the UK authorities had not achieved a fair balance between the right to respect of family life and the maintenance of public order and public safety, the ECJ has consistently applied heightened scrutiny when family life is at issue as well as when the interests of children are at stake.[115]

Similar considerations seem generally to be at play in the EU context in these cases as under the ECtHR, when it comes to defining the width of the margin, or the intensity of judicial scrutiny, where important national interest relating to public policy and public security may lead to a wide normative margin for the national authorities.[116] Important individual interests may, however, provide countervailing considerations.[117] These considerations, and the balance sought by the EU institutions and Member States, have been codified in secondary law,

113 Case C-353/06 *Grunkin-Paul* [2008] ECR I-7639, para. 38. Advocate General (Sharpston) recognised the necessity for deference in para. 41 of her Opinion: 'This is clearly an area in which it behoves the court to tread softly, and with care. But just because it must tread softly, that does not mean that it must fear to tread at all.'

114 Case C-391/09 *Runevič-Vardyn and Wardyn* [2011] ECR I-3787 (protection of official language); Case C-208/09 *Sayn-Wittgenstein* v. *Landeshauptmann von Mann* [2010] ECR I-13693 (constitutional identity).

115 Case C-60/00 *Mary Carpenter* v. *Secretary of State for the Home Department* [2002] ECR I-6249, para. 43. See also for example Case C-200/02 *Zhu and Chen* v. *Secretary of State for the Home Department* [2004] ECR I-9925, paras 33 and 45 on financial conditions for the right of residence and the residence right of the child's parent respectively and Case C-127/08 *Metock and Others* [2008] ECR I-6241 (paras 70–74) on the entry of family members being determined by EU law, as interpreted by the ECJ, with only a residual margin applicable in individual cases.

116 *Tsakouridis* (n. 37) (wide margin in relation to determining when criminal activity (drug dealing) constitutes a threat to the fundamental interests of society, justifying a restriction on free movement and residence); Case C-348/09 *PI* (Judgment 22 May 2012) (wide margin in relation to restrictions on free movement and residence due to committing a heinous crime).

117 See the ECJ's guidance to the national court in both *Tsakouridis* (n. 37) para. 53 and *PI* (n. 116) para. 32. See also Case C-249/11 *Byankov* (Judgment 4 October 2012), para. 47.

currently Directive 2004/38/EC.[118] Heightened scrutiny in cases relating to the protection of family life often goes hand in hand with the strengthening of the status of Union citizenship.[119] That is not always the case, however.[120] Recent case law on the interpretation of the Family Reunification Directive also shows the ECJ leaving a narrow normative margin to the national authorities when interpreting the Directive in light of Article 7 EUCFR.[121] Again, the Directive itself, as interpreted by the ECJ, confines the margin left to the Member States.

Finally, cases relating to the right to asylum in Article 18 EUCFR provide examples of systemic and normative restraint alike. While the ECJ has determined broadly the 'scope of EU law' and consequently examined issues relating to Member States' decisions relating to applications for asylum under the Charter,[122] the ECJ nevertheless respects the boundaries set by the relevant harmonisation measures. With the exception of cases relating to reception conditions for asylum seekers, where substantive guidance and a narrow normative margin may be identified,[123] most cases concern the division of responsibility between Member States under the Dublin II Regulation.[124] Here the Court refers to the Member States' obligations to exercise their discretion with due respect for the objectives and effectiveness of the Common European Asylum System, only engaging with a normative assessment under the Charter if and when particular core rights are at issue in that context.[125]

118 Directive 2004/38/EC of 29 April 2004 on the right of citizens of the Union and their family members to move and reside freely within the territory of the Member States [2004] OJ L 158/77 (Citizens' Rights Directive).

119 Such as in *Carpenter* (n. 115) where, as commentators have pointed out, EU law guaranteed better rights than could have been established under ECHR in a comparable case, see Helen Toner, *Partnership Rights, Free Movement and EU Law* (Hart Publishing, 2004) 158–161.

120 See for example Case C-451/11 *Dülger* (Judgment 19 July 2012), paras 52–53. In *Dülger*, a third-country national spouse of a Turkish national was refused residence in Germany. The ECJ found that limitation of 'family members' to Turkish nationals would undermine the objective of the provision of Decision 1/80 and would be contrary to the right to respect for private and family life under Article 7 EUCFR.

121 See for example *O and S* v. *Maahanmuuttovirasto* (n. 37) and *Chakroun* (n. 43).

122 Case C-411/10 *NS* [2011] ECR I-13905, para. 69.

123 Joined Cases C-199–201/12 *X, Y and Z* (Judgment 7 November 2013) (sexual orientation and fear of persecution); Joined Cases C-71 and 91/11 *Germany* v. *Y and Z* (Judgment 5 September 2012) (freedom of religion and fear of persecution) and Case C-465/07 *Elgafaji* [2009] ECR I-921 (individual threat in situations of armed conflict). The ECJ interpreted the provisions of Directive 2004/83/EC (on the minimum standards for the qualification and status of third-country nationals or stateless persons as refugees [2004] OJ L 304/12) in light of the Charter; however, provisions of the Directive set out in detail the obligations of the Member States in these cases.

124 Regulation (EC) No. 343/2003 establishing the criteria and mechanisms for determining the Member State responsible for examining an asylum application lodged in one of the Member States by a third-country national [2003] OJ L50/1.

125 See for example Case C-245/11 *K* v. *Bundesasylamt* (Judgment 6 November 2012) (family life) and Case C-648/11 *MA and Others* v. *Secretary of State for the Home Department* (Judgment 6 June 2013) (unaccompanied minors).

3.4 Overlap between systemic and normative elements of restraint

The dividing line between the two forms of judicial restraint is by no means clear-cut and the widest normative margins indicating lenient review may in fact be hard to distinguish from the systemic margin where the relevant court defers altogether on certain elements of assessment. This is particularly so in the ECHR context. Sometimes, of course, it is clear that the relevant court relies on systemic rationales to exclude certain issues from the scope of its review, while proceeding to applying the normative margin to those elements that still remain within that scope. But the fact that both courts may in certain circumstances cross the jurisdictional boundaries otherwise dictated by systemic elements complicates the picture. Thus, the ECtHR generally retains the power to abandon judicial restraint and perform its own assessments if 'manifest deficiencies' present themselves in the conduct of the national (or EU) authorities otherwise deferred to.[126] And in order to give a 'useful answer', the ECJ may for its part reformulate the questions or legal context posited by the referring court.[127]

It is also possible that the use of judicial restraint ranges from the systemic to the normative in respect of the same or similar issues, notably in cases where the division into interpretation of norms and their concrete application is at issue. This results in a picture of different shades of grey as opposed to bright-line contrasts.[128] In cases involving competing individual interests under the ECHR, it is of course quite possible that calibration of the scope of review under the systemic margin renders the outcome that there is in fact a 'strong reason' to substitute the Court's full review (interpretation *and* application/balancing) for that of the national courts.[129] But the Court otherwise also often seems to couple deference to national courts with some normative commentary of its own, thus combining deference and own assessments.[130] In such instances, the invocation of the systemic rationale nevertheless creates a protective layer indicating a relatively large scope for manoeuvre before any Strasbourg reassessment takes place.

126 The aptly descriptive phrase 'manifest deficiencies' is taken from *Bosphorus Airways* v. *Ireland* (n. 63), para. 156, but applies across the board in cases involving the systemic margin of appreciation.

127 For example *Tsakouridis* (n. 37), para. 26.

128 *Animal Defenders* v. *United Kingdom* ECHR 2013, is a case in point from the ECHR context. While attaching 'considerable weight to [the] exacting and pertinent reviews, by both parliamentary and judicial bodies, of the complex regulatory regime governing political broadcasting in the United Kingdom' (para. 116), the Court also performed a detailed own review of the measure in question (paras 117–124). It is, thus, difficult to distinguish whether the systemic or the normative margin carried the day. Dissenting, Judges Ziemele, Sajó, Kalaydjieva, Vučinić and de Gaetano opined that the Court did not perform 'full analysis' and left too wide a margin to the state. In the EU context see, *Familiapress* (n. 36) and the 'outcome' cases discussed by Eeckhout (n. 9).

129 For example *Fáber* v. *Hungary* (n. 70).

130 For example *Axel Springer AG* v. *Germany* (n. 69); compare paras 98–100 and 101; *Verlagsgruppe News GMBH and Bobi* v. *Austria* App. No. 59631/09 (ECtHR, 4 December 2012), compare paras 82, 83 and 86.

Similarly, as we have seen, the ECJ frequently crosses the lines between 'guidance' and 'outcome' and even abandons the systemic deference implied by the preliminary reference procedure to give interpretative guidance that extends to the national courts' final assessments relating to fact and the application of law. In *DEB* the ECJ left the concrete assessment to the national court, relying in that sense on systemic restraint, but in its engagement with the scope of Article 47 EUCFR, the Court drew on criteria established under ECtHR case law on Article 6 ECHR, guiding the national court in its balancing under proportionality.[131] Case law on Article 7 EUCFR shows the same tendency, in particular where Union citizenship is at stake,[132] as does case law relating to intellectual property rights under Article 17(2) EUCFR. The demarcation between the systemic and normative is not always clear under the Framework Directive on Equal Treatment, where the ECJ has sometimes relied on systemic deference,[133] but sometimes engaged normatively with the balancing of interest.[134] In cases on the right to asylum, the competence is explicitly left with the Member States to grant asylum on humanitarian or other discretionary grounds, but in certain cases the ECJ may step in to enforce a particular Charter right within that context.[135]

In sum, it is clear that the two types of judicial restraint may overlap to varying degrees in both systems. The difference between the two is, nevertheless, important as the two approaches have different implications in terms of the extent to which the relevant court engages normatively with setting out the parameters of 'European rights'. In the final analysis, an overall assessment of the court's reasoning and the outcome of the judgment will be required to ascertain which of the two approaches (normative engagement or systemic deference), or which kinds of combinations between them, were applied and to which parts of the case as a whole.

4 Conclusions

The jurisdiction of the two courts vis-à-vis the national authorities, and their scope of review of national law are prima facie different. Systemic elements relating to the composite EU legal order, most notably the preliminary rulings proceedings, create a protective layer, which formally restricts judicial intervention by the ECJ when it comes to the implementation and application of EU law, including Charter provisions, in the national context. In contrast, the ECtHR's jurisdiction reaches all matters concerning the interpretation *and* application of Convention norms (Article 32 ECHR). This will generate different presentation of core

131 *DEB* (n. 74) para. 61.

132 As to the ECJ detecting arbitrariness or inconsistency in the national context, see in particular *Grunkin-Paul* (n. 113), para. 37 and *Runevič-Vardyn* (n. 114), para. 92.

133 See in particular Case C-411/05 *Palacios de la Villa* [2007] ECR I-8531, paras 71–72 (for the competent authorities to find the right balance) and Case C-341/08 *Petersen* [2010] ECR I-47, para. 64. See also Case C-476/11 *HK Denmark* (Judgment 26 September 2013), paras 64–65.

134 *Sabine Hennigs* (n. 86) and (n. 88).

135 See text to (n. 126).

systemic issues and possibly also diverging case law. At the same time, however, both courts recognise that the establishment of facts and the interpretation of national law are in principle within the mandate of the national courts. Importantly also, both courts exercise a certain control over defining their jurisdiction and the use it has been put to exhibits clear tendencies towards a closer resemblance between the two systems. The ECJ has, thus, in some instances adopted approaches that resemble the ECtHR's full jurisdiction under Article 32 ECHR and the ECtHR has sometimes opted for a self-imposed systemic restraint resembling the interpretative dialogue of the preliminary rulings proceedings under Article 267 TFEU.[136]

When it comes to normative elements of restraint, relating to the content and outer limits of rights within the substantive jurisdiction of each court, similarities are even more pronounced, subject to the specific characteristics of the composite legal order of the EU and the scope and nature of positive harmonisation. In light of how the two systems are to a certain extent normatively integrated, with ECHR provisions explicitly mentioned as normatively relevant for the interpretation of Charter rights in Article 52(3) EUCFR, it seems quite possible that the case law might develop towards a clearer common language for when and how a margin of appreciation or judicial restraint in the normative sense is appropriate and for how to calibrate its width in light of various influencing factors.

For a clearer understanding of the dynamics of human rights adjudication across Europe, it is important to distinguish between systemic and normative elements influencing the intensity of judicial intervention. As has been shown, there are different underlying rationales and different consequences in practice. In the 'limited and shared' jurisdiction emerging in the integrated system of fundamental human rights protection in Europe, it will become increasingly important that the courts are able to explain the reasons behind any dissimilarity in their case law. While we have identified commonalities in approaches and trends towards increased affinity between systems, we do not at this point make any normative claims as to how approaches to judicial restraint should evolve in each system. What we do claim, however, is that the development of a common language is an important step in order to navigate the similarities *and* differences between the systems. It would be helpful, therefore, if both courts developed a clearer approach to the calibration of the scope and intensity of judicial intervention, while making the difference between systemic and normative elements of restraint more explicit in their reasoning.

136 Further exhibiting the trend towards closer resemblance between systems, Protocol 16 to the ECHR will also, once it takes effect, construct an advisory opinion procedure under the Convention where the jurisdiction of the Court will be expressly confined to interpretative dialogue, see Protocol No. 16 to the Convention on the Protection of Human Rights and Fundamental Freedoms (adopted 2 October 2013) CETS No. 214.

11 Squaring the circle at the battle at Brighton: is the war between protecting human rights or respecting sovereignty over, or has it just begun?*

Andreas Follesdal

1 Introduction

How should the European Court of Human Rights best 'balance' respect for 'the sovereignty of Contracting Parties with their obligations under the Convention [on Human Rights]'?[1] Long simmering conflicts about this aspect of the European Court of Human Rights (ECtHR, the Court) came to a boil prior to the 2012 high-level conference at Brighton. The result at Brighton was an innocuous-looking addition to the Preamble of the European Convention on Human Rights (ECHR), now expressed in Protocol 15 to the Convention:

> [T]he High Contracting Parties, *in accordance with the principle of subsidiarity*, have the primary responsibility to secure the rights and freedoms defined in this Convention and the Protocols thereto, and … *in doing so they enjoy a margin of appreciation*, subject to the supervisory jurisdiction of the European Court of Human Rights established by this Convention.[2]

Will these references to subsidiarity guide the Court's attempt to respect both the Treaty and its sovereign creators by granting the latter a certain scope of discretion – a margin of appreciation (the margin) which differs from its current practice?

Some parties, including the UK government, appealed to subsidiarity in order to secure broad discretion for states' domestic human rights review in the form of a wide

* This chapter was written under the auspices of ERC Advanced Grant 269841 MultiRights – on the Legitimacy of Multi-Level Human Rights Judiciary; and partly supported by the Research Council of Norway through its Centres of Excellence Funding Scheme, project number 223274 – PluriCourts – The Legitimacy of the International Judiciary. I am particularly grateful to Oddný Mjöll Arnardóttir and Antoine Buyse for extensive helpful comments including several references to relevant cases. A previous version was presented at the conference Shifting Centres of Gravity in European Human Rights Protection, Reykjavik, 6–7 March 2014.

1 Ronald St. J. Macdonald, 'The Margin of Appreciation', in Ronald St. J. Macdonald and F. Matcher (eds), *The European System for the Protection of Human Rights* (Springer, 1993) 123.

2 Protocol No. 15 amending the Convention for the Protection of Human Rights and Fundamental Freedoms (adopted 24 June 2013) CETS No. 213 (my emphasis).

margin of appreciation. By other, arguably better justified conceptions of subsidiarity, the Court should grant a narrower, more circumscribed margin. To give a sense of the conflict, consider the UK government's draft proposal for the Brighton meeting which outlined implications of what I shall term a 'state-centric' conception of subsidiarity:

> Each State Party enjoys a *considerable* margin of appreciation in how it applies and implements the Convention. This reflects that *national authorities are in principle best placed to apply the Convention rights in the national context.* The margin of appreciation implies, among other things, that it is the responsibility of democratically-elected national parliaments to decide how to implement the Convention in reasoned judgments. The role of the Court is to review decisions taken by national authorities *to ensure that they are within the margin of appreciation.*[3]

The Brighton negotiations yielded a declaration with small yet crucial differences. The margin only applies to a limited set of apparent rights violations, and the Court remains authorised to review states' assessments. The parties agreed that:

> The jurisprudence of the Court makes clear that the States Parties enjoy a margin of appreciation in how they apply and implement the Convention, depending on the circumstances of the case and *the rights and freedoms engaged.* This reflects that the Convention system is subsidiary to the safeguarding of human rights at national level and that national authorities are in principle better placed than an international court *to evaluate local needs and conditions.* The margin of appreciation goes hand in hand with supervision under the Convention system. In this respect, the role of the Court is to review whether decisions taken by national authorities are compatible with the Convention, having *due regard* to the State's margin of appreciation.[4]

In the literature, 'subsidiarity' appears to be used in different ways to support divergent implications for how powers should be allocated and used between states and the Court. Thus general appeals to 'subsidiarity' will neither settle the balancing between sovereignty and human rights protection, nor provide much guidance to the Court's attempts in the cases brought before it. Instead of resolving these issues, we should expect that Protocol 15 will fuel more attention to the Court's interpretation of subsidiarity. Indeed, we may hope that the Court draws on a well-reasoned conception of subsidiarity to further develop the margin of appreciation doctrine (the doctrine). Thus the battle at Brighton may be over, but

3 UK Government, 'Draft Brighton declaration on the future of the European Court of Human Rights – second version' <http://adam1cor.files.wordpress.com/2012/02/2012dd220e.pdf> accessed 6 August 2015, 17 (my emphasis).

4 High Level Conference on the Future of the European Court of Human Rights Brighton Declaration, 19–20 April 2012, <www.echr.coe.int/Documents/2012_Brighton_FinalDeclaration_ENG.pdf> accessed 5 November 2014, para. 11 (my emphasis).

the work has barely begun. The present chapter defends this analysis and points to parts of the future agenda for the Court in its jurisprudence – and parts of the research agenda for those who study the Court.

Different conceptions of subsidiarity have in common that the burden of argument rests with those who seek to move decisions away from the fundamental units towards more centralised bodies. This chapter partly explores what version of subsidiarity should be brought to bear, since some such versions themselves rest on normative premises that are difficult to defend. I shall suggest that the Brighton Declaration's account of the role of the Court fits better with a 'person-centred' conception of subsidiarity, and that it is such a conception that should be brought to bear when the Court continues to elaborate and specify its margin of appreciation doctrine. Such a defensible principle of subsidiarity can alleviate the fears that human rights protection is at serious risk by a more developed doctrine by the Court – while expressing due deference to legitimate domestic decisions – or so I shall argue. In contrast, such fears may hold against a state-centric conception of subsidiarity.

I then address some contested and salient aspects of the doctrine, in particular the proportionality test and the narrowed margin of appreciation when the ECtHR identifies an 'emerging European consensus'.

Section 2 lays out some relevant features of the margin of appreciation doctrine. Section 3 reports popular criticism of the present doctrine, focusing on the fear that human rights protection suffers from it. Section 4 presents a modest defence of the current practice by indicating that some objections miss their target. Section 5 presents competing principles of subsidiarity more fully, which in section 6 are applied to the doctrine to suggest areas to be maintained, changed or specified. Section 7 concludes by considering whether the changes to the Preamble and the person-centred conception of subsidiarity will help alleviate the criticisms.

2 The margin of appreciation doctrine

The so-called margin of appreciation doctrine of the ECtHR grants a state the authority, within certain limits, and on certain conditions, to determine in a particular case whether the rights of the ECHR are violated. Hitherto the doctrine is not found in the Convention text proper, but is a long-standing practice of the Court. The doctrine is claimed by the Court to be appropriate for at least three main issue areas:

- 'Balancing' private human rights against public interests such as emergencies, public safety, the economic well-being of the country, etc. – as permitted for several rights (Article 8 on private life, Article 9 on religion, Article 10 on free expression, Article 11 on peaceful assembly). Indeed, many trace the doctrine back to the 1958 *Cyprus* case where the (then) Commission asserted that the UK authorities could enjoy a certain measure of discretion to assess the extent to which derogation from the Convention under Article 15 was strictly required by the exigencies of the situation – which in this case was a state of public emergency.[5]

5 *Greece* v. *United Kingdom* App. No. 176/56 (1958–9) Y.B. Eur. Conv. on H.R. 182.

- 'Balancing' or 'trade-offs' among different private human rights in the Convention – such as between freedom of expression (Article 10) and privacy (Article 8) – including conflicts between private interests in the same right.[6]
- How to apply the European norms to the specific circumstances of a state, which may depend on shared values and traditions within the state in question, or perceived threats to it.

These three may overlap, e.g. when the Court must balance several private human rights and public interests.[7]

One element of the current doctrine is that in order to grant a margin of appreciation, the Court often requires that the accused state has undertaken a 'proportionality test'. The state must have made a good faith check to ascertain whether the rights violation could have been avoided by other policies in pursuit of the same social objectives.

3 Criticism of the present margin of appreciation doctrine

The doctrine has received much praise and much criticism, some of both are well deserved. On the one hand, it expresses some respect for sovereign democratic self-government – within some limits. But a key objection to the current doctrine is that it is too vague: it is hardly a 'doctrine' in the sense of a principle or position that forms part of a legal system. There are at least three kinds of concern.

Firstly, the doctrine creates legal uncertainty, because states are unable to predict and hence cannot avoid violations of the ECHR.[8] Indeed, even the judges of the Court disagree about the doctrine to such an extent that legal certainty seems at risk. To some extent the uncertainty is due to the legal norms, rather than the doctrine itself. Consider Article 10, which protects freedom of expression – but

> subject to such formalities, conditions, restrictions or penalties as are prescribed by law and are necessary in a democratic society, in the interests of national security, territorial integrity or public safety, for the prevention of disorder or crime, for the protection of health or morals, for the protection of the reputation or rights of others, for preventing the disclosure of information

6 *Godelli* v. *Italy* App. No. 33783/09 (ECtHR, 25 September 2012), para. 53.

7 *Evans* v. *United Kingdom* ECHR 2007-I, para. 74.

8 Anthony Lester, 'The European Court of Human Rights after 50 Years' (2009) 4 *European Human Rights Law Review* 461; cf. Jeffrey A. Brauch, 'The Margin of Appreciation and the Jurisprudence of the European Court of Human Rights: Threat to the Rule of Law' (2004) 11 *Columbia Journal of European Law* 113, 125; Patrick Macklem, 'Militant Democracy, Legal Pluralism, and the Paradox of Self-Determination' (2006) 4 *International Journal of Constitutional Law* 488; Yutaka Arai-Takahashi, 'The Margin of Appreciation Doctrine: A Theoretical Analysis of Strasbourg's Variable Geometry', in Andreas Follesdal, Birgit Peters and Geir Ulfstein (eds), *Constituting Europe. The European Court of Human Rights in a National, European and Global Context* (Cambridge University Press, 2013).

> received in confidence, or for maintaining the authority and impartiality of the judiciary.

The Court often – but not always – grants states a margin in determining whether such interests override the right. Thus in the *Sunday Times* case, a majority of 11 judges found against the United Kingdom in holding that Article 10 protected newspapers reporting on a case. But nine dissenting judges held that this should have been left to the domestic judiciary, reasoning that '[t]he difference of opinion separating us from our colleagues concerns above all the necessity of the interference and the margin of appreciation which, in this connection, is to be allowed to the national authorities'.[9]

Similar disagreements among judges are legion.[10] One upshot of this criticism is that the doctrine should be made more precise, *and* should be more consistently applied, than is presently the case.

A second concern is that the vague doctrine leaves too much discretion to the judges. The above quote from *Sunday Times* illustrates this point. Similarly, scholars note that 'the Court leaves itself vulnerable to the charge that it manipulates the consensus inquiry to achieve an interpretation of the Convention that it finds ideologically pleasing'.[11] It would seem that one main response is to make the rules of the doctrine more precise.

However, a more precise doctrine does not automatically avoid other objections: that such discretion entails a failure of the ECtHR to protect human rights in the short and long run. This is the point of Benvenisti's criticism:

> By resorting to this device [of a margin of appreciation], the [European Court of Human Rights] eschews responsibility for its decisions. But the court also relinquishes its duty to set universal standards from its unique position as a collective supranational voice of reason and morality. Its decisions reflect a respect of sovereignty, of the notion of subsidiarity, and of national democracy. It stops short of fulfilling the crucial task of becoming the external guardian against the tyranny by majorities.[12]

The Court thereby 'side-step[s] its responsibility as the ultimate interpretative authority in the Convention system.'[13] Indeed, '[t]he essence of the international

9 *Sunday Times (No. 1)* v. *United Kingdom* Series A, dissenting opinion of judges Iarda, Cremona, Thór Vilhjálmsson, Ryssdal, Ganshof van der Meersch, Sir Gerald Fitzmaurice, Bindschedler-Robert, Liesch and Matscher, para. 4.

10 *Observer and Guardian* v. *United Kingdom* Series A no. 216; *Wingrove* v. *United Kingdom* ECHR 1996-V.

11 Laurence R. Helfer, 'Consensus, Coherence and the European Convention on Human Rights' (1993) 133 *Cornell International Law Journal* 141, 154.

12 Eyal Benvenisti, 'Margin of Appreciation, Consensus, and Universal Standards' (1999) 31 *International Law and Politics* 843, 852.

13 Howard Charles Yourow, *The Margin of Appreciation Doctrine in the Dynamics of European Human Rights Jurisprudence* (Kluwer, 1996) 181.

control mechanism may evaporate if there is in fact no effective check upon national power'.[14] Thus there is a risk that a broad margin threatens the role of the Court as protector of the Convention.

4 A modest defence of the current doctrine

Are these criticisms to the point? I grant that if the margin were to become very wide, the value added of ECtHR review diminishes: it would leave each state to be judge in its own case.

However, as practised, the margin is limited. And it will remain circumscribed with the Brighton declaration, which specifies in para. 11 that the Court remains responsible for assessing states' compliance with the Convention:

> the States Parties enjoy a margin of appreciation in how they apply and implement the Convention, depending on the circumstances of the case and the rights and freedoms engaged … the role of the Court is to review whether decisions taken by national authorities are compatible with the Convention, having due regard to the State's margin of appreciation.

The margin does not apply in a general way to the non-derogable rights to life (Article 2), against torture (Article 3), or to slavery or forced labour (Article 4).[15] Moreover, recall that the margin often concerns a 'balancing' among private rights stated in the ECHR. Such 'balancing' does not entail *less stringent* human rights protection, but rather that the state gives some rights a certain weight compared to other rights. Furthermore, national courts enjoy such a margin only when the ECtHR is satisfied that the national court has duly considered several conditions – in the form of a proportionality test – in good faith.

I submit that a more specified margin can reduce several of the concerns stemming from vagueness, and not risk its objective unduly. But such specification must be guided by an understanding of why a margin of appreciation should be accepted at all. This is the question for which a principle of subsidiarity may be thought to offer guidance.

Considerations of subsidiarity may help to specify the doctrine so as to prevent human rights abuses over citizens from their own domestic authorities, *and* to prevent unchecked discretion by international judges. One way to limit such discretion is to specify the doctrine, in light of a general account of what the margin is for. This in turn can best be assessed by considering what the role of the ECtHR is, guided by a principle of subsidiarity.

14 Ibid.

15 Though the ECtHR has referred to the margin of appreciation concerning positive obligations with regard to some aspects of Article 2 (*Budayeva* v. *Russia* ECHR 2008, para. 156) and Article 3 (*M.C.* v. *Bulgaria* ECHR 2003-VII, paras 153–154 and *Berganovic* v. *Croatia* App. No. 46423/06 (ECtHR, 25 June 2009, para. 80)). Thanks to Oddný Mjöll Arnardóttir for these and other references.

5 Subsidiarity

Several authors, including Benvenisti and others, hold that a principle of subsidiary supports 'the' margin of appreciation doctrine.[16] I submit that there is some truth to this claim, mainly in that appeals to subsidiarity indicate the sorts of arguments that may be made.

The 'principle of subsidiarity' is a principle of political ordering which regulates the allocation and use of political or legal authority, typically among a centre and member units. In the history of political thought the principle has a variety of versions, each with long historical roots. Thus, we find a 'protestant' version based on Althusius, a Catholic version expressed in various papal encyclicals; arguments by the 'Anti-Federalists', and economists' arguments favouring fiscal federalism.[17] For our purposes what unites the various traditions is the assumption that the burden of argument lies with attempts to centralise authority. The different principles of subsidiarity express a commitment to leave as much authority as possible to the more local authorities, consistent with achieving the objectives being considered – be it human rights protection, economic efficiency, human flourishing of a certain kind, or some other goals. Different versions disagree on important issues, including:

- whether it is the member units or the centre that should have the final say for determining those objectives – be it human rights or trade liberalisation – or whether central action is needed to achieve them;
- whether central action should be permitted or required under certain conditions; and
- whether central action should aim to empower the member units, supplement them, or replace them.

For our purposes, it is helpful to distinguish a 'state-centric' principle of subsidiarity from 'person-centred' versions of the principle.[18] The former matches a standard presumption of international law, and may best be supported by the Althusian tradition of subsidiarity.[19] Sovereign units – here states – are taken to be free to decide whether they have shared objectives, and whether these objectives are better secured by delegating some of their authority to some central body – such as

16 Benvenisti (n. 12); Dean Spielman, 'Allowing the Right Margin: The European Court of Human Rights and the National Margin of Appreciation Doctrine: Waiver or Subsidiarity of European Review?' (2011) 14 *Cambridge Yearbook of European Legal Studies* 381; Jan Kratochvil, 'The Inflation of the Margin of Appreciation by the European Court of Human Rights' (2011) 29 *Netherlands Quarterly of Human Rights* 324; Ignacio de la Rasilla del Mortal, 'The Increasingly Marginal Appreciation of the Margin-of-Appreciation Doctrine' (2006) 7 *German Law Journal* 611, 614.

17 Andreas Follesdal, 'Subsidiarity' (1998) 6 *Journal of Political Philosophy* 231.

18 Andreas Follesdal, 'The Principle of Subsidiarity as a Constitutional Principle in International Law' (2013) 2 *Global Constitutionalism* 37.

19 Johannes Althusius, *Politica Methodice Digesta* (Liberty Press, 1995); Johannes Althusius, *Politica Methodice Digesta of Johannes Althusius* (Harvard University Press, 1932).

an international court. Such arguments may be based on states' inability or unwillingness to achieve sufficient coordination absent some centralised body, or simply the need for mutual trust that each state actually carry out their obligations. Such pooling of sovereignty may thus differ across issue areas depending on the interests of states, the nature of their collective problem, and the new risks induced by a centralised authority.

Generally, this version of subsidiarity would support as broad a margin as possible, consistent with these objectives, to ensure that the state retains maximal authority and immunity from interference. Three challenges to this version of subsidiarity merit mention, concerning the status of the states in this account. Firstly, there is no clear standard within this account to determine whether any state is beyond the pale with regard to internal legitimacy. Secondly, this account will not allow any other authority to override the domestic bodies' assessment of the objectives and the need for common responses. Thus standard coordination problems or collective action problems abound: often joint benefits can be achieved only if every participant is sanctioned for defection from certain common standards – e.g. concerning low trade barriers, non-aggression agreements, etc. To require universal consent for such common standards to be maintained may often be impossible, while the benefits to all – even to those who withhold consent – are clear. Thirdly, the normative justification for such a principle is unclear: what reasons are there to accept this primacy of states, especially if we take as a normative starting point that it is individuals and their interests that are the units of ultimate normative concern. We witness all three flaws in our current system of states, which includes several rogue states who mistreat their citizens, yet are still immune from various kinds of interference. From the perspective of such a state-centric conception of subsidiarity, the central puzzle of international human rights courts is: if they are the solution, what exactly is the problem states have? – and in light of the answer, what scope should a domestic court retain for adjudicating the state's compliance with the human rights treaty? From this point of view, *democratic* states may want to 'self-bind' to a regional or international human rights court in order to be more credible in the eyes of their own citizens to promote more willing compliance, or to hinder a takeover by undemocratic political forces. A state may also seek credibility in the eyes of other states for instance to convince them to pool sovereignty – such as in the EU. But heads of non-democratic states may not have such needs, and thus should not agree to any curtailment of immunity beyond what the government's self-interest dictates. Thus, the general tendency on the side of many non-democratic states may be to promote as broad a margin as possible.

A 'person-centred' version of subsidiarity does not give such primacy to the state and the interests of states, but instead insists that subsidiarity goes 'all the way down' to the interests of individuals. The states are not the 'natural' reservoir of sovereign authority, but should only have such legal powers and immunities as needed to secure the shared interests of its members: the communities and municipalities – and ultimately the citizens whose states they are. Such accounts of subsidiarity are found *inter alia* in the Catholic or fiscal federal tradition.[20] Among the central problems of these accounts are how to avoid abuse of the centralised authority's power to identify and specify the objectives to be pursued. Thus, in the Catholic tradition consider how the Church authorities have identified some ideals for human flourishing which determine the proper composition and objectives of families – with contested implications. There is also a risk that the centre seeks its own interests rather than those of the citizens or sub-units. Moreover, even if the problem of deliberate ill will is checked, the centre will often be unable to remain sufficiently attuned to local variations in needs and feasible solutions. For our case these risks may be smaller: the human rights standards are agreed by state consent, and the aim is only to secure a minimum threshold.

From this point of view, an important design challenge of international human rights courts and the doctrine is to grant the state enough authority to promote the interests of its citizens and of foreigners, while preventing the abuse of such powers in the form of human rights violations. Regional or international human rights courts can provide such protection, and bolster the protection provided by independent domestic courts. At the same time, citizens run the risk that all these courts – domestic, regional and international – will misuse or even abuse their power due to incompetence or ill will. In particular, no court should limit *democratic* and other forms of self-governance unduly, especially when the governments are sufficiently responsive to the best interests of their and other citizens.

For our purposes here – namely human rights protection performed primarily by the domestic courts, supported by regional human rights courts – I submit that the 'person-centric' principle of subsidiarity is more plausible. There seems to be no sound reason to insist that the principle of subsidiarity should stop at the state level, nor that states should retain a final veto. This is particularly so concerning human rights protection.

A 'state-centric' conception of subsidiarity will presumably support a broader margin. The person centred version, in contrast, will require more detailed delineation of the margin. Indeed, a person-centred account must include complex arguments for the doctrine, showing that certain interests of individuals require centralised authority above the state, e.g. human rights protected and promoted by the ECHR, but that a margin is still permitted or even required.

Why allow a margin at all, on a person-centred principle of subsidiarity? It would seem to re-create the problems for which international courts were the solution, namely to prevent the state from being judge in its own case – be it human rights violations or arbitration disputes. We now turn to consider why individuals' interests may require that international human rights judicial review be constrained by a margin. This requires us to look at the ECtHR as part of a multilevel legal order.

20 Pope Pius XI, 'Quadragesimo Anno (1931)', in Carla Carlen (ed.), *The Papal Encyclicals 1903–1939* (McGrath, 1981); and R. A. Musgrave, *The Theory of Public Finance: A Study in Political Economy* (McGraw-Hill, 1959), Wallace E. Oates, *Fiscal Federalism* (Harcourt, Brace & Jovanovich, 1972), respectively.

6 Applying subsidiarity to the margin of appreciation doctrine

I shall suggest that the Court when following a duly specified margin of appreciation doctrine can help to prevent human rights abuses of citizens from their own domestic authorities, *and* that the doctrine can help to prevent domination by international judges. Some versions of a principle of subsidiarity can help to specify the doctrine in more defensible directions. To apply a person-centred principle of subsidiarity properly to the doctrine, we first consider the objectives of individuals that are better secured by establishing ECtHR than by domestic authorities alone; then consider the role of the ECtHR; and then the particular role of the doctrine as part of this complex.

6.1 The objective of the ECtHR

The presumed objective of the ECtHR can be read out of the Preamble to the ECHR: the aim is to protect

> those fundamental freedoms which are the foundation of justice and peace in the world ... [which] are best maintained on the one hand by an effective political democracy and on the other by a common understanding and observance of the human rights upon which they depend.

There are several aspects of this objective and function of the multilevel human rights judiciary worth noting.

States' main objective with human rights treaties is often to bind themselves. Some treaties serve primarily to bind all states to solve shared problems, and each state only binds itself as a necessary burden to convince other states to do likewise. Compared to such 'other-binding' conventions, some of the main aims for states that sign human rights treaties are different. The state binds itself in order to enhance its own credibility as a 'rule of law', human rights respecting political system. This self-binding is a feature these treaties share with investment treaties to attract foreign investors, unlike treaties concerning trade liberalisation to gain access to foreign markets.[21] One implication is that treaty interpretation and adjudication should not obviously be made so as to minimise the curtailment of state sovereignty – as is often the case for 'other-binding' conventions which each state signs in order to make other states commit likewise for common gains.[22] It follows that a margin should not necessarily be as broad as possible.

The protection of citizens against certain kinds of avoidable abuse or neglect by means of the laws and policies of their government require detailed knowledge about the local culture and circumstances, the risks individuals face due to complex interplay between majority culture and institutions – and about a range of feasible

21 Karen Alter, 'Delegating to International Courts: Self-Binding vs. Other-Binding Delegation' (2008) 71 *Law and Contemporary Problems* 37.

22 Andrew Moravcsik, 'The Origins of Human Rights Regimes: Democratic Delegation in Postwar Europe' (2000) 54 *International Organization* 217.

alternatives. The abstraction of human rights may thus be among their virtues, since they can be specified in different ways to reflect such differing circumstances.[23]

Also note that the objective of the ECHR is human rights protection, not harmonisation across all states. Certain treaty objectives require harmonisation of regulations across jurisdictions, for instance to facilitate international trade. Different rules for tariffs would easily create suspicion that some states were seeking to free ride on other more compliant states, and would challenge the objective of the treaty. For human rights protection, the same concern for harmonisation does not apply. The aim is to secure some of the important interests of individuals against standard threats mainly stemming from their own state organs, whatever institutions and policies are in place. There are only few problems that arise by some states seeking to free ride on others' strict compliance – for instance, there may be a 'race to the bottom' for labour rights. But, in general, the concern to protect important interests is compatible with a range of different institutions in different states, all of which are compatible with human rights. Consider, for instance, how different European states regulate the relationship between religions and the state: some states such as the United Kingdom maintain a state church, while others such as France insist on a sharp divide. Both of these arrangements, suitably tailored, are compatible with the ECHR. One implication is that some alleged problems of fragmentation are not as challenging as one might have thought, and that the role of an international court for human rights protection may be less intrusive into domestic regulations.

6.2 *The role of the ECtHR as a regional court in a multilevel order*

In the following I leave aside interesting 'de lege ferenda' questions concerning which role would be best for the Court to have. This is not only of theoretical interest given the current discussions e.g. about how to reconfigure the European legal order as regards the relationship between the Court and the EU's Court of Justice of the European Union.

According to the ECHR, the states remain the primary responsible actors to respect and protect human rights in the complex multilevel European legal order. The express objective of the ECtHR is to *assist* states in securing this objective, not to replace them: its task under Article 19 is limited to 'ensur[ing] the observance of the engagements undertaken by the High Contracting Parties'. Thus its role is really 'subsidiary' or supportive and supplementary in the promotion of human rights. Subsidiarity is also taken to be expressed in Articles 1, 13 and 35. The Court interprets its own role in this light:

> The Court observes that within the scheme of the Convention it is intended to be subsidiary to the national systems safeguarding human rights … The

23 Adam Etinson, 'Human Rights, Claimability and the Uses of Abstraction' (2013) 25 *Utilitas* 463.

> Court must be cautious in taking on the role of a first-instance tribunal of fact, where this is not rendered unavoidable by the circumstances of a particular case. As a general rule, where domestic proceedings have taken place, it is not the Court's task to substitute its own assessment of the facts for that of the domestic courts and it is for the latter to establish the facts on the basis of the evidence before them … in normal circumstances it requires cogent elements to lead [the Court] to depart from the findings of fact reached by the domestic courts … Nonetheless … it is the Court's role definitively to interpret and apply the Convention.[24]

The impact of the ECtHR in the multilevel European legal order is profoundly shaped by the fact that it is a permanent court which interprets the Convention authoritatively. Its judgments thus have a certain 'erga omnes' effect and thereby shape states' expectations and future behaviour. Domestic courts must consider relevant decisions by the ECtHR even about cases in other states – thus, for instance, the ECtHR's decision about balancing of freedom of expression against privacy in one case in Germany is generally heeded by all domestic courts when they decide similar cases.[25] This also applies to the ECtHR's claims about when it grants states a margin of appreciation. Thus the practice of the margin of appreciation shapes states' behaviour broadly: domestic courts appear to argue cases in ways which the Court has recognised elsewhere as sufficient to grant a margin of appreciation, in the expectation that the Court will grant them a similar margin if the case goes to the ECtHR.[26]

6.3 Why a margin of appreciation? An argument from subsidiarity

If the ECtHR is set up to support and strengthen the domestic judiciary's protection of human rights, why should its support be reduced by introducing a margin of appreciation? This practice appears to reduce the protection of human rights, since the ECtHR thereby hands back authority to the domestic judiciary which it was supposed to monitor and override if necessary.

From the perspective of a person-centred conception of subsidiarity, the state organs should retain the final authority when the international human rights court *cannot* or is *unlikely* to provide extra protection. That is: the ECtHR should apply a margin of appreciation, under certain conditions, in so far and for those objectives where the domestic courts and other authorities are at least as well suited to determine whether there is a breach. What arguments of this kind may be offered to assess and specify the current doctrine?

24 *Austin and Others* v. *United Kingdom* App. Nos 39692/09 etc. (ECtHR, 15 March 2012), para. 61.

25 *Von Hannover* v. *Germany* ECHR 2004-VI and *Lillo-Stenberg and Sæther* v. *Norway* App. No. 13258/09 (ECtHR, 16 January 2014), respectively.

26 See *Lillo Stenberg and Sæther* v. *Norway* (n. 25) paras 44–45.

Consider several features of the doctrine. The Court hardly grants any margin when certain rights are at risk, regardless of what states claim, namely rights against torture and slavery, and the right to life.

The state may be better able to apply the ECHR to complex local circumstances than will an international court. Thus the Court often claims that domestic authorities are in principle better placed than an international court to evaluate local needs and conditions.[27] But when is a state more *likely* than an international court such as the ECtHR to evaluate the situation correctly, in ways that promote the objective of human rights protection *against* the state itself? I submit that this is more likely when the domestic laws and policies are sufficiently responsive to the best interests of all citizens, and where the domestic authorities have mechanisms of self-correction. This is arguably often the case for democratic rule under the rule of law.

Under functioning democratic mechanisms and the rule of law the population deliberates about alternative policies and legislative proposals in light of their implications for all affected parties, so as to promote broadly shared interests while avoiding harm to anyone. In so far as this argument holds, the ECtHR should allow a very narrow margin for rights concerning political participation, freedom of expression and other rights required for well-functioning democratic decision-making. And indeed, this appears to be a pattern of the practice.[28]

Furthermore, the majoritarian democratic mechanisms are not particularly reliable in securing the vital interests and equal respect for those who are likely to be in the minority when decisions are taken by majorities. For this reason, the ECtHR should not grant a wide margin for rights which protect interests of minorities which may likely be outvoted by persistent majorities – such as the curtailments of freedom of religion for religious minorities – even in well-functioning democracies. In such cases, the Court should at least engage in strict scrutiny as to whether the state has indeed carried out a proportionality test. Again, this pattern appears to be in accordance with the current doctrine.[29]

Finally, even democratic deliberative majoritarian decision-making is not always well functioning. For instance, there are limits to the general claim that the domestic authorities are closer to the specific circumstances and *thus* in a better position to assess proportionality and judicial review. The domestic authorities may know more about the domestic setting, but there is no reason to believe that they are particularly well placed to know the Convention and the case law of the Court. Nor are they particularly well placed to assess the best set of policies to

27 *Hatton and Others* v. *United Kingdom* ECHR 2003-VIII, para. 97.

28 Andrew Legg, *The Margin of Appreciation in International Human Rights Law: Deference and Proportionality* (Oxford University Press, 2012) 90–92; and Benvenisti (n. 12) 847, citing *inter alia United Communist Party of Turkey* v. *Turkey*, ECHR 1998-I.

29 Legg (n. 28) 93; Alexandea Timmer, 'A Quiet Revolution: Vulnerability in the European Court of Human Rights', in Martha Albertson Fineman and Anna Grear (eds), *Vulnerability: Reflections on a New Ethical Foundation for Law and Politics* (Ashgate, 2013) 145. I owe these references to Oddný Mjöll Arnardóttir.

secure their social goals. The latter requires a comparative perspective which domestic authorities may be too myopic to discern. Thus it makes sense to have a proportionality test when certain human rights appear to be at stake, to ensure that state authorities have not overlooked less invasive alternatives, and have not ignored the impact on some groups – and at the same time ensure that the population can be sure that this is fact the case.

Such deliberation about alternatives and their impact is of course what well-functioning democratic decision-making should secure. In so far as such proportionality testing has not been carried out at all – in well-functioning democracies and elsewhere – the ECtHR has no reason from deference for democratic decision-making to refrain from reviewing a decision. On the contrary, the Court may seek to nudge the domestic authorities to perform a thorough proportionality test, by letting it be known that the Court only grants a narrow margin, if at all, when there is no evidence of such testing by domestic organs – be it by the judiciary or the legislature. Indeed, this is the reason why the Court refused to grant the UK a margin of appreciation in the *Hirst* case and likewise in the case *Lindheim and Others* v. *Norway*.[30]

On this basis, I submit that a margin of appreciation doctrine with these features, with exception for the rights mentioned, seems compatible with and even required by the rationale for placing some authority with an international court to adjudicate human rights – when this *supplements* review by domestic courts. When constrained in this way, the doctrine serves the particular objectives of the ECtHR: to bolster the domestic protection of human rights. Note that it is not obvious that similar features and conditions should be part of a margin of appreciation doctrine for other international courts: they may have different relations to other actors in the multilevel regional or global system, and with other objectives with different normative weight than human rights.

A final aspect of the practice is more contentious. The Court may restrict the margin, or require better arguments from the accused state, when the Court detects a consensus in policies or regulation in Europe.[31] This is referred to by the Court in terms of 'the existence or non-existence of common ground between the laws of the Contracting States'.[32] The Court's attention to emerging consensus may be a good way to constrain the judges' discretion when they engage in dynamic or 'evolutive' interpretation of the ECHR. The Court might only interpret dynamically in areas where it detects common ground, and/or be particularly

30 *Hirst* v. *United Kingdom (No. 2)* ECHR 2005-IX, paras 79–82; *Lindheim and Others* v. *Norway* App. Nos 13221/08 and 2139/19 (ECtHR, 12 June 2012), paras 128–130. In *Animal Defenders* v. *United Kingdom* ECHR 2013, paras 108–109, this approach was confirmed by granting a wide margin of appreciation when a thorough proportionality assessment had been performed.

31 Laurence Helfer and Anne-Marie Slaughter, 'Toward a Theory of Effective Supranational Adjudication' (1997) 107 *Yale Law Review* 314.

32 *Rasmussen* v. *Denmark* Series A no. 87, para. 40; cf. Eva Brems, 'The Margin of Appreciation Doctrine in the Case-Law of the European Court of Human Rights' (1996) 56 *Heidelberg Journal of International Law* 240, 248, 276.

critical only when a state deviates from such a consensus. However, the Court does not appear to have an established procedure to ascertain the requisite consensus. Several scholars claim that 'emerging consensus' is very much in the eyes of the beholder.[33] These and other critics also claim that the weight of the consensus factor is indeterminate, opening up for too much judicial discretion. Indeed, this respect for a majority consensus seems to run counter to some of the central arguments for the Court: that the majority may well be in the wrong, and subject those in the minority to tyranny. More fundamentally, it appears unclear why an emerging consensus among other states should reduce the margin granted one state on issues where it faces particular dilemmas in balancing two Convention-protected rights against each other and has established its own routines to handle them – routines that hitherto have appeared unobjectionable?

7 Conclusion: criticisms reconsidered

We have considered whether the proposed changes to the Preamble of the ECHR wrought by Protocol 15, with references to subsidiarity, can guide the Court's attempt to respect both the Treaty and its sovereign creators by means of a margin of appreciation. I have argued that general appeals to 'subsidiarity' neither help the balancing nor guide the Court's attempts in the particular cases. We should indeed expect Protocol 15 to focus attention on the Court's interpretation of subsidiarity. I have argued that a person-centred conception of subsidiarity is to be preferred over a state-centric conception. The former can alleviate some of the criticisms voiced against the doctrine of the margin of appreciation.

The doctrine of the margin of appreciation should be specified *not* in light of a state-centric conception of subsidiarity which would tend to grant all states a wide margin to be judge in their own case as long as trust in the state by their citizens or other states is not at risk. Rather, I have laid out some implications of a *person-centred* subsidiarity principle, which seems to support some of the alleged features of the current practice, in particular no margin for violations of the right to life and the right against torture, slavery or forced labour; and a very narrow margin where rights central to the well-functioning of a democratic order are at stake. Then the person-centric version supports a presumption that domestic democratic procedures can ensure that the domestic courts can be trusted to monitor whether the discretion of the state complies with the ECHR. But this presumption must be defended, not least when the rights of minorities are at stake, by requiring that the domestic authorities have indeed performed a proportionality test in good faith.

These aspects of the doctrine should thus be elaborated, and if guided by a subsidiarity principle then certainly a person-centred one. The arguments I have laid out do not challenge the widespread criticism that the current margin of appreciation 'doctrine' is very vague and partially inconsistent. Moreover, I have questioned the Court's reliance on an observed 'emerging consensus'. However, I

33 Benvenisti (n. 12); Helfer and Slaughter (n. 31); but cf. George Letsas, 'Two Concepts of the Margin of Appreciation' (2006) 26 *Oxford Journal of Legal Studies* 705, 713.

have suggested that one plausible response is to make the rules of the doctrine more precise. I submit that this task will be even more urgent, and become more of a public concern, with the changes wrought by Protocol 15. It is only by making the substantive criteria of the doctrine more precise that the margin of appreciation 'doctrine' becomes worthy of that name. This is required if the Member States of the Council of Europe are to become and remain worthy of their citizens' trust and deference – by showing more clearly that these authorities work to the best interest of all.

Index

For Product Safety Concerns and Information please contact our EU representative GPSR@taylorandfrancis.com
Taylor & Francis Verlag GmbH, Kaufingerstraße 24, 80331 München, Germany

www.ingramcontent.com/pod-product-compliance
Ingram Content Group UK Ltd.
Pitfield, Milton Keynes, MK11 3LW, UK
UKHW011008180926
475701UK00004B/635

* 9 7 8 0 3 6 7 5 9 7 0 1 6 *